KEY IDEAS IN *Sociology*

3 EDITION

For Susan

KEY IDEAS IN *Sociology*

3 EDITION

Peter Kivisto
Augustana College, Rock Island, IL
University of Turku

SAGE | PINE FORGE
Los Angeles | London | New Delhi
Singapore | Washington DC

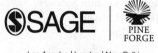

For information:

Pine Forge Press
An Imprint of
SAGE Publications, Inc.
2455 Teller Road
Thousand Oaks,
California 91320
E-mail: order@sagepub.com

SAGE Publications India Pvt. Ltd.
B 1/I 1 Mohan Cooperative
Industrial Area
Mathura Road, New Delhi 110044
India

SAGE Publications Ltd.
1 Oliver's Yard
55 City Road
London EC1Y 1SP
United Kingdom

SAGE Publications Asia-Pacific Pte. Ltd.
33 Pekin Street #02-01
Far East Square
Singapore 048763

Printed in the United States of America

Library of Congress Cataloging-in-Publication Data

Kivisto, Peter, 1948-
Key ideas in sociology / Peter Kivisto. — 3rd ed.
p. cm.
Includes bibliographical references and index.
ISBN 978-1-4129-7811-8 (pbk.)
1. Sociology—History. 2. Social change. I. Title.

HM435.K58 2011
301.09—dc22 2009047960

This book is printed on acid-free paper.

10 11 12 13 14 10 9 8 7 6 5 4 3 2 1

Acquisitions Editor: David Repetto
Editorial Assistant: Nancy Scrofano
Production Editor: Catherine M. Chilton
Copy Editor: Heidi Crossman
Typesetter: C&M Digitals (P) Ltd.
Proofreader: Caryne Brown
Indexer: Diggs Publication Services
Cover Designer: Candice Harman
Marketing Manager: Erica DeLuca

Contents

Preface

This book, in presenting a brief account of the sociological vocation and promise, is designed to serve as a text particularly well suited for courses in which students are also expected to read from primary texts.

I had two specific goals in mind when setting out to write *Key Ideas in Sociology*. First, I intended for it to provide students with a general overview of the ways in which a number of important ideas have helped sociologists to better understand contemporary societies and human social relations in those societies. I wanted to show how those ideas have been continually reformulated by social theorists attempting to respond to the ongoing impact of social change.

The second reason for writing the book is related to this last point, for it is an effort to illustrate the value of social theory beyond the classroom. I want students to come to appreciate that theories are not arcane intellectual exercises but, in fact, invaluable interpretive guides helping them in the ongoing quest to understand complex and ever-changing social conditions. These ideas have relevance for sorting out issues related to the world of work. They speak to problems and possibilities shaping what it means to be a citizen today. They have much to offer in thinking about the shifting nature of social relations even at the most intimate levels involving lovers, friends, and neighbors. In short, the purpose of the book is to reveal the relevance of sociological thinking for everyone concerned about their public and private lives.

In the second edition of the book I took more seriously than I had in the earlier version the challenges that globalization poses for sociological thought. As will be clear, some of the scholars discussed herein had an awareness of globalization before the term was common, whereas others operated with a problematic tendency to equate society with the nation-state. The concluding chapter of the book surveys promising developments in social theory today that build on the past while simultaneously attempting to grapple with new challenges posed by the advent of a global society.

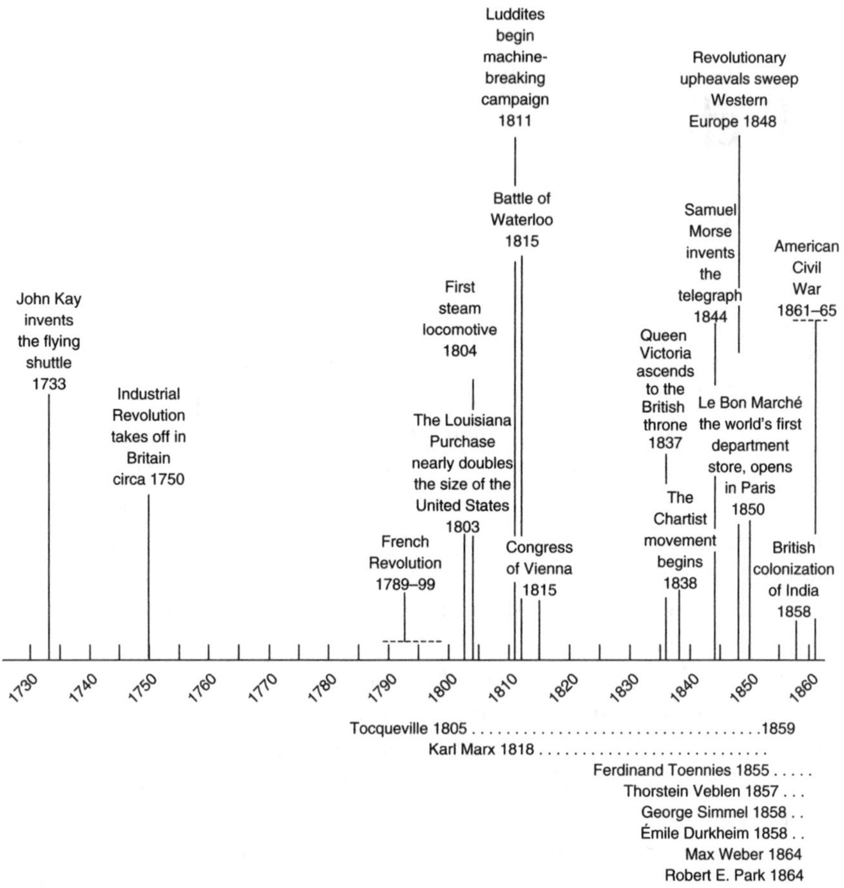

This new edition is intended to reflect on my earlier analyses, making use of scholarship that has been produced in the first decade of the 21st century. This includes new studies of the classics, some of which are biographical and some of which offer new and challenging interpretations of aspects of their work. It also includes new currents in theoretical thinking, seen, for

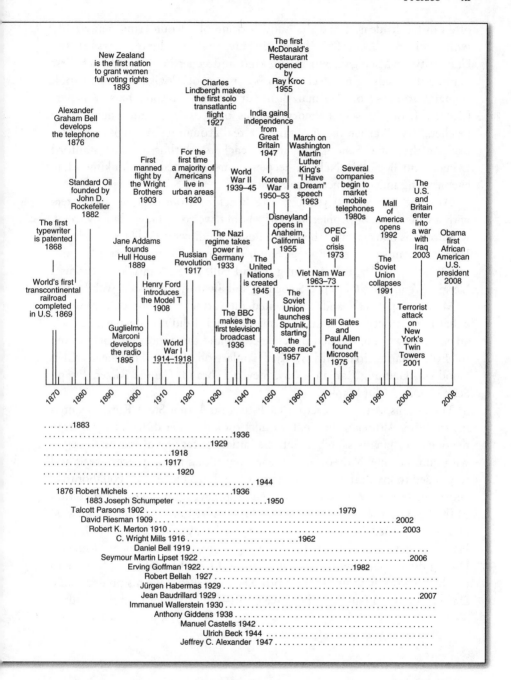

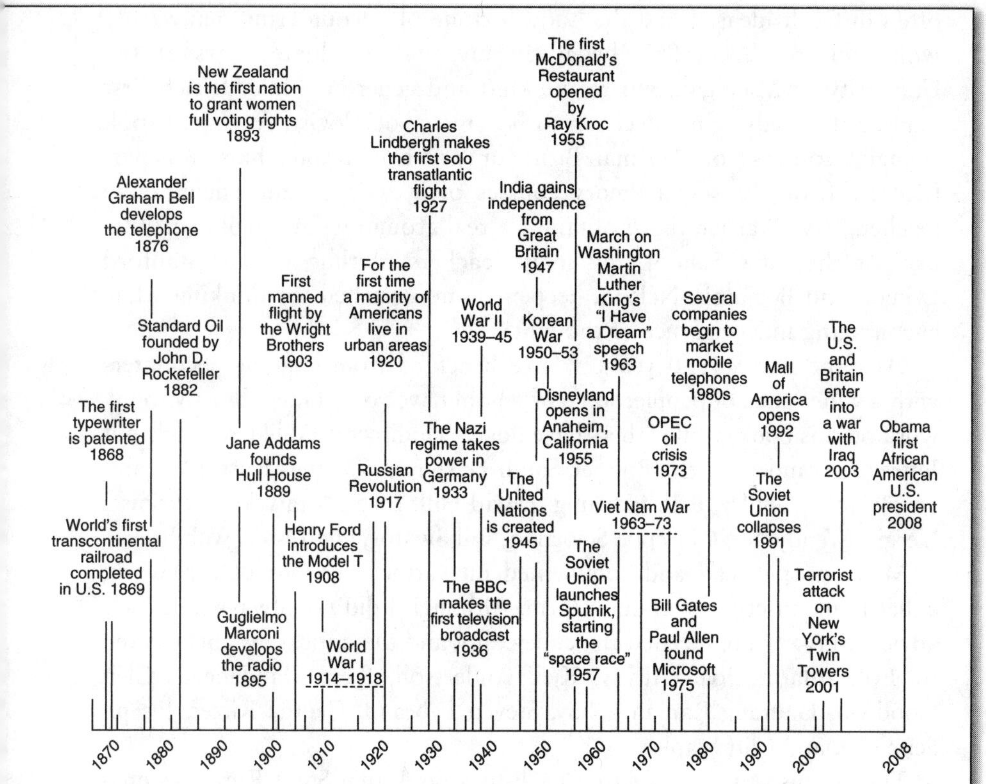

example, in Jeffrey Alexander's development of the idea of the civil sphere and in Zygmunt Bauman's introduction of the idea of liquid modernity.

In preparing this work, I came to realize how important some of my former teachers were in convincing me of the vitality and significance of the sociological imagination. In coming to understand what are admittedly often difficult ideas, I had the good fortune of encountering many truly wonderful teachers. This began in my undergraduate years at the University of Michigan, where the kind and generous Max Heirich first planted the seeds of my decision to become a sociologist. At Yale, I took engaging courses from Norman Birnbaum and David Apter, but it was particularly from the social theory courses of a dynamic and encouraging teacher, Steve Warner, that I obtained a real grounding in sociological theory. At the New School, my main teachers, Arthur Vidich, Stanford Lyman, and Benjamin Nelson, deepened and enriched my thinking while encouraging independence of thought.

Over the past several years, I have benefited from ongoing encounters with a wide range of people, some of whom have contributed directly to my work on this book, while others have done so indirectly. I'd like to single out Jeffrey Alexander, Martin Bulmer, Samir Daspupta, Thomas Faist, Margaret Farrar, John Guidry, Beth Hartung, David Hill, Ewa Morawska, Devrimsel Nergiz, Wendy Ng, Giuseppe Sciortino, Bill Swatos, and Östen Wahlbeck.

Many people read and commented on various versions of this work, either in manuscript or in book form. Although I did not always take their advice, I greatly appreciated the collegiality and the critical insights offered by Erik Allardt, Joan Alway, Kjell Andersson, Steve Dandaneau, Glen Goodwin, Gaurang Ranjan Sahay, Steven Lybrand, George Ritzer, Joseph Scimecca, and Cliff Staples.

The origins of this project go back to a book that Steve Rutter wanted me to write. Although the final product took a rather different form from the one he originally sketched out, the initial conception of this book began with him, not me. Moreover, at every stage along the way, Steve read and responded to my drafts, thus making the final product a truly collaborative endeavor. Jerry Westby was instrumental in developing the second edition of the book. Since our initial partnership, I have gotten to know him well and have learned to appreciate his reasoned judgments about book publishing and to be thankful for his insights and general encouragement. During the preparation of this new edition, I have had the good fortune to be able to work with yet another pro, Dave Repetto. Like his predecessors, Dave made this a truly collaborative effort—and for that I am thankful.

Acknowledgments

SAGE Publications would like to thank the following reviewers:

Anne F. Eisenberg
SUNY–Geneseo

Vincenzo Mele
Monmouth University

Kristen Myers
Northern Illinois University

Kevin T. Leicht
The University of Iowa

Jenifer Kunz
West Texas A&M University

1

Key Ideas About the Social World

If you pay attention to recurring messages in the popular media, you might easily get the idea that our world is in the process of changing dramatically. You might sense that the past is rapidly disappearing as we cross the threshold into an entirely new era. From cheerleaders of the future, the message we get is that on one side of the divide are all the old, bankrupt ideas that have made our world so messy and dangerous, whereas on the other side are the brilliant new ideas that will usher us into utopia. From the prophets of doom, you get the opposite sense of where we have been and where we are heading. They usually have a positive, if romanticized, view of the past and its presumed values (commitment to family, community spirit, work ethic, etc.), and they envision a future devoid of such virtues. Not surprisingly, they view what is ahead with considerable foreboding.

Both views have many popularizers. And the issues these popularizers speak to have attracted the attention of a number of perceptive commentators. Perhaps you have seen the following titles on library shelves, in bookstores, or online:

Runaway World

Hot, Flat, and Crowded

Consumed

Democracy Incorporated

The Clash of Civilizations

The End of Work

War Without End

The End of History and the Last Man

The Age of Discontinuity

The Age of Unreason

The Jobless Future

The Twilight of Common Dreams

The Twilight of American Culture

The New World Order

The Coming Information Age

The Closing of the American Mind

Powershift

Bobos in Paradise

Jihad vs. McWorld

Do titles such as these make you feel curious, a little excited, or apprehensive? Realize that the authors intended to provoke such responses, in part because they help sell books. Realize, too, that you and your contemporaries are not the first to feel this way about trends in the social world. Over 150 years ago, the intellectual forerunners of contemporary sociology began examining the rapid and far-ranging changes occurring in their world and wondered why those changes were happening and where they were heading. This was the beginning of a tradition of sociological searching for answers to questions about social change.

Each succeeding generation was stimulated by the ways its predecessors attempted to understand their own particular historical situations. Those generations borrowed ideas from those who came before them, adapting those ideas to the new circumstances that characterized their own times. In fact, the ideas expressed in the preceding titles are essentially variations and extensions of, and reactions to, contemporary social events as well as a tradition of social thought. This book is about some of the major ideas that have developed out of that tradition. It examines their origins, their development, and their relevance at the dawn of the 21st century.

Conceptualizing Contemporary Society

In this book, we examine four key ideas that have played a central role in discourse about the nature of society. Specifically, in Chapters 2 through 5, we explore the meaning and significance of the following ideas: industrial society, democracy, individualism, and modernity. In the final chapter, we turn to the significance of globalization and suggest ways in which sociology is called upon to reorient its historic tendency to treat "society" as a reference to the nation-state by moving beyond this perspective to grasp the significance of an emerging global order (or, as some would describe it, disorder). These ideas can be seen as key because they help supply us with insights into major social trends and assist us in seeing how those trends influence all facets of our lives (Williams 1976; Elias 1978; Shils 1981; Seidman 1983; Wolfe 1995; Bauman and May 2001).

These ideas, of course, cannot stand alone. First, they are interconnected. Thus, for example, we cannot appreciate the nature of democracy in American society today without an awareness of the nature of individualism. Some versions of individualism, which encourage the single-minded pursuit of self-interest, can work against people acting collectively in political life to advance the common good. This, obviously, has significant implications for the way democracy will look and function.

Second, these four central ideas have been further refined and shaped by a variety of other consequential ideas. In each chapter, ancillary ideas that are closely related to the four master ideas, and that have added new dimensions of understanding, are also discussed. Among the concepts that are examined are alienation, technology, capitalism, socialism, social class, citizenship, civil society, bureaucracy, and community.

With an awareness of both the interconnections of the four key concepts and the role played by a number of other important ideas, a brief preview of Chapters 2 through 5 follows.

Industrial Society

Chapter 2 introduces the ways in which a number of important sociological thinkers from the 19th century to the present have attempted to make sense of industrial society, identifying both its promise and its problems. As you will see, the Industrial Revolution signaled the advent of a new type of economic system that proved to be extraordinarily innovative, dynamic, and productive. In its relatively short history, industrial society has transformed work, the class structure, communication and transportation systems, leisure, patterns of consumption, our homes—in short, all facets of our lives. Most of us would not want to return to a preindustrial world because we realize that our lives are far more comfortable because of industrialization.

We also realize, however, that industrialization has a downside. Workers frequently view their employers as exploiters and their jobs as degrading and alienating. At the same time, they fear that, because of the dynamism of this type of economic system, their livelihoods are never secure. Industrial society has generated serious environmental problems and new kinds of risks. There is a wasteful and destructive side to industrial society. The purpose of Chapter 2 is to explore the dual-edged nature of industrial society in the context of how the thinking about it has evolved during the past two centuries.

Democracy

The American and French revolutions marked the beginning of a shift in the way people thought about government and its relation to the governed. The democratic era marked the end of the age of absolutism, in which monarchs identified themselves with the state and in which the people were seen merely as subjects of the crown. Democracy changed this by investing ultimate authority in the citizenry, with government being redefined as an institution intended to reflect and represent its interests. Throughout the 19th century, democracy took root and expanded in the countries of Western Europe and in North America—precisely those countries that were also witnessing the emergence of capitalist industrial society. By the 20th century, democratic ideals were sufficiently powerful so that even manifestly undemocratic political regimes such as the former Soviet Union claimed to be democratic. Democracy, however, did not manage to take root in some places, and, in nations where it did, antidemocratic forces sometimes undermined it, as in the case of Nazi Germany.

The political history of the past two centuries has prompted sociologists to attempt to ascertain the preconditions that make democracy possible as well as to discover the major threats to democratic systems. In trying to address these issues, they have also dealt with many related questions: Are ordinary people actually fit to govern? What is their proper role in the political arena? What kinds of leaders are needed in a democracy? Can democracy survive contemporary challenges to it? How has democracy shaped gender relations and vice versa? Similarly, how has democracy shaped race relations and vice versa? Sociologists have been pondering these and related questions since the 19th century, and we examine the insights of some of the most prominent of these thinkers in Chapter 3.

Individualism

Chapter 4 shifts ground from large, macrolevel concerns to the social psychological realm. As you will learn, America was the birthplace of contemporary ideas about individualism, and because of this we tend—often unwittingly—to view the world through the lens of an individualistic worldview. Individualism in our culture is generally seen in a positive light, conjuring up notions of personal autonomy and self-reliance. Individualism, however, also has a darker side.

Individualism recasts the way people define their ties to community and to other people outside the orbit of family and friends. This has broad implications. An example of this is seen in a letter that Robert Bellah, one of the sociologists discussed in Chapter 4, sent to former President Clinton, criticizing him for signing a new welfare bill into law. The bill was designed to prevent people from remaining on welfare for extended periods of time. According to its proponents, the rationale for this legislation was that poor people need to take responsibility for their own lives. In his letter, Bellah (1996), assuming the mantle of a public sociologist, contended, "We know that this punitive legislation is popular because it resonates with the radical individualism that has long been part of our culture" (p. 65). Why did he believe this legislation was punitive, and in what ways did he see individualism as a culprit? Chapter 4, by providing an overview of the history of individualism, provides a clearer sense of what Bellah is claiming and will help you judge whether you agree with him.

Modernity

In Chapter 5, we build on the preceding chapters and return to the big picture, this time focusing on culture. It is not always easy to define what it means to be modern, but at the outset of the chapter, we work through a provisional understanding of the central features of modern culture. As you will see, modern culture cannot be understood without appreciating the way it has been shaped by industrialization, democracy, and individualism. As you will also see, however, modern culture is more than the result of these influences, and it has a reciprocal impact on them.

The topic of modernity is approached from several angles, including money, fashion, urban life, the mass media, and mass entertainment. Moreover, by entering into the controversial debates about postmodernism, you will get a sense of how modernity has evolved and how contemporary social theorists are attempting to make sense of the cultural transformations we are living through.

After reading these four chapters, you will appreciate the importance of these key ideas in their own right and have a better understanding of how they are interconnected. Furthermore, you will realize that these ideas not only were useful in understanding the past but also have contemporary relevance.

Careers of Ideas

Although we understand that people have careers, it is not so obvious that ideas about the nature of society do also. As you will see, ideas have careers insofar as they are used over an extended period to help us comprehend major social trends. Ideas are formulated, elaborated, refined, and revised by particular individuals, but the ideas nonetheless manage to take on lives of their own. Thus, they need to be understood on their own terms.

The individuals who developed these ideas inhabited particular times and places. In return, the ideas developed in partial response to the immediate intellectual and social concerns and interests of those individuals. This book traces the careers of the four ideas identified previously as they have been articulated by several eminent thinkers. I have not attempted to include everyone who has ever written anything of importance about industrial society, democracy, individualism, or modernity. Nor am I suggesting that the work of any particular person discussed in this book can be reduced simply to one of the four ideas. In fact, it is fair to say that for Karl Marx, Max Weber, Émile Durkheim, Georg Simmel, and their intellectual heirs, all four master ideas are woven in one way or another into the overall fabric of their work (Becker 1971; Giddens 1971; Hawthorn 1976; Aron 1985; Mazlish 1989; Wallerstein 1991). This should not be surprising because, as noted previously, these ideas are indeed interconnected.

To demonstrate the enduring significance and relevance of these ideas, I frequently discuss the circumstances in which they were formulated. The focus on particular thinkers' lives is not intended to provide comprehensive biographies of these individuals but, rather, to highlight some of the events that may have affected the meaning and significance attached to particular ideas over time. In other words, the ways ideas are modified, transformed, and reappropriated is a matter of central concern when we decide to investigate their careers (Hughes 1961, 1975; Williams 1976; Kivisto 1989; Sica 1989; Bourdieu 1993).

Reappropriated is an important word to consider. The previously mentioned four seminal thinkers are proverbial dead white males, as indeed is true for most of their peers. Succeeding generations of scholars instrumental in shaping the course of the discipline were also largely white and male, and when they looked to the sociological canon, they looked especially to this quartet. Without denigrating the significance of their work, this is also an expression of the legacy of sexism and racism that contemporary sociology inherits. It is, fortunately, also a legacy that the discipline is combating and gradually overcoming. One way it is doing so is by seeking at last to begin the process of appropriating the thought of long-neglected people of color and women. I think, for example, of scholars such as Harriet Martineau, Jane Addams, Charlotte Perkins Gilman, W. E. B. Du Bois, and C. L. R. James. Second, in the wake of the civil rights movement and the women's movement of the 1960s, both people of color and women have begun to achieve places of prominence in the discipline where they have been so long denied. They are at this moment writing a new chapter in the history of sociology.

Key Ideas and the Field of Sociology

The key ideas discussed in this book have significance beyond the confines of sociology. For example, industrialization has special meaning for economists, whereas literary scholars are keenly interested in the impact of modernity on literature. We, however, are primarily interested in these ideas because they have played a central role in sociology. In fact, the four individuals most associated with the four key ideas—Marx, Weber, Durkheim, and Simmel—are often considered the classic founders of the field of sociology (Bannister 1987; Ross 1991; Horowitz 1993; Giddens 1995a).

The scope and persistence of these central concepts demonstrate the fact that sociology is the most ambitious of the social sciences. Its self-appointed task is nothing less than to add to our understanding of the major trends that have given shape to the modern world. Its subject matter includes the institutions singled out for attention by economics and political science as well as the family, religion, education, or, in short, the entire realm of what is frequently referred to as civil society (Therborn 1976; Gurnah and Scott 1992; Wolfe 1993, 1995; Edwards 2004; Alexander 2006). Like psychology, sociology attempts to understand the individual, but sociology does so by locating the person in social settings and by attempting to understand the complex ways in which society and the individual impinge on and reciprocally shape each other.

Sociology is also ambitious methodologically. Sociologists sometimes pattern themselves after natural scientists, using quantitative methodologies in the hopes of establishing a genuinely predictive science (Haskell 1977; Vidich and Lyman 1985; Bannister 1987; Giddens 1987; Ross 1991). These sociologists have frequently been interested in offering the findings of social research to political leaders with the intention that research results will be used to formulate public policy (Halliday and Janowitz 1992).

Other sociologists emphasize interpretation rather than prediction (Brown 1989; Wolfe 1993). These sociologists take into account the conceptual undergirdings of the people they are investigating, employing a variety of qualitative methods. Some of their work, such as the best writing produced by ethnographers, bears a distinct affinity with literature or narrative history (Nisbet 1976; Lepenies 1988; Brown 1989). Thus, it is fair to say that, from this perspective, sociology is a social science with one foot in the humanities.

The first flowering of a science of society occurred during a period of dramatic social change. The founders of the discipline lived in what is customarily referred to as the "age of revolution," the period during which economic and political change swept first across Europe and North America and then throughout the globe. Political revolutions produced a new democratic sensibility and, with it, an awareness of what it meant to be a citizen. The Industrial Revolution spelled the end of the feudal era and the triumph of capitalist market economies. The age of revolution, however, spilled over into other areas of life: science, art, literature, religion, social institutions, and human relations (Hobsbawm 1962).

The founders of the sociological enterprise sought to make sense of this transition from one social order to another while living through it. In this undertaking, they are no different from contemporary sociologists or, for that matter, you and me. We are all attempting to understand the dynamics of present-day trends and, in so doing, perhaps glimpse what the future holds.

Tools for Understanding Social Trends

Sociologists seek to explain why, how, and in what circumstances certain phenomena do or do not occur. For this task, they use tools called theories. Theories are simply mental constructs; they are assemblages of words. Whether we are aware of it or not, we all use theories in everyday life. Everyday theories and sociological theories, however, are different. Everyday theory is formulated off-the-cuff as we go about our daily lives. This type of theory is often formulated only implicitly and is taken for granted rather than subjected to critical questioning. We do not try to scientifically determine whether our theory holds up in all circumstances. In contrast, sociological theory strives (a) to be as explicit as possible, (b) to avoid logical contradictions or absurdities, and (c) to ascertain whether the ideas square with empirical reality. Sociological theories are held only provisionally, pending evidence that proves them right or wrong, and are viewed with a critical eye (Wolfe 1996).

One becomes a social theorist when something is askew in the realm of knowledge, when current explanations are perceived to fail, or when existing theories appear to be inadequate tools in the task of comprehension. Theoretical work is simply an attempt to explain, and thus to assist in understanding, the social world. Sociology's central concern is to view societies at any particular point in their history in terms of the distinctive structures and processes that shape their character at that moment. These were the concerns of the four classic sociologists whose ideas are discussed in this book. They witnessed social change that could not be explained by existing theories and set out to find workable explanations.

For such inquiry, social theorists rely on others' ideas, which provide the basis for common understanding and produce a genuinely collective enterprise. In other words, theories are constructed by individuals operating within a community of scholars, including not only their contemporaries but also theorists from the past. Marx, Weber, Durkheim, and Simmel built their theories on the thought of their predecessors and were continually influenced by the theories of their contemporaries.

Similarly, as we today try to understand the major trends of our time, we need to take into account industrial society, democracy, individualism, and modernity—key ideas articulated initially in the 19th century and continually developed and reshaped throughout the 20th century. We need to be knowledgeable about the past, including past efforts at understanding, if we are to comprehend the present (Seidman 1983; Sztompka 1993). We can profit greatly by considering the four key ideas discussed in this book, building on the insights of generations past and present who wanted to understand their own societies and who shaped the tools of inquiry to assist in that task. At the same time, in the early years of the 21st century, we are increasingly aware of the varied impacts of globalization. As Chapter 6 illustrates, this complex and contested phenomenon is forcing us to reconfigure our key ideas in significant ways. Our task is to build on the sociological tradition to assist us in making sense of the profound changes that will confront us in the future.

2

Industrial Society

From the Satanic Mills to the Digital Age

Imagine a world without automobiles, telephones, microwave ovens, personal computers, the Internet, and the numerous other technological inventions that have become an integral part of our everyday lives. A little reflection will make you realize how dramatically different such a world would be and may lead you to wonder how we got to where we are today. How do we account for the machine age and, recently, what has popularly been referred to as the "information age"? These are the central questions addressed in this chapter.

During the past two centuries, a world historical process has been under way that has succeeded in transforming the entire globe. We refer to this process as industrialization and the type of societies that are produced by this process as industrial societies. Not only were early industrial societies markedly different from the preindustrial societies they replaced, contemporary industrial societies are considerably different from industrial societies of the past. Just as the steam engine and the organization of work in factories—seen by critics as "satanic mills"—signaled a decisive break with the past, so today we are witnessing a profound transformation of industrial society brought about by computers and related information technologies. Industrial society has proven to be remarkably dynamic and ever-changing, keeping sociologists busy trying to understand those changes.

In this chapter, we first discuss the work of Karl Marx, the preeminent theorist of the formative period of the industrial age. His ideas inspired revolutionary theorists long after his death, critics of society who found in his thought a vision of a more cooperative and egalitarian society. We next discuss some of the most consequential of these Marxist theoreticians, after which we turn to three highly influential thinkers—Joseph Schumpeter, Thorstein Veblen, and C. Wright Mills—who, although they were not Marxists, discovered that it was important to take Marx's ideas seriously even though they disagreed with him. After discussing these theorists, who analyzed capitalist industrial society as it evolved during the first half of the 20th century, we conclude the chapter by examining Daniel Bell's claim that in recent decades we have entered into a new type of society that he has described as postindustrial.

The Industrial Revolution

Beginning primarily in one nation—Great Britain—the Industrial Revolution constituted one of the turning points in world history, marking the transition from predominantly agricultural economies to industrial economies. As part of this great transformation, a profound demographic shift took place as ever-increasing numbers of rural dwellers moved to urban areas in search of employment (Ashton 1948; Hobsbawm 1969).

The Industrial Revolution was made possible by the rapid expansion in the use of machine technology in economic production. Thus, during the second half of the 18th century, the British textile industry, the emblematic industry in this initial stage of industrialization, was transformed by innovations in spinning machines, particularly James Hargreaves's spinning jenny (patented in 1770), and in weaving machines, especially John Kay's introduction of the flying shuttle in 1733.

Industrialization, however, was shaped only in part by technological developments. It was also defined in terms of new ways of organizing manufacturing operations and new modes of social control. Thus, industrialization gave birth to the factory, taking workers out of their homes and into a setting in which the owners of industry could institute administrative policies that would maximize productivity. The factory would replace domestic cottage industries because the work process would be increasingly characterized by rationalizing strategies designed to enhance calculability, efficiency, and control.

A key symbol of rationalization was the introduction of the clock into the work process. Whereas in the past, work schedules and the pace of work were influenced by nature and custom, this would no longer be the case. Instead of determining when and how to work based on the weather or season, or tolerating the continued participation in numerous tradition-based holidays (e.g., "St. Monday" was an unofficial way of extending the weekend by a day), the industrial order demanded a routinization of work, which, as labor historian E. J. Hobsbawm (1969) noted, workers experienced as the "tyranny of the clock" (p. 85).

New modes of surveillance and control were part and parcel of a new configuration of social classes and social relations. Clearly, there were those who were the beneficiaries of industrialization, whereas others were losers. The major beneficiaries were the owners of industrial enterprises and the financiers who provided the capital for business ventures. This era witnessed the expansion of the middle class in general, and the standard of living of members of this class improved considerably.

Among the losers were the land-owning aristocracy, who did not sink into oblivion but in the political struggles of the era saw their dominance erode. Their declining political power vis-à-vis the industrialists was most evident in the agitation regarding the Corn Laws. These were a series of laws that had been passed by Parliament from the 1400s to the early 1800s to protect the interests of the landlords by controlling the price of grains. They were seen by the growing middle class, with its livelihood determined by industry, as detrimental to its interests because they kept the cost of food higher than would be the case in the free market. After a long and protracted battle, the landlords lost the political campaign as the Corn Laws were repealed in 1846. This marked a decisive shift from a primarily agrarian economy to one based on industrial capitalism.

The economic viability of artisans and journeymen was undermined by industrialization. This was vividly seen in the case of the Luddites, a loosely bound group of displaced textile workers who in the second decade of the 19th century, lacking legitimate channels of political redress, undertook a secretive campaign of destroying the machines that were undermining their economic well-being. These machine breakers clearly perceived that they were not the beneficiaries of industrial change. The entrepreneurs who were generating substantial profits and the middle-class consumers who could count on cheaper goods benefited by economic change, but they did so at the expense of the Luddites.

The birth of sociology occurred during this epoch, as intellectuals sought to make sense of the dramatic changes that were sweeping across Western Europe. Among the progenitors of modern sociology—including Henri Saint-Simon, Auguste Comte, and Herbert Spencer—one person stands out for the singularly far-reaching impact his thought would have on subsequent efforts to grapple with industrial society: Karl Marx.

Karl Marx: The Permanent Exile

The seventeen mourners at Karl Marx's funeral could hardly have predicted the subsequent role his ideas would have in the 20th century. According to Marx's recent biographer, Francis Wheen (1999), "Not since Jesus Christ has an obscure pauper inspired such global devotion—or been so calamitously misinterpreted" (p. 1). Another biographer, Vincent Barnett (2009), contends that Marx "is probably the most influential philosopher, historian, and social theorist of modern times" (p. 1). This was not evident during his lifetime. Indeed, when Marx died in 1883, his ideas were just beginning to take on a life of their own. Marx's burial plot in London's Highgate Cemetery—the resting place for many famous literary, intellectual, and social figures of the 19th century—highlights some interesting features of his life and his subsequent reputation after his death (Figure 2.1). First, Marx is buried in England and not in Germany—the land of his birth—despite the fact that Marx, like many immigrants, appears to have lived on the margins during his 34 years in England. Thus, Marx remains in death what he was in life: a permanent exile (Derrida 1994; Manuel 1995).

Second, Marx's grave site is large and well maintained more than a century after his death. Visitors today will find freshly cut flowers on the ground next to the monumental bust of Marx. This is in stark contrast to the grave of Herbert Spencer directly across the path from Marx's. This important early British sociologist, who was the major exponent of Social Darwinism, appears to be all but forgotten because his marker is virtually hidden by the vines that have engulfed it. This, despite the fact that he was famous during his lifetime, having been, for example, wined and dined at New York's Delmonico' by prominent American business elites during his sole visit to the United States. Indeed, sociologist of science Steven Shapin (2007) contends that "Spencer was, arguably, the single most influential systematic thinker of the nineteenth century, but his influence . . . was short-lived" (p. 75). As a reflection of this obscuring of his name, only a few decades after Spencer's death, the social theorist Talcott Parsons (1937)

Figure 2.1 Marx's Grave at Highgate Cemetery

began his first book with the rhetorical question, "Who now reads Spencer?" (p. 3). Unlike Spencer, not only is Marx's work read, but most major academic bookstores have on display a large body of recent commentary devoted to Marx and the ideas he spawned.

Indeed, Marx's reputation grew considerably after his death. When he was first buried, his grave was located at the bottom of a hill. Subsequently, the family plot was relocated to higher ground, which was considered to be a more prestigious part of the cemetery. In effect, Marx experienced upward social mobility after death—a testament to the subsequent reception of his life's work.

With the dismantling of communism in Eastern Europe and the collapse of the Soviet Union in 1991, it has become commonplace for commentators to claim that ideas that originated with Karl Marx, the key 19th-century social theorist of revolutionary change, should also be consigned to the dustbin of history. At the same time, sociologists continue to view Marx as one of the important progenitors of contemporary social thought, and his work continues to be widely read (Wolff 2002). For some, Marx's thought led inevitably to the horrors of the totalitarian regimes of the 20th century: Stalin's reign of terror in the Soviet Union, Mao's in China, Pol Pot's in Cambodia, and numerous others. For others, Marx was a humanist who was committed to combating economic exploitation and promoting the virtues of democracy and equality—a thinker whose ideas were an invaluable contribution to the establishment of the welfare state in Western European democracies (Manuel 1995).

Marx's legacy is, in short, ambiguous and controversial. In fact, near the end of his life, Marx became aware of widely divergent interpretations of his work at the hands of those who called themselves Marxists. At one point, he protested what he considered to be misinterpretations of his ideas by some followers, stating bluntly that if these were accurate representations of "Marxist" ideas, then "I for one am not a Marxist" (Manuel 1995:vii).

Although this book will not attempt to unravel the Marxian legacy with an eye to discovering the "real" Marx—a probably futile task—I shall try to untangle some of the complexity and ambiguity of his thought in an effort to indicate why it is that I think Marx is the first great theorist of industrial society. To begin this task, it is important to understand Marx's intellectual trajectory in terms of his biography, locating the three main strands of his thought—philosophy, politics, and economics—in relation to the nations in which they originated. In undertaking such a task, it is important to remember that Marx was not always consistent and what he wrote was often open to varied interpretations. It's also useful to be reminded, as the eminent philosopher Leszek Kolakowski (2008) has written, that Marx's thought was shaped by his historical context and if he had lived much longer than he actually did "he would have had to alter his views in ways that we have no way of conjecturing" (p. 6).

The Intellectual Context of Marx's Ideas

Born in 1818 in Trier, in Germany's Rhineland, Marx was a member of a comfortable middle-class Jewish household. Although he could trace a number of rabbinical ancestors from both his maternal and his paternal families, Marx's father was a rather comfortable lawyer who converted to Christianity not out of religious conviction but to circumvent a ban that prohibited Jews from practicing the law. Unlike his son, Heinrich was gifted at the art of compromise and actively sought out means of accommodation with those in power. The result was that, despite the role of anti-Semitism in German society, he had a successful and esteemed career (McLellan 1975:1–2; Padover 1978:1–20).

Marx was proud of his father, and as a student, he planned to follow in his father's footsteps. After one year as a law student at Bonn University, however, characterized by diligence in the classroom and boisterousness outside (e.g., his parents were dismayed by his drinking and his arrest for disorderly conduct), he transferred to Berlin University, where, abandoning legal studies, he turned to philosophy. In giving up the idea of becoming a lawyer, he also appears to have left behind his family and the life they envisioned for him. Wheen (1999) reports that when his father died in 1838, Marx "did not attend the funeral. The journey from Berlin would be too long, he explained, and he had more important things to do" (p. 30).

This transition marked the beginning of the first major stage in Marx's intellectual development because it was in his native Germany that Marx developed a philosophic orientation that would inform his thinking throughout his life. He immersed himself in the philosophy of G. W. F. Hegel, becoming associated with a philosophic movement known as the Young Hegelians, whose key figures included David Friedrich Strauss, Bruno Bauer, and Moses Hess. These young philosophers were united in their critical attitude toward German politics and in their desire to infuse philosophy with political significance. Thus, Marx's turn toward Hegel was simultaneously a turn toward radical leftist politics (Berlin 1963:62–81; Padover 1978:77–81).

After completing his doctorate in philosophy, Marx was unable to obtain an academic appointment, mainly because of his critical stance toward the political establishment. Thus, he turned to journalism, writing for the left-wing paper *Rheinische Zeitung* in 1842 and 1843. The latter year marked a major turning point for him because he both married Jenny von Westphalen and, with her, moved to Paris after the authorities shut down the newspaper (Padover 1978:138–160).

Owing to the relatively tolerant atmosphere during the rule of Louis Philippe, Paris was a mecca for dissident intellectuals from throughout Europe, and Marx found in Parisian café society an inviting and stimulating cadre of social critics and apostles of revolutionary change. What was significant about his sojourn in France was that in this nation that had experienced a major political revolution a half century earlier, his political thought moved in new directions. It was shaped particularly by the various currents of socialist thought associated with such diverse thinkers as Henri Saint-Simon, Charles Fourier, Louis Blanc, and Pierre Joseph Proudhon (Berlin 1963:82–121; Padover 1978:172–199).

Marx's own ideas emerged in reaction to these and other thinkers, whose work was subjected to critical—and often ruthless—scrutiny. Thus, in response to Proudhon's "The Philosophy of Poverty" (1969), Marx wrote a scathing book-length rebuttal sarcastically titled *The Poverty of Philosophy* (Marx [1847] 1963). Marx was especially critical of what he considered to be utopian socialism and of anything that smacked of moralistic appeals. Although Marx's own work can be read as a moral indictment of the existing socioeconomic order—and at times his writing style is reminiscent of that of the Old Testament prophets—he nonetheless wanted his work to be viewed as rigorously rational and scientific (actually, the desire to create a scientific understanding of capitalism would become more overt later in his life).

It was in Paris that he met his friend and future collaborator, Friedrich Engels. Engels, the son of a wealthy industrialist and the sometime manager of his father's factory in Manchester, was instrumental in Marx's turn toward socialism—or communism. Although Marx's acerbic attacks on others made him many enemies, Engels would remain an intellectual ally—and financial benefactor—throughout the remainder of Marx's life. In the year prior to the aborted revolutionary upheavals of 1848, Marx and Engels coauthored their famous economic prognosis and call to arms, *The Communist Manifesto* ([1848] 1967).

A changing political climate in France made it necessary for Marx to remain on the move. He resided for short intervals in Brussels and Cologne, returning briefly to Paris. In the end, however, he departed the continent in 1849 for London, where he remained for the rest of his life.

If Germany had shaped his philosophic orientation and France his initial understanding of socialism, England would be the place where his economic thinking would come to fruition. It is not that he had ignored economics prior to his arrival in London. To the contrary, Marx had laid out the contours of his thinking on economic matters early on in France in a series of essays that were not published until after his death and that are known today as the *Economic and Philosophic Manuscripts of 1844* (1971). Nonetheless, it is not surprising that in the cradle of the Industrial Revolution his understanding of the underlying economic character of contemporary industrial society would deepen, resulting in *The Grundrisse* ([1857/1858] 1974) and *Theories of Surplus Value* ([1862/1863] 1963, [1862/1863] 1968) and culminating in his magisterial multivolume work, *Capital* ([1867] 1967).

The early London years were difficult for Marx's family. The only income Marx received during this time was for articles he wrote on European affairs for the American radical newspaper *The New York Daily Tribune*. He considered such work to be at best a nuisance, distracting him from his real labors, which involved mastering the thought of British political economists, such as Adam Smith, Thomas Malthus, and David Ricardo, and becoming intimately familiar with the workings of industrial capitalism. Typically,

Marx would be found daily in the reading room of the British Museum while his family languished in a small apartment in Soho.

For years, the family lived in abject poverty, a condition relieved periodically by financial support from Engels. One of the consequences of this impoverished state was that the entire family was frequently ill, Marx included. Three of his children died young, two of them only a year after they were born (Barnett 2009:70). This took a heavy psychological toll on Marx and his wife, but nonetheless he persisted in his relentless intellectual endeavors rather than attempting to find employment that would alleviate the family's economic distress (Berlin 1963:180–219).

In summary, despite his early involvement in London with a secret society known as the Communist League, Marx primarily lived the life of a scholar and not that of a revolutionary political organizer (Barnett 2009:53). He wrote about economic and political matters but remained aloof from activists for well over a decade. This changed by 1864, when he undertook an instrumental role in the foundation of the working-class movement known as the First International. Nonetheless, it is for his ideas and not his actions that he is best remembered. During his last years, his reputation grew. When his mother died, his inheritance made it possible to move to a pleasant middle-class home. Appropriately, he died not on the barricades but in his favorite armchair (Wheen 1999:381).

The Analyst of Capitalist Industrial Society

The distinctiveness of Marx's thought is due to the way in which he wove the disparate strands of Hegelian philosophy, socialist political theory, and economic thought into a relatively coherent synthesis that was at once an analysis and a critique of capitalist industrial society. Crucial to appreciating Marx's thought is an awareness of its emphasis on understanding the unique dynamics of capitalism rather than understanding industrial society in general. Moreover, what makes it distinctive is its unique combination of an aspiration to be rigorously scientific while at the same time offering both a powerful moral critique and a notion of what human development might look like in a world freed from capitalism.

Marx's goals were twofold. First, he sought to provide a scientific—rather than a moralistic or philosophical—account of the underlying dynamics of capitalism. This aspiration to the status of scientific inquiry was evident, for instance, when he attempted to dedicate Volume 2 of *Capital* (Marx [1867] 1967) to Charles Darwin, who politely declined the offer (Padover 1978:363–364). Second, Marx sought to articulate what he viewed as a revolutionary theory or, in other words, a theory that would assist in the radical transformation of society. He thought that by making it possible to adequately comprehend capitalism, his theory would provide the conceptual tools for overcoming it—for freeing industrial society from the presumed impediments imposed on it by the peculiar nature of capitalism. In Marxian terminology, he wanted to translate theory into praxis.

Marx was a product of the Enlightenment, embracing its call to replace faith by reason and religion by science. He was convinced that social relations should be guided by reason rather than by the blind force of tradition. Far from harboring a romantic yearning for the past, Marx looked to the future. From his early work to his most mature, as the inheritor of Hegel's progressive philosophy of history, Marx was convinced that capitalism was linked to the future. Insofar as this was the case, it had a progressive role to play in human history. Although capitalism would establish the preconditions for a postscarcity society in which economic exploitation ceased, it would become an impediment to the realization of such a society. Thus, capitalism was necessary, but after its full development it needed to yield to a new form of industrial society, which Marx variously called socialism or communism.

Capitalism and Exploitation

Long before Marx's extended excursions into political economy at the British Museum, he was convinced of capitalism's problematic character, which is rooted in the fact that capitalism is an economic system based on private property. Capitalism, in Marx's view, is a type of industrial society characterized by the private ownership of the "means of production"—by which he meant the machines, factories, raw materials, and finished products that comprise the entire economic ensemble. Ownership is in the hands of one social class—the capitalist, or bourgeoisie.

In his early writings, Marx posed the problem of capitalism in terms of alienation rather than exploitation. Marx's thought was shaped by a philosophical anthropology that viewed humans as active agents in the creation of their world and their place in it. In his view, unfettered labor is an essential means by which humans come to realize their individual potentials while simultaneously establishing an organic connectedness with the natural world and with others (Marx 1964; Mészáros 1970).

Alienation does not describe the human condition at all times, but it is a specifically historical phenomenon that emerges out of what Marx considered to be the inherent contradictions of capitalism. These contradictions are manifest in the class divisions that emerge in this economic system—most important, in the relationship between private property and its capitalist owners against wage labor and the industrial working class.

For Marx, according to Shlomo Avineri (1968), "The most obvious phenomenal expression of alienation is the worker's inability in capitalist society to own the product of his work" (p. 106). By selling their labor for wages, workers simultaneously lose connection with the object of labor and become objects themselves. Workers are devalued to the level of a commodity—a "thing"—through the process Marx describes as "universal salability." They become alienated from the objects created by their creative activity as those products are expropriated by their employers, the capitalist owners of industrial enterprises. Marx (1964) articulated this philosophically in his essay "Alienated Labor":

> This fact simply implies that the object produced by labor, its product, now stands opposed to it as an alien being, as a power independent of the producer. The product of labor is labor which has been embodied in an object and turned into a physical thing; this product is an objectification of labor. . . . The performance of work appears in the sphere of political economy as a vitiation of the worker, objectification as a loss and a servitude to the object, and appropriation as alienation. (p. 122)

Far from realizing themselves through their labor, from fulfilling essential human needs through productive activity, workers experience labor as a forced rather than a voluntary activity. As a result of the institution of wage labor, workers' activities are no longer the result of their own autonomous decisions. Work becomes an alien activity, one that no longer serves the needs of *homo faber* (i.e., the human "maker" or self-creator) but can only be a means for satisfying others' needs. Marx (1964) concluded,

> We arrive at the result that man (the worker) feels himself to be freely active only in his animal functions—eating, drinking, and procreating, or at most also in his dwelling and in personal adornment—while in his human functions he is reduced to an animal. The animal becomes human and the human becomes animal. (p. 125)

At approximately the same time Marx was composing this philosophic critique of private property in capitalism, his future collaborator, Engels, was writing what would become a classic sociological documentary, *The Condition of the Working Class in England* ([1844] 1968). Engels vividly described the negative impact of rapid industrialization on cities such as Manchester, portraying the foul pollutants emanating from factories, the squalor of overcrowding, and the social problems generated by impoverishment. In the bleak industrial landscape he described, human relations were seen as distorted and pathological. People increasingly became self-seeking, isolated, and brutally indifferent to the suffering of others. In short, this empirical account dovetails with the philosophical critique proffered by Marx.

Although Marx never repudiated this earlier, philosophical criticism of capitalism, situated at the center of his later and more explicitly economic work was the concept of exploitation rather than the basic theme of the fragmentary *Economic and Philosophical Manuscripts* (1971)—alienation (Althusser 1970; Seigel 1978; Elster 1986). In his later writings, which culminated in *Capital* ([1867] 1967), Marx attempted to prove that capitalism necessarily exploited one social class in the interests of another.

Marx's economic theory is complex and at times convoluted, but central to it is the understanding that capitalism is driven by the quest for profits. Capitalists invest money not to produce something of use value—although they do produce useful goods—but to make more money. Indeed, capitalists who fail to realize a profit are driven out of the market. Marx considered the capitalists' economic motives to be unique in this regard.

To illustrate the contrast, in Volume 1 of *Capital* ([1867] 1967:78), Marx used the example of a weaver who produces linen and wants to obtain a Bible. How is this acquisition accomplished? Quite simply, the weaver sells his linen for money, which is then used to purchase a Bible. Marx inherited what was known as the labor theory of value from British political economists such as Adam Smith and David Ricardo (a theory few economists embrace today). This theory held that the value of a commodity is derived from the labor invested in it. Value is not created by machines, or what Marx called *fixed capital;* it is solely determined by the socially necessary labor time required to produce the commodity. Money, in the case of the weaver, is a medium of exchange that is used as a measure of the value of each of the commodities involved in the exchange. Thus, the transaction can be depicted as follows: C-M-C.

Capitalists, Marx argued, do not operate in this way. They succeed insofar as they end up with more money (i.e., not a Bible) than they originally invested. Thus, the basic formula for capitalism is M-C-M′, where M′ is greater than M. How does this occur? Classical economics contends that profit comes at the point of exchange in the marketplace. In other words, the capitalist produces a commodity at a certain cost and sells it at a price in excess of that cost. The difference constitutes the source of profit.

Marx disputed this understanding of the origin of profit by invoking the labor theory of value. He contended that it is not the capitalist but, rather, the worker who creates the commodity and thus who creates value. The worker produces value but by being a wage laborer has lost control of the fruits of labor. It is not the exchange between the capitalist and the consumer that creates profit but, rather, the nature of the exchange that transpires between the capitalist and the worker.

Classical economists such as Adam Smith presupposed that this exchange was an equitable one. The employer obtained the worker's labor power in exchange for wages. Marx argued that for capitalism to function, the exchange necessarily had to be unequal because the capitalist actually got more in the bargain than the worker. Beginning with *The Grundrisse* ([1857/1858] 1974) and developed considerably in Volume 1 of *Capital* ([1867] 1967), Marx saw in this difference the source of what would become the linchpin of a distinctively Marxist economics: surplus value (for useful summaries of the significance of this idea, see Giddens 1971:46–52; Seigel 1978:309–312).

Surplus value, the ultimate source of profit, is calculated as the ratio of what Marx termed necessary labor time and surplus labor time. We need not discuss the highly abstract argument Marx advanced on behalf of this concept to understand the singular importance of surplus value, which, according to Barnett (2009), Marx thought was "his most important discovery" (p. 161). It is, in the first place, intended to be a measure of what he refers to as the "rate of exploitation" (Marx [1867] 1967:171). Suffice it to say that the following powerful image adequately summarizes his view of the inherent relationship between the capitalist and the worker: "Vampire-like, [the capitalist] only lives by sucking living labor, and lives the more, the more labor it sucks" (p. 257; see Francis Wheen's 2008 "biography" of *Das Kapital* for an analysis of the "Gothic novel" elements of Marx's classic work). Moreover, as he asserted in Volume 3 of *Capital* (p. 47), the exploitation of workers is the ultimate source of profit (although he does not totally discount the role of consumer demand in shaping prices). Note that most economists today have rejected the labor theory of value. However, this does not necessarily undermine Marx's characterization of capitalism as exploitative. Erik Olin Wright (2000) makes a persuasive case that exploitation—the key to a distinctly Marxist class analysis—is not dependent on the labor theory of value and, in fact, can be better understood if the concept is abandoned.

Crisis Tendencies of Capitalism

Marx thought that he had not only unearthed the dynamics of capitalism, exposing the fact that it is built on the systematic exploitation of one class in the interests of another, but also found in these dynamics the source of the limitations of a capitalist economy. Because capitalists compete with other capitalists, they are forced to constantly upgrade the means of production. Stated simply, this competition among capitalists results in perpetual technological innovation. This accounts for the incredible productivity of capitalism, but it also creates a crucial problem in relation to the extraction of surplus value and thus profit (Marx [1867] 1967, 1974).

Marx identified the problem by distinguishing between two types of capital: variable and constant. Variable capital was that portion of investment that went into the acquisition of labor power. Constant capital referred to the investments in machines and raw materials. Over time, technological innovations resulted in an increase in constant capital and a decrease in variable capital as machines came to play a greater role in production while workers played a smaller role. At a relatively early stage in industrial development, he was describing what would become known in the 20th century as automation. What made Marx's assessment of this process unique was that he saw this change as having an adverse impact on workers who were being displaced by machines as well as on the ability of capitalists to generate profits.

The reason for this, recall, is that Marx saw profit as being made possible by the extraction of surplus value. Because surplus value does not derive from machines, but rather only from labor, to the extent that labor becomes a small part of the production equation, the more difficult it becomes for the capitalist to realize profit. Built into this economic system is a tendency for the rate of profit to fall. Capitalists are forced to contend with this tendency, and they do so by attempting to find ways to enhance the rate of exploitation, including slashing wages, increasing the hours of the work day without increasing wages, and speeding up the pace of work. Needless to say, these efforts serve to intensify the conflict between capitalists and laborers.

A Theory of Revolutionary Change

Throughout his career, Marx mounted a frontal assault on capitalism, accusing it of causing alienation, being based on exploitation, and generating crisis tendencies that result in the impoverishment of vast sectors of the population. Not surprisingly, he was intent on finding a way to eliminate capitalism by replacing it with an economic system that would overcome its destructive features.

Indeed, one cannot appreciate Marxian social theory unless one recognizes that it constitutes a fusion of an existential ("what is") dimension and a normative ("what ought to be") dimension. Marx, especially in his mature writings, tended to obscure the latter dimension by attempting to provide a scientific analysis while distancing himself from a moralistic critique. Nonetheless, like the economists sympathetic to capitalism, whose thought he both appropriated and challenged, Marx was at once a social theorist and a moral philosopher (McCloskey 1994).

Marx was convinced that if industrial society was to become nonexploitative, it would necessarily need to be radically transformed into another economic system, which he referred to either as socialism or communism. Although Marx was not very clear about what this kind of economic system would look like, the key difference between it and capitalism is that it would be a classless society. In other words, class divisions would be eradicated in socialism. Contrary to a common misconception of Marxian thought, he did not think that all people would become equals by being reduced to the lowest common denominator.

He also did not think that socialism would mark the end of all conflict. History would not come to a screeching halt, and the world would not become a utopia or paradise. The social order would be unique, however, insofar as all people would be, for the first time in history, afforded the opportunity to develop their full potential, and a society of scarcity would be replaced by one of abundance.

Social Classes

Central to comprehending Marx's articulation of a theory of revolutionary change is an appreciation of the crucial role of social classes. Indeed, in his view, class divisions constitute the most essential divisions in capitalist society just as in other economic systems. In various works, Marx discussed the importance of class divisions in what he referred to as the Asiatic, ancient, and feudal modes of production (Marx [1857/1858] 1965). Marx accorded a privileged role to social classes, and in so doing he downplayed the significance of other key social divisions, such as gender or race and ethnicity.

Despite the centrality accorded to social classes, it is somewhat surprising that Marx failed to provide a systematic analysis of the entire range of social classes that were to be found in modern capitalism. He began to address the matter in the final chapter of Volume 3 of *Capital* ([1867] 1967:885), but because he died before completing it, the passage remains a fragment. For this reason, Marx's discussions of social classes in capitalism varied considerably. Thus, in *Class Struggles in France* ([1895] 1970), he depicted subdivisions within classes, seen, for example, in his discussion of the conflict between industrial and financial capitalists. In *The Communist Manifesto* (Marx and Engels [1848] 1967), he enumerated four classes, whereas in "The Eighteenth Brumaire of Louis Bonaparte" ([1852] 1996), his list expanded to include the aristocracy of finance, the industrial bourgeoisie, the middle class, the petit bourgeoisie, the lumpenproletariat, the intellectual lights, the clergy, the rural population, and the proletariat. Elsewhere throughout his writings, he cited a long list of classes, including the feudal nobility, the bourgeoisie, the petit bourgeoisie, the upper and middle peasantry, the free lower peasantry, the slave peasantry, the agricultural laborers, and the industrial proletariat.

What is clear from this is that Marx believed that there were many different classes existing in capitalist economies without being able to consistently specify them. At the same time, in articulating the principal basis of conflict and the primary cause of social change, he examined the class character of capitalism in essentially dichotomous terms. Thus, in the famous introductory passage of *The Communist Manifesto*, which introduced the discussion of the respective positions and roles of the bourgeoisie and the proletariat, Marx and Engels ([1848] 1967) wrote,

> The history of all hitherto existing society is the history of class struggles. Free man and slave, patrician and plebeian, lord and serf, guild master and journeyman, in a word, oppressor and oppressed, stood in constant opposition to one another, carried on an uninterrupted, now hidden, now open fight, a fight that each time ended either in the revolutionary reconstitution of society at large or in the common ruin of the contending classes. (pp. 13–14)

Marx thought that although there were many classes in any particular mode of production, two were always most important (Table 2.1): the dominant or hegemonic economic class and the oppressed class that most directly and immediately confronts the dominant class. Built into the system is the potential for conflict between these two central classes. The idea of the clash of warring interests takes on a uniquely Marxist hue insofar as it is indebted to the Hegelian dialectic. The idea of the dialectic involves the assumption that although history moves in a directional, progressive way, it does so through conflict between competing forces (Bernstein 1972:21). Marx attempted to apply this concept concretely to class relations, thereby treating class conflict as the main source of social change.

Table 2.1 Main Classes in Marxist Theory

Bourgeoisie	Owners of the capitalist "means of production"
Proletariat	Working class, wage laborers
Petit bourgeoisie	Small shopkeepers, tradespersons
Landowners	Owners of agricultural lands
Peasants	Landless agrarian laborers
Lumpenproletariat	Structurally unemployed

The Proletariat as Agent of Social Change

In capitalism, the proletariat is construed both as the victim of exploitation and as the agent of historical change. The proletariat has a mission, and this mission provides the answer to the question regarding how it was possible to move from capitalism to socialism. The transition is possible, according to Marx, only if the members of the industrial working class achieve class consciousness, which involves a heightened understanding of their situation due to their class location and a realization that they can attempt to remedy their oppressed condition only by collective action. This action would, in most instances, entail armed insurrections because the capitalist class would likely attempt to hang on to power. In those countries in which workers had the right to vote, however, the transition to socialism might be achieved peacefully at the ballot box.

A classless socialist society would overcome the inequalities and injustices inherent in capitalism and would make the benefits brought about by industrialization available to all. In short, Marx was enthusiastic about industrial society's potential for improving the material conditions of people and establishing the context for individuals to create lives that are richly meaningful and rewarding.

Capitalism plays a key role in making this possible. Although seeking to transcend the limitations of capitalism, Marx nonetheless thought that it was a force of progress. Indeed, he depicted capitalism as the most dynamic economic system that had ever existed. The reason for this, as we have seen, is that to survive in the competitive market, capitalists are compelled to constantly revolutionize the instruments of production (Elster 1986:70–74).

Thus, in *The Communist Manifesto* (Marx and Engels [1848] 1967), capitalism is praised rather than being roundly condemned. The bourgeoisie are described as being, in their own way, revolutionary. They have served to dramatically improve communication and transportation networks. They have undermined parochialism by making the world more cosmopolitan. They have challenged the traditions that, out of sheer habit, have ruled people's lives. The bourgeois worldview strips away the mysteries of religious beliefs and replaces them with the insights of reason. The bourgeois class has stimulated scientific and technological changes: the result being that in its short existence this class has "accomplished wonders far surpassing Egyptian pyramids, Roman aqueducts, and Gothic cathedrals" (Marx and Engels [1848] 1967:19; for a perceptive discussion of this passage, see Berman 1982).

The previous passage suggests that Marx viewed the full development of capitalism as a prerequisite for the emergence of socialism. It creates the potential for a society of abundance, but because of the way that capitalism necessarily skews the distribution of wealth, the hegemonic class benefits from this generation of wealth at the expense of others.

When a class-conscious and organized proletariat challenges the domination of capitalism, it does so as a universal class. As with his understanding of the dialectical character of historical progress, Marx derived this notion from Hegel. A universal class is one that acts in the interests of society as a whole. Hegel saw the state bureaucracy as the universal class insofar as it was deemed to be capable of mediating and reconciling differences among competing interests and classes, thereby promoting the common good. Marx disputed this view of the state bureaucracy, which he saw as operating to preserve and enhance dominant economic interests (Giddens 1971:236–237; Seigel 1978:103–106).

According to Marx, what was distinctive about the proletariat, and thus made it a genuinely universal class, was the fact that it was the one class with no interest in preserving itself as a class. When the proletariat acts in its own self-interest, it is not to strengthen its position in capitalist society but to eliminate itself as a class by destroying the socially antagonistic class relations that characterize capitalism. As the late French philosopher Jean-Paul Sartre (1976) noted, this entailed "negation of the negation." If the proletariat succeeds in this effort, it creates the basis for a classless society. Because he thought revolutionary change was possible, Marx proved to be remarkably optimistic about the future and continued throughout his life to be an enthusiastic supporter of a vision of industrial society liberated from class divisions. Like Moses, however, Marx did not live to see the Promised Land.

Marxism After Marx

The history of Marxist thought after Marx's death is long and convoluted (Anderson 1976; Gouldner 1980). It also reveals the extent of its appeal. Tony Judt (2008) was certainly correct when he wrote that the "combination of economic description, moral prescription, and political predication proved intensely seductive—and serviceable." Moreover, that history has illustrated "the sheer versatility of his theories when invoked by others to justify the political systems to which they gave rise" (p. 133). Despite the rise of militant labor organizations during the latter part of the 19th century in the most developed industrial nations—Britain, France, Germany, the United States, and other Western states—a revolutionary overthrow of capitalism did not take place in any of them. Rather, the first successful Marxist-inspired revolution occurred in Russia, which at the time had only begun to industrialize and lacked the highly class-conscious proletariat that Marx saw as essential for radical change to occur. In other words, revolution occurred in a country that had not witnessed the flowering of capitalist development and the establishment of an industrial base that would make socialism viable by establishing the preconditions for economic abundance.

Nonetheless, the hope of Marxist theoreticians and activists, including such luminaries as Vladimir Ilyich Lenin, Leon Trotsky, Rosa Luxemburg, Antonio Gramsci, and Georg Lukács, was that this weak link in the capitalist chain would prove to be the beginning of the end for capitalism because revolutionary struggles, inspired by the Russian Revolution, would emerge in the more advanced capitalist countries. This did not prove to be the case because these nations turned out to be the ones that were most immune to the appeals of communism.

The result was that until the success of the Chinese Revolution, approximately three decades later, the Soviet Union stood alone. After the death of Lenin and the bloody power struggle that resulted in the tyrannical rule of Josef Stalin, it would serve as an alternative to, rather than an outgrowth of, capitalism. It suggested the possibility of a new road to industrialization, one that circumvented capitalism altogether. In combination, the Russian and Chinese Revolutions served simultaneously as stimuli for and models of economic development in what became known as the Third World. As the Chinese case in particular revealed, however, their claim to be Marxist is suspect. Far from being a revolution of the urban industrial proletariat, it was primarily a peasant revolution, ironically the class that Marx singled out as being inherently conservative. Moreover, the Chinese Revolution, more so than the Russian Revolution, served as the template for numerous Third World revolutions.

In place of the competitive market, a command economy emerged in the Soviet Union in which a highly centralized state apparatus was responsible for economic decision making. This meant that government planners in the state bureaucracy claimed to understand and speak for the interests of the public. Lenin (1969) once asserted that this alternative to the presumed anarchy of the market in capitalist economies was in part modeled after a capitalist state bureaucracy that he admired: the U.S. Post Office. Industrial development began in the 1920s with the implementation of a series of five-year plans that focused on the expansion of heavy industry. Although industrial output did increase dramatically, this bureaucratized mode of economic decision making proved in the long term to be inefficient and unresponsive to consumer demands (Nove 1972; Rittersporn 1991).

In the economically developed Western nations, capitalism proved to be more resilient and, because of its productivity, capable of satisfying the economic needs of the citizenry better than Marx's notion of the crisis tendencies of capitalism could have predicted. The result was that much of the working class was willing to accommodate itself to capitalism rather than seeking to overthrow it. In such a situation, the Marxian idea of the historical mission of the proletariat looked increasingly like a myth. Rather than creating a revolutionary labor movement, workers were willing to create what Lenin (1969) pejoratively referred to as "bread-and-butter trade unions" or organizations designed to improve the conditions of workers within the parameters of capitalism.

The unwillingness of the working classes to assume the task of revolutionary transformation articulated by Marx forced subsequent Marxists to wrestle with this gulf between the proletariat of theory and flesh-and-blood workers who, as Frank Parkin (1979)—a critic of Marxist class theory—noted, were seen as "suffering from a kind of collective brain damage" (p. 81) that prevented them from realizing the necessity to engage in revolutionary struggle.

Two of the most original Marxist theorists of the 20th century who proved to have a lasting impact—the Hungarian philosopher Lukács and the Italian theorist Gramsci—confronted the dilemma posed so vividly by Parkin. The former is best known for *History and Class Consciousness* ([1923] 1971), published shortly after the Russian Revolution and the creation of the Soviet Union. Lukács served as the People's Commissar for Culture in the short-lived Hungarian Soviet Republic and subsequently spent time in Berlin, Vienna, and Moscow before returning to Hungary after World War II and the establishment of a communist government in that country. Given his complex, convoluted, and compromised relationship with the Soviet regime and with Stalinism, he has aptly been described as an "orthodox heretic" and a "romantic Stalinist" (Pachter 1984:295).

His distinctiveness arose from his ability to go to behind Marx to rediscover the Hegelian origins of Marx's thought, doing so at a time that Marx's early writings were not readily available. He did so, in his own words, by reading Marx "through spectacles tinged" by the thought of two of the theorists who will figure significantly in subsequent chapters—Simmel and Weber (Lukács 1971:ix). Alex Callinicos (2007) observes that "his most striking intellectual achievement was to take over their interpretations of modernity as a process of, respectively, objectification and rationalism, and to integrate them into the Marxist critique of the capitalist mode of production" (p. 205). Reification was the parallel concept to those of his mentors, one that treats the commodity character of capitalist production as leading inevitably to alienation.

True to Marx's understanding of the historical mission of the proletariat, Lukács contends that Marxism's historical materialism offers a key to comprehending capitalism as a totality—a key concept in his philosophy. For him, that comprehension can only result through action or praxis, which is construed in terms of the self-conscious collective actions of the proletariat, not in terms of individuals. He was convinced that the proletariat was the sole historical subject capable of uniting theory and praxis in a way that would result in eliminating itself as a class by destroying the socially antagonistic relations inherent in capitalism. Posed in dramatic terms, Lukács (1971) argues that the proletariat must become class conscious, for "the fate of mankind will depend . . . on its class consciousness" (p. 70).

But he was aware of Parkin's observation about the gulf between the proletariat in theory and in reality. His solution was to embrace Lenin's view of the vanguard party as "the bearer of the class consciousness of the proletariat" (Lukács 1971:41), a position that led him, despite what appears to be ambivalence and criticism at various points in his life, to consistently support and defend the Bolshevik party despite the horrors that it was responsible for both before Stalin assumed the reins of power and most dreadfully during the long era of Stalinist rule.

Unlike Lukács, who lived in a communist society, Gramsci helped to create one of the largest Communist parties outside of the Soviet bloc (Cammett 1967). His political activism resulted in his imprisonment once the fascist regime of Benito Mussolini took power in Italy. His most influential writings, contained in English translation under the title *Selections from the Prison Notebooks* (1971), were composed during this time, a fact that accounts for the often cryptic language he used in order to get his work past prison censors. The work is often fragmentary and suggestive, with many arguments remaining underdeveloped. What is clear is that he rejected the economic determinism he found in positivist versions of Marxism and argued for the centrality of culture, a view that accounts for its current appeal among those within sociology and related disciplines that have made what has become known as the "cultural turn."

Two key concepts in his work that have gained considerable currency are hegemony and civil society. By the former, he means a form of domination that is not based solely, or perhaps even primarily, on force but rather on consent. This consent comes about to the extent that a particular ideological description of how social relations operate is seen as natural and normal. Gramsci thought that in bourgeois capitalist society, two major competing ideological constructs exist, that of the ruling class and that of the working class. The ruling class is able to maintain its control only insofar as its particular ideological worldview is capable of being hegemonic. Thus, part of the task of achieving proletarian class consciousness must take place at the level of culture—of ideology.

The struggle occurs in civil society, which he construes as a sphere located between the economy and the political system, a sphere of public life where matters of culture are articulated, debated, and determined (Gramsci 1971:206–276). Gramsci argues that an organized working class must engage in a battle for the ideological control of civil society. Using the language of warfare, he suggests that this should amount to a "war of position" rather than a "war of maneuver"—or in other words as the slow chipping away of bourgeois hegemony rather than a frontal attack on it.

Like Lukács, Gramsci thought that this struggle would not materialize without the strong leadership of the Communist Party. In his case, referring to Machiavelli's famous treatise *The Prince*, he argued that rather than the leadership of a powerful individual, in the contemporary world, the "modern prince" takes the form of a political party (Gramsci 1971:125–205). Although he didn't manage to work out a fully articulated theoretical account of the relationship between the party and the proletarian masses, his writing exhibits sensitivity to the complexity of the era he lived in in general and in Italy in particular. Thus, he wrestled with such matters as how the party ought to deal with the peasantry, which Marx had written off as being inherently conservative; the role of intellectuals, including a category he refers to as "organic intellectuals"; and the significance of spontaneous actions arising from workers outside the structure of the party. In all this, there is, as Callinicos (2007) puts it, "enough conceptual looseness in his writings" (p. 214) to permit varied readings, ranging from concluding that, like his Hungarian counterpart, he would have remained devoted to the Soviet Union (he died in 1937), to the view expressed by many in the 1970s, when a reformist vision of Marxism known as Eurocommunism was in vogue. But there is nothing in his work to suggest that he questioned the idea that the proletariat would be the vehicle for the transformation of society that would result from overcoming capitalism.

Of all the 20th-century thinkers emerging out of the Marxian tradition, those associated with what became known as the Frankfurt School (most important, the influential trio of original members, Theodor Adorno, Max Horkheimer, Herbert Marcuse, and the central figure of the second generation, Jürgen Habermas) were willing to call into question not only the transformative role of the proletariat but also other basic tenets of the tradition, such as the labor theory of value, the belief in the inevitable progressive impoverishment of the proletariat, the underlying economic explanation of the crisis tendencies of capitalism, and the view that the state is nothing more than the ruling arm of the capitalist class (Jay 1973; Anderson 1976; Tar 1977; Bottomore 1984; Wiggershaus 1994; Alway 1995). At the same time, the Frankfurt School made a valuable contribution to a cultural critique of capitalism (Nealon 2002).

Horkheimer, the director of the Institute for Social Research, the official name of the Frankfurt School, and his associate Adorno, who has been described by several commentators as a genius, were unprepared to see the proletariat as the subject of history. This led them, in their advocacy of "Critical Theory," to construct a critique of social life without recourse to a "real historical subject" (Jay 1973:43). Thus, in stark contrast to those who sought to maintain a fundamental tenet of Marx's work, this duo severed any attempted linkage between theory and praxis, and thus their work was devoid of any obvious political goal of transcending capitalism.

They lived through dark times, witnessing the triumph of the Nazi regime and the subsequent horror of the Holocaust. They were forced into exile in the United States, and as such were homeless intellectuals, living comfortably (indeed, for a time they lived in Pacific Palisades among an affluent community of German émigrés working in Hollywood) though feeling alienated in a culture they disdained. During this period, they wrote *Dialectic of Enlightenment* ([1948] 1972), a complicated diagnosis of our times that Thomas Wheatland (2009) has aptly described as "strange and despairing" (p. 162). Horkheimer and Adorno ([1948] 1972) contend that "in the most general sense of progressive thought, the Enlightenment has always aimed at liberating men from fear and establishing their sovereignty. Yet the fully enlightened earth radiates disaster triumphant" (p. 3). This, as we shall see in the next chapter, is an argument that bears an uncanny resemblance to Weber's assessment of the consequences of rationalization. Just as he is seen as a profound pessimist, so they have been characterized as prime examples of the "melancholy Left."

Their fear, in a nutshell, was that reason—"true" reason—had been perverted in the process of being used as a mode of domination. In their sociological work—which included both theory development and empirical research—they focused their energies on the forces at play in shaping contemporary domination. Like Gramsci, their specific emphasis was on culture. In particular, they were among the pioneers in the study of what they termed the "culture industry," which constituted the institutions responsible for producing the entertainment and leisure pastimes that were characteristic of mass culture. This was linked to their analyses of authority, in which they concluded that there was a decided tendency on the part of ordinary people to submit to authority (Adorno was the lead author in the classic study of *The Authoritarian Personality* [1950]), and this contributed to conformism.

In its preoccupation with the deleterious consequences of mass society, their work dovetailed with that of a number of contemporary American sociologists, some of whom will be discussed elsewhere in this book, including C. Wright Mills. Thomas Wheatland's (2009) recent study, *The Frankfurt*

School in Exile, chronicles the relationships that members of the school had with American intellectuals and academics. For example, the independent scholar Dwight Macdonald attempted to establish an alliance, but was rebuffed. Similar potential linkages did not develop as they might have given the shared concerns of the Frankfurt School and their American counterparts. Part of the reason for this failure had to do with Horkheimer's insistence that members of the group refrain from engaging in politics. However, Wheatland (2009) points to another, perhaps more fundamental, reason that has to do with differing attitudes toward liberal democracy. Whereas Americans, including the New York intellectuals they had the most contact with, embraced democracy, he claims that the group "betrayed a lack of faith in liberalism as both creed and a practice" and that it "maintained an antidemocratic paternalism that was condescending and overly pessimistic" (p. 133).

Not surprisingly, Horkheimer and Adorno returned to Germany after the war. It is worth noting that Marcuse remained in the United States, perhaps a reflection of the fact that Wheatland's characterization did not quite apply to him. Marcuse had long ago given up on the revolutionary potential of the working class, but he continued to look for new social actors capable of challenging what he came to see as an overly administered society. In describing what is distinctive about the nature of domination in contemporary advanced industrial societies, the panache of his critique of contemporary society is on display at the very beginning of *One-Dimensional Man* (1964): "A comfortable, smooth, reasonable, democratic unfreedom prevails in industrial civilization, a token of technical progress" (p. 1). In his search for social movements that might challenge this situation, he turned in the 1960s to the student movement. While he did not necessarily see that movement as revolutionary in the old Marxist sense, he did think—or at least hope—that it might lead to progressive change.

Despite these obvious differences within the ranks of the Frankfurt School, in their willingness to challenge Marxist orthodoxy, they pointed to the problematic features inherent in Marx's thought in conjunction with initiating an analysis of industrial society that in key respects dovetailed with theoretical developments taking place outside of Marxism, although by thinkers who also took Marx seriously.

Counterimages of Capitalist Industrial Society: Shifts in the Class Structure

Many social theorists operating outside of the Marxist tradition agreed that industrial society is composed of a number of important class divisions, and that the precise character of these divisions has a profound effect on the social relations in such a society. Like the Frankfurt School theorists from within the tradition, however, they disagreed with Marx's characterization of these class divisions. In the view of many of these theorists, industrial society had developed in directions not fully anticipated by Marx, and as a result new classes emerged that would become more influential in shaping the future of industrial society than the industrial proletariat. Next, we examine three theorists whose ideas have influenced subsequent theorists of advanced industrial societies: Joseph Schumpeter, Thorstein Veblen, and C. Wright Mills.

Joseph Schumpeter and the Achilles' Heel of Capitalism

Joseph Schumpeter was not a Marxist. Indeed, as one commentator stated, "Schumpeter abhorred the ideology of Marxism; yet he had a keen understanding of the analytical value of Marx's work" (Dahms 1995:6–7). Marx's and Schumpeter's lives could not have been more different because Schumpeter was not an outsider but, rather, a successful academic insider. Indeed, after a number of successful academic appointments in Europe, he immigrated to the United States, where he ended up at Harvard University. Moreover, he had hands-on experience that provided him with keen insights into the workings of capitalist economies, having served briefly as the minister of finance in the Austrian Republic (though not successfully) and as president of a private bank after World War I (McCraw 2007).

Like Marx, Schumpeter viewed capitalism as a historically specific economic system that had built into it certain tendencies that over time undermined its foundations. In other words, both agreed that in the long term, capitalism could not sustain itself and thus would inevitably come to an end. They differed about how this was to occur and what the future likely held.

Schumpeter's unique contribution to our understanding of industrial society is woven throughout his entire body of writing (Schumpeter 1928), but his clearest assessment of the fate of capitalism and the possibility of socialism is contained in a book written during the last decade of his life, *Capitalism, Socialism, and Democracy* (1942). In the prologue to the book's second part, Schumpeter laid out his central thesis in no uncertain terms. He wrote, "Can capitalism survive? No. I do not think it can" (p. 61). The prologue to the following section proceeds to address socialism's chances: "Can socialism work? Of course it can" (p. 167).

What led him to these conclusions, and in what sense should his thought be seen as converging with or diverging from Marx's theory of capitalism? Although Schumpeter tended to emphasize certain similarities, in fact, they diverged considerably. Marx saw capitalism's collapse in terms of its failure: its inability to contend with the mounting crisis brought about by the growing tendency for the rate of profit to decline. In contrast, Schumpeter viewed the problem—the "Achilles' heel of capitalism"—as a product of the success of capitalism (Stolper 1968:70).

Second, in Schumpeter's writings, the working class played no role in either terminating capitalism or ushering in socialism. Quite the contrary was the case. In his ironic view, "The true pacemakers of socialism were not the intellectuals or agitators who preached it but the Vanderbilts, Carnegies, and Rockefellers" (Schumpeter 1942:134). This rather remarkable claim arises out of Schumpeter's view of the prime mover of capitalism: the business entrepreneur.

In capsule form, his argument is as follows. This entrepreneurial class is mainly responsible for the powerful productive capacity of capitalism. Due to its willingness to take risks in the competitive market, this is the class that has spawned the development of new and improved goods and continues to introduce new and enhanced methods of production via the continual introduction of new technologies (Rosenberg 2000). For this reason, it is appropriate to view capitalists as the vehicles of economic progress.

In this connection, capitalism is characterized by its capacity for what he terms "creative destruction" (McCraw 2007). Schumpeter thought that capitalism has a unique ability, due to competition, to eradicate established but declining economic sectors in order to make way for new ones. As Robin Blackburn (2007) has noted, "While admitting that such competition brings ruin to whole industries and regions, he stressed that the accompanying rise of innovative industries will bring new goods within reach of working men and women" (p. 36).

One of the dramatic achievements of the entrepreneurial class to emerge in the 20th century was the modern bureaucratic corporation. In these enterprises, economic decisions were made by a new and increasingly influential stratum in the corporate hierarchy: the administrators or managerial class. The ultimate outcome of this development was that the entrepreneur increasingly became irrelevant, replaced in importance by the managers, who succeeded in institutionalizing methods that ensure economic progress. Schumpeter (1942) described this process as follows:

> Since capitalist enterprise, by its very achievements, tends to automatize progress, we contend that it tends to make itself superfluous—to break to pieces under the pressure of its own success. The perfectly bureaucratized giant industrial unit not only ousts the small or medium-sized firm and "expropriates" its owners, but in the end it also ousts the entrepreneur and expropriates the bourgeoisie as a class which in the process stands to lose not only its income but also what is infinitely more important, its function. (p. 134)

This being the case, the end of capitalism for Schumpeter differs considerably from the Marxist perspective. For Schumpeter, capitalism's demise did not entail the end of the market or the emergence of a classless society. It simply meant that the entrepreneurial class, having outlived its usefulness, ceased to exist, being supplanted by the managers of the corporate bureaucracies.

In addition, his definition of socialism was not synonymous with Marx's view. Schumpeter offered a pithy definition of socialist society. It was construed to be "an institutional pattern in which the control over the means of production and over production itself is vested with a central authority" and with this centralization, "the economic affairs of society belong to the public and not to the private sphere" (Schumpeter 1942:167). In other words, economic decisions would be made by centralized authorities on behalf of the interests of the public. This conclusion parallels the Marxist version, but rather than the workers or the "people" making key economic decisions, the decisions are made by the managers. Thus, Schumpeter concluded that if a revolution has taken place in industrial society, it is what James Burnham (1941) called a "managerial revolution," the ascendance to power of a class of people equipped with the expert knowledge necessary to make a modern industrial society function and expand.

The Iconoclastic Social Theory of Thorstein Veblen

Thorstein Veblen, the American-born son of Norwegian immigrants, was one of the most original social thinkers of the late 19th and early 20th centuries. Although rightly appreciated for his creativity, his thought has often been misunderstood. This is in no small part due to its mode of presentation. Veblen was perhaps the most acerbic social critic of his era, but his criticism was couched in irony and sarcasm. In part because his views ran against the grain of conventional social thinking, and in part because he was a somewhat difficult and unorthodox person, Veblen lived on the margins of American academic life, despite the fact that during the course of his career, he had appointments at such prestigious institutions as the University of Chicago and Stanford University.

These positions did not last. First of all, Veblen's teaching left something to be desired. He appeared ill-prepared, and he mumbled through his lectures. Although his wit was often evident, students had a difficult time making sense of his classes. According to biographer Joseph Dorfman (1934), "Judged by conventional standards, he was the world's worst teacher" (p. 250). At the same time, Veblen attracted and was attracted to women, and although he was married he carried on numerous amorous relationships. Indeed, his extramarital affairs were the primary reason he was forced to leave both Chicago and Stanford.

After a stint at the University of Missouri, he worked briefly for the federal government in Washington, D.C., and as an editor of *The Dial*. He joined the faculty of the innovative New School for Social Research in New York City, where he remained until 1926. At that time, he returned to California, choosing to live the life of a semihermit in a mountain cabin. He died three years later (Dorfman 1934; Riesman 1953).

Veblen was raised in rural Minnesota in a Norwegian immigrant enclave characterized by hard work and an ascetic atmosphere that viewed ostentatious displays of wealth and prestige as distasteful. This was the world shaped by the piety of the Lutheran tradition and by American populism, a political movement that had a particular appeal to midwestern farmers and laborers. Populists sought to challenge the economic power of giant industrialists and banks, advancing a more radical vision of democracy and economic justice (Goodwyn 1976). Populism, not Marxism, would inform the radicalism of Veblen. This was the cultural milieu that infused Veblen's fertile mind, and one can see in his life work the dual impact of these two intellectual traditions. This is evident in the central themes and concerns developed in a series of major works, beginning with *The Theory of the Leisure Class* ([1899] 1924) and continuing through such books as *The Theory of Business Enterprise* (1904), *The Engineers and the Price System* (1921), and *The Higher Learning in America* ([1924] 1993).

In his most famous book, *The Theory of the Leisure Class* ([1899] 1924), Veblen's pen dripped with sarcasm in his characterization of the owners of business enterprises. Unlike Schumpeter, he did not appear to view these "captains of industry" as having been an innovative, progressive force responsible for the dynamism and innovativeness of industrial society. Rather, he viewed their position as the dominant class in capitalist industrial society as due to their success in the struggle for survival—a position he appears to have adopted from his Social Darwinian professor at Yale, William Graham Sumner.

Indeed, although the business owners lived off of the success of industrial society, they did little to contribute to that success. For this reason, he referred to them as the "leisure class." In his view, "The leisure class lives by the industrial community, rather than in it. Its relations to industry are of a pecuniary rather than an industrial kind" (Veblen [1899] 1924:246). Veblen viewed the giant industrialists of his era—Carnegie, Rockefeller, Vanderbilt, and so on—as predators and survivors from an earlier era. As such, he found it most appropriate for them to be dubbed, as critics at the time did, the "robber barons" (Riesman 1953).

Much of the book focuses on the culture of the leisure class. Veblen introduced a term that has since gained widespread usage, *conspicuous consumption*, and its counterpart, *conspicuous leisure*. By these interrelated terms, he meant that the consumption patterns of the leisure class are designed not to fulfill genuine needs but to advance prestige claims. They are predicated on waste—the waste of time, effort, and goods. Thus, he saw them as acts of consumption that do nothing to enhance human well-being (Veblen [1899] 1924:85–98).

It is not, as Marx and Schumpeter believed, that this class has outlived its historical purpose. Rather, the leisure class has never had a genuinely beneficial role to play in industrial society; it exists in a parasitical relationship to what are actually the productive classes. Veblen was not entirely explicit on which classes were mainly responsible for industrial productivity, but they certainly included workers involved in the actual creation of goods (Veblen [1899] 1924, 1904).

Veblen was suspicious of notions of progress and of inevitable laws of social evolution. He did, however, tend to treat technological developments as a major—perhaps the major—source of social change. Advances in a society's level of technology made necessary cadres of workers with the expert knowledge required to make the economic system function effectively and efficiently. Not surprisingly, Veblen placed great emphasis on these knowledge experts, whom he referred to as the "engineers and technicians" (Veblen 1921).

Thus, industrial society was characterized by a dichotomy between business and industry or, in Veblen's words, between "pecuniary" interests and "industrial" interests. Although the owners were motivated by the desire to make money, it was only the experts who were capable of producing socially useful goods. They could do so, however, only when they were not dependent on the owners for their own livelihoods. Industrial society would continue to be "wasteful" and would fail to meet actual human needs as long as business owners constituted the dominant economic class. In this regard, biographer John Patrick Diggins (1999) claims that among the significant American social scientists of the early 20th century, Veblen offered the most important non-Marxist economic critique of capitalism.

The solution to this situation revolved around the ability of the engineers and technicians—today we might call them "technocrats"—to wrest control of the economy from the owners. This class of experts, and not the proletariat, was crucial to any possibility of liberating industrial society from the impediments of its capitalist moorings. Soon after the Russian Revolution, in *The Engineers and the Price System* (1921), Veblen borrowed from the language of the Bolsheviks and called for a "soviet of engineers and technicians." It is not entirely clear that he was serious about this suggestion. Rick Tilman (1992), for example, suspects that this was a "perhaps tongue-in-cheek proposal" (p. 62).

Veblen did not view the engineers and technicians as a revolutionary class in the way Marx viewed the proletariat. He valued the idea of a knowledge elite, and this would suggest that there were limits to the ability to create a more egalitarian society. He also did not explore the likelihood that these knowledge experts would be either willing or able to organize collectively to usurp control of the economy from the owners. Indeed, the general tone of his writing would lead one to conclude that Veblen was dubious about the chances for bringing an end to the tension between business and industry.

C. Wright Mills: The Academic Outlaw

C. Wright Mills's intellectual legacy in some respects resembled that of Veblen. This is not to say that Mills was a latter day Veblenian. He definitely was not. Certain similarities between the two, however, are evident. Both sought to combine scholarship with partisanship, and as penetrating critics of their society they generated considerable controversy. Both were radicals, although neither was a Marxist. Indeed, like Veblen, Mills was primarily influenced by American populism. Both, however, were convinced that the problems they had identified were incapable of resolution. Although Veblen, at least in his writing, hid his reaction to this realization, Mills's publications became increasingly pessimistic over time (Horowitz 1983; Tilman 1984:61–106).

The differences between Mills and Veblen are equally evident. Whereas Veblen had little use for or interest in Marx, the same was definitely not the case for Mills. Mills described his view of Marx in a letter to the magazine *Commentary* in the following way: "I happen never to have been what is called 'a Marxist,' but I believe Karl Marx to be one of the most astute students of society modern civilization has produced." (Mills 2000:237). While reading his work offers abundant evidence that he both knew Marx's work and took it very seriously, it is also clear that the classic theorist who most profoundly shaped his intellectual legacy was Weber. In this regard, he can appropriately be described as a Left Weberian.

Mills was born on August 28, 1916, into a middle-class Catholic household in Waco, Texas. After receiving both a bachelor's degree and a master's degree in philosophy from the University of Texas, he studied sociology at the University of Wisconsin, where he came under the influence of the German émigré scholar Hans Gerth. Far from the usual student-professor relationship, they engaged in a series of collaborative works focusing on social psychology and introducing the work of the German sociologist Max Weber to an English-speaking audience.

While completing his PhD in sociology and continuing to work on collaborative projects with Gerth, Mills taught for a time at the University of Maryland. Given its close proximity to the nation's capital, he was able to gain a sense of the political life in the corridors of power. Mills, however, was a man in a hurry. Not content with the life of the academic in the cloistered surroundings of the university, Mills sought to become a public intellectual. To accomplish this, he headed for the nation's cultural capital, New York City, where, as he stated, he was intent on "taking it big" (Dandaneau 2001). With the assistance of the then editor and ex-socialist, New York intellectual Daniel Bell, Mills moved into an apartment in Greenwich Village and began to pursue his goal of combining a life of scholarship with that of the partisan intellectual (Jamison and Eyerman 1994:30–63). He landed an academic position at Columbia University. During this time, he wrote for various, at that time left-wing, journals, such as Bell's *The New Leader, The New Republic, Partisan Review,* and the union journal *Labor and Nation* (Scimecca 1977).

Early on, he forged a relationship with the independent radical Dwight Macdonald, who defined their camaraderie in terms of shared temperaments. Macdonald (1974) wrote, "We had in common a peculiar . . . mixture of innocence and cynicism, optimism and skepticism. We were ever hopeful, ever disillusioned" (p. 300).

Mills had an uncanny ability to irritate people who had befriended him. His life comprised a series of fallings-out with such people, beginning with Gerth, whom he used and then abandoned (Oakes and Vidich 1999). This pattern continued throughout his life and included Bell, Macdonald, and other luminaries in the New York intellectual scene, and his sociology colleagues at Columbia. His growing marginality within these intellectual circles did little to temper his positions. If anything, his writing became more vitriolic with the passage of time. The balance between the scholar and the partisan broke down in his later works, which were devoted to issues related to the prospects of another world war, this time with the threat of nuclear weapons, and to revolutionary upheavals in the Third World.

This is not to suggest that he was a loner. He was not (Geary 2009). Over time, he expanded his relationships with European intellectuals, particularly in Britain. Thus, he had an enduring friendship with Ralph Miliband, a democratic socialist professor at the London School of Economics. His son David, the Labour Party's Foreign Secretary under Prime Minister Gordon Brown, bears the middle name Wright—testimony to the depth of the friendship (Birnbaum 2009:34). In addition, during the latter part of his life, the signs of what might have been an intriguing relationship with leaders of what became known as the New Left were evident.

Indeed, Tom Hayden, one of the founders of the Students for a Democratic Society (SDS), and in that capacity the primary voice in that organization's call for democratic renewal, "The Port Huron Statement," was thoroughly immersed in Mills's work. Though Hayden never met Mills, he wrote his MA thesis on Mills's work, published recently for the first time as *Radical Nomad: C. Wright Mills and His Times* (2006). Reflecting on his youth, Hayden (2006) wrote that "none of us in SDS knew him, though many were followers. After Albert Camus and Bob Dylan, Mills ranked as the most pervasive influence on the first generation of SDS" (p. 56).

In a trilogy published during an eight-year period beginning in 1948, Mills provided his clearest expression of his sense of the changes that had occurred in capitalist industrial society since the turn of the century. In so doing, he also provided an appraisal of the contributions and the limitations of earlier theorists, including Marx, Schumpeter, and Veblen.

Changes in the Class Structure

Mills was interested in comprehending the new forms of stratification that were arising in a novel phase in the history of industrial societies, one that involved a reconfiguration of the class structure. Mills shared with his predecessors discussed in this chapter a position that accorded a place of singular importance to class divisions. Mills parted company with this trio, however, over differences about how best to construe the relationship between economics and politics. For Mills, politics was far more consequential and more interconnected with economics than any of the other theorists appreciated. Thus, his intellectual efforts were simultaneously studies in social class and studies in political power.

The first book in the trilogy, *The New Men of Power* (1948), is a study of the American labor movement. In this work, Mills comes to terms with Marx, criticizing what he refers to as Marxism's "labor metaphysic." By this he meant that Marxism is wrong to view the working class as a revolutionary class capable of overthrowing capitalism. Indeed, as his analysis of labor leaders in postwar America indicated, the leadership had been thoroughly co-opted by business and government. Rather than viewing themselves as the leadership vanguard of societal transformation, labor leaders were content to become "thoroughly integrated into the main power system as a junior partner" (Tilman 1984:21; see also Hayden 2006:136). Mills did not believe that the rank-and-file workers were a militant force; they were quite willing, as Lenin had feared, to be content to pursue "bread-and-butter" issues, seeking to obtain a larger piece of the economic pie within capitalism rather than desiring the establishment of socialism.

Advanced industrial society had also signaled the numerical decline of the blue-collar workforce and with it the dramatic expansion of the middle class (Figure 2.2). It was the emergence of the new middle class that Mills discussed in his next book, *White Collar* (1951). By writing about a "new" middle class, Mills had in mind something quite different from the traditional—or "old"—middle class. The latter was composed of small businesspersons, farmers, and independent professionals, such as doctors and lawyers. The former constitutes the white-collar class. According to Mills (1951), "The white-collar people slipped quietly into modern society" (p. ix).

In contrast to the self-employed members of the old middle class, the new and rapidly expanding segment of the class consisted of salaried professionals working in corporate or government bureaucracies. In contrast to the manual work of blue-collar laborers, these are white-collar occupations relying on mental labor. This class segment incorporated a wide range of occupations, including middle managers, technicians, administrators, civil servants, salaried supervisors, clerks, and salespersons. Those at the top of the class are well paid, whereas those at its lower rungs receive far less. Like their blue-collar counterparts, the new middle class worked in the employ of the owners. They contributed to a situation in which, as Rick Tilman (1984)

Figure 2.2 Class Structure of Advanced Capitalism

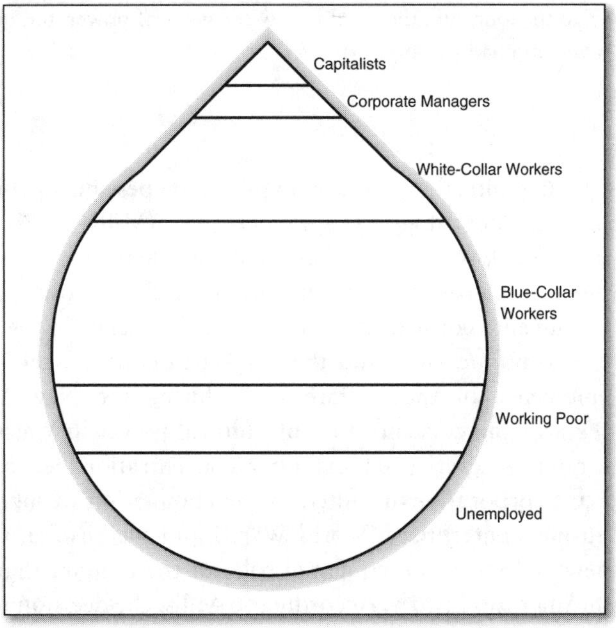

noted, "the United States had become a nation of employees for whom independent property ownership was no longer a viable option" (p. 25).

In chapters with such provocative titles as "The Managerial Demiurge," "Brains, Inc.," "The Great Salesroom," and "The Enormous File," Mills (1951), in a style reminiscent of that of Veblen, examined the social psychology, the cultural orientations, and the political proclivities of the new middle class. Although conceding that it was premature to draw many conclusions about the character of the new middle class, Mills nonetheless suspected that their location in the middle of the class structure inclined them to be moderate, careful, and conformist in matters cultural and political. The dramatic growth of this class encouraged the homogenizing tendencies of mass society.

In politics, the new middle class seemed unlikely to band together collectively to promote their interests, unlike their unionized blue-collar counterparts. Here, their conformist tendencies—their fear of rocking the boat—meant that despite their numbers, they were inclined to be part of what Mills (1951) referred to as a "politics of the rearguard." The book ended with the following unflattering description of the political orientation of this class:

> They are a chorus, too afraid to grumble, too hysterical in their applause. They are rearguarders. In the short run, they will follow the panicky ways of prestige; in the long run, they will follow the ways of power, for, in the end, prestige is determined by power. (p. 354)

Rise of the Power Elite

The political orientation explains the pessimism voiced in the third volume of the trilogy, *The Power Elite* (Mills 1956). Mills had become increasingly convinced that American democracy was being undermined due to the growing concentration of political power in the hands of a tripartite elite consisting of high-ranking officials in the federal government, the corporate elite, and the highest ranking officers in the military. The emergence of the welfare state during the New Deal contributed to the growing concentration of political power in Washington, whereas the economy experienced a similar concentration because the expansion of giant corporations resulted in the elimination of increasingly more small business enterprises. World War II and the ensuing Cold War signaled a new and more consequential role for the military than at any other point in American history. According to Mills, the decision makers in these three institutional arenas experienced a dramatic expansion in their power as they increasingly worked cooperatively. The result was a highly coordinated and remarkably unified power elite.

American economic prosperity and the repressive political climate of the Cold War period conspired to prevent any significant challenge to this ominous shift from democratic to elite rule. Indeed, the two previous books had concluded that neither the working class nor the new middle class was likely to oppose this trend. According to Norman Birnbaum (2009), this accounts for the fact that "Mills became angry—an anger that grew with time. It drove him in a relentless search for actors who could reset the historical clock" (p. 35). In his view, only the most marginalized segments of American society—Mills had in mind racial minorities—might resist, but they were seen as fundamentally lacking the clout to stem the tide. Thus, Mills saw little reason not to conclude that the future would entail a general acquiescence by the mass of the populace to the domination of the new elite.

The challenges to the existing social order that burst onto the cultural and political landscape in the 1960s—the civil rights movement, the antiwar movement, and the counterculture—called into question Mills's pessimistic assessments. He did not have an opportunity, however, to grapple with these dramatic forces of social change. The man in a hurry died of a heart attack in 1962; he was only 45 years old.

Daniel Bell on the Advent of Postindustrial Society

Daniel Bell, who was appointed the Henry Ford II Professor of Social Science at Harvard University in 1980, has gone beyond the trio discussed previously in arguing that as a consequence of the changes they had identified, industrial society was in the process of being replaced by something qualitatively new, which he dubbed "postindustrial society" (Bell 1973).

The conviction that we had crossed what Michael Piore and Charles Sabel (1984) called the "second industrial divide" and entered a new stage in the history of industrial society was shared by many others, and a wide range of labels have been suggested, including Peter Drucker's "knowledge society," Ralf Dahrendorf's "service class society," Zbigniew Brzezinski's "technetronic era," and a number of "posts," such as postbourgeois, postmodern, postscarcity, postcivilized, and posteconomic. It is obvious that Bell was not alone in thinking that we had entered or were about to enter a novel age that in some substantial way moved beyond industrial society. The term Bell chose to employ, *postindustrial*—a term also adopted by the French sociologist Alain Touraine (1971) at approximately the same time—would catch on as the most commonly used term to depict advanced industrial society (Kivisto 1980/1981, 1981, 1984).

Bell is a paradigmatic example of the New York intellectual who so fascinated C. Wright Mills (recall that Bell helped Mills find an apartment when the latter arrived in New York City). His intellectual career took place both inside and outside the university. It has been aptly characterized by Douglas G. Webb as a gradual journey from socialism to sociology, a journey that Bell (1980) characterized as a "winding passage."

The son of Jewish immigrants, Bell was born in New York City in 1919. When he was 13 years old, he joined the Young People's Socialist League. Bell (1981) described the reason for this decision as follows:

> I had grown up in the slums of New York. All around me I saw the "Hoovervilles," the tin shacks near the docks of the East River where the unemployed lived in makeshift houses and rummaged through the garbage scows for food. Late at night I would go with a gang of other boys to the wholesale vegetable markets on the West Side, to swipe potatoes or to pick up bruised tomatoes in the street to bring home, or to eat around the small fires we would make in the street with the broken boxes from the markets. I wanted to know, simply, why this had to be. It was inevitable that I would become a sociologist. (p. 532)

In the late 1930s, he attended the City College of New York along with numerous other second-generation ethnics. During the Depression, City College was home to an array of radical students, who congregated in the alcoves of the school's cafeteria along radical sectarian lines: the Stalinists, Trotskyites, Cannonites, Shachtmanites, and various other obscure groupings. Bell was very much a part of this world (Bender 1987; Jacoby 1987).

During the 1940s and 1950s, Bell worked primarily as a journalist and editor, first as managing editor of the labor periodical *New Leader* and later for *Fortune* magazine. Working for Henry Luce at *Fortune* was an indication that Bell had moved closer to the mainstream in matters related to economics and politics. Nonetheless, he continued to view himself as a socialist, by which he meant that he remained committed to the idea that a community's resources must first be used to meet everyone's basic human needs (Bell 1981:550). During this time, he wrote books on Marxism and on right-wing extremists, culminating in a book titled *The End of Ideology* (1965), in which he argued that old political ideas could no longer account for the changed circumstances after midcentury.

On the Transition to Postindustrial Society

The idea that we were entering a distinctly new period in the development of industrial society was related to Bell's earlier work on ideologies, reaching its full expression in his influential *The Coming of Post-Industrial Society* (1973). His central thesis in this book is that whereas industrial society was a "goods-producing society, . . . postindustrial society is organized around knowledge for the purpose of social control and the directing of innovation and change" (p. 20). In making this contrast, it is clear that Bell's thinking bears a family resemblance to that of both Schumpeter and Veblen.

A postindustrial economy requires the existence of a highly educated professional class that possesses the scientific, technical, managerial, and administrative training needed to ensure that the economy will function well. Moreover, this class should be capable of making decisions independently. The success of postindustrial society depends on whether it is in a position to ensure that rational decisions are made, ones that stress efficiency, calculability, and control (Bell 1973, 1980).

A postindustrial economy also requires more highly centralized coordination than was the case in industrial society—coordination that can occur only in the political arena. Thus, a new interconnection arises between the economy and the political system. Bell considers government to be the "cockpit" of the new industrial order, and insofar as this is the case, the knowledge class needs to assert itself in government planning and policy formulation as well as in decision making in economic firms (Bell 1973:267–337; see also Galbraith 1967; Table 2.2).

At times, Bell seems to be saying that the driving force of change is technology and, like such optimistic cheerleaders for technology as Alvin

Table 2.2 Contrasting Industrial and Postindustrial Societies

	Industrial	Postindustrial
Key resource	Machinery	Knowledge
Key institution	Business firm	University
Key decision makers	Businessperson	Professional/expert
Power base	Property	Knowledge/skill
Role of politics	Laissez-faire	Government/corporate partnership

and Heidi Toffler, that technology will lead us into a brave new world (Kumar 1988:73–99). For instance, he claims that one of the consequences of technological developments during the past 200 years is "a steady decrease in the disparity among persons" (Bell 1973:451)—in other words, that technology has reduced the levels of inequality. He writes of a future in which, because of advances in knowledge, compared to the past we have far greater control over, and thus the ability to change for the better, our social world. He envisions, for example, a postscarcity society in which all human needs can be met (p. 466).

Bell, however, does not think that postindustrial society signals the end of social divisions and conflict. Far from it, because one of the characteristic features of postindustrial societies is a lack of coherence and unity across three key sectors of society: the economy, the polity, and the cultural realm. Problems arise insofar as each operates on the basis of what Bell calls differing axial principles, by which he means different norms and rules (Bell 1973, 1980; Touraine 1977).

As noted previously, the economy is guided by axial principles based on instrumental rationality. In contrast, the polity is guided by principles that promote equality and an expansion of citizen involvement. What emerges out of this is a tension between (1) the need to accord the knowledge class considerable say in the running of the economy and (2) the polity and the demand on the part of the larger sectors of the population for an expansion of democratic participation. This built-in tension can at various times lead to conflict regarding how power is allocated (Waters 1996:124–147).

In *The Cultural Contradictions of Capitalism* (1976), Bell seeks to illustrate that there is also a tension between the axial principles guiding the economy and those informing the culture. In this book, Bell was in no small part responding to the cultural changes that swept the United States during the 1960s. In his view, the youth counterculture of that period epitomized the new cultural sensibility, which placed a premium on feelings, self-expression, and the quest for individual fulfillment. Decidedly antirational, this youth subculture promoted a hedonistic worldview made possible by an affluent consumer society. This shifting cultural sensibility constituted a marked departure from the culture of previous generations, a shift "from the Protestant ethic to the psychedelic bazaar" (Bell 1976:54–84). Despite the book's catchy title, Bell skirts the issue of the role that capitalism might play in generating these contradictions.

The implications of these divisions are not entirely clear, but Bell is convinced that we are entering a period of great uncertainty and instability. Although he is not unduly pessimistic, Bell's apprehensions about the future of postindustrial society stand in sharp contrast to the exuberance about future prospects that can be found in the writings of the first great theorist of industrial society, Karl Marx.

Critical Responses to Bell

Critics of Bell have frequently accused him of overemphasizing the differences between earlier capitalist industrial society and its postindustrial version (Giddens 1973; Kivisto 1980/1981). Indeed, the choice of terms to describe contemporary society implies a disjuncture or break between the two. It can be seen to imply that the problems of earlier industrial society have been surmounted. In recent years, however, the resurgence of serious levels of poverty is strikingly reminiscent of the scenes from Bell's youth. We clearly have not entered a postscarcity society in which everyone's human needs are being met, which raises anew the sociological question Bell posed as a youth regarding why this has to be. It also raises a question about whether social theorists should, like Marx, focus increased attention on capitalism and not simply on industrial society—on the differences between the past and present as well as the continuities.

Although at times it appeared that capitalism evaporated from Bell's work, at other points it was clearly still there—as his study of the cultural contradictions of capitalism makes clear. In this regard, intellectual historian Howard Brick (2006) observes that "Bell consistently resisted the inference some readers drew that his postindustrial society could no longer be understood as 'capitalist'" (p. 198). It has certainly been placed center stage by a variety of theorists who have sought to identify changes in the character of capitalist economies during the past century. This is, for example, evident in discussions initiated by British neo-Marxists about what they characterize as the shift within the sphere of production from "Fordism" to "post-Fordism." Fordism refers to the mechanized production methods associated with the assembly line introduced by Henry Ford and the use of scientific management techniques developed by Frederick Winslow Taylor. The interventionist state that Bell argued was integral to postindustrial society was clearly necessary for Fordist production, entailing both the implementation of Keynesian economic policies and the administration of an expanding welfare state to ensure societal stability. However, changes brought about by automation and the global exportation of manufacturing operations to less developed nations where labor costs were considerably lower led to the process of deindustrialization, which Barry Bluestone and Bennett Harrison (1982) describe as "the widespread, systematic disinvestment" (p. 6) in the manufacturing sector.

Deindustrialization set the stage for the advent of post-Fordism, a somewhat imprecise term referring to new manufacturing techniques that rely on flexible, decentralized, specialized, and just-in-time production methods. Industrial enterprises, increasingly reliant on new information technologies, require expanded cadres of knowledge experts while at the same time need a much smaller blue-collar workforce. In this regard, there is agreement with Bell. In a post-Fordist economy, however, the state does not assume the role of pilot in the cockpit, coordinating economic activities. Rather, the introduction of neoliberal economic policies—seen most explicitly in the regimes of Margaret Thatcher in Britain and Ronald Reagan in the United States—signaled a new relationship between state and economy. Neoliberalism involved a frontal assault on the welfare state, promoting, in the words of Alain Touraine (2001), a situation in which "the market had replaced the state as the principal regulatory force" (p. 9) in the economy and throughout the rest of society. His French counterpart Pierre Bourdieu (2003) forcefully made a similar case when he wrote that "Neoliberalism aims to destroy the social state . . . which . . . safeguards the interests of the dominated, the culturally and economically dispossessed, women, stigmatized ethnic groups, etc." (pp. 34–35).

With these trends in mind, Scott Lash and John Urry (1987) contend that we have moved into a third stage in the history of capitalism. If the era of Marx can be seen as the period of liberal capitalism, and the era of Fordist methods can be viewed as the period of organized capitalism, Lash and Urry suggest that since the 1960s this second stage has been giving way to "disorganized capitalism." Moreover, disorganized capitalism resonates with the culture of postmodernity (discussed in Chapter 5) rather than being at odds with it. In other words, contrary to Bell, who views these changes as the consequence of the culture, economy, and polity operating according to different axial principles, Lash and Urry and similar commentators, such as David Harvey (1996) and Fredric Jameson (1991), see them as reflections of the functional requisites, or the "cultural logic," of contemporary capitalism.

Whatever the misgivings various critics have expressed about Bell's postindustrial society thesis, there is nonetheless a consensus among scholars that the task of sociological inquiry—staked out by Marx and continued on through to Bell and contemporaries—remains. Sociologists seek to explore the continuities and changes that characterize capitalist industrial society and to make sense of the complex ways that the economy reciprocally shapes and influences democratic politics, individual identities, communal attachments, and modern culture. We discuss these topics in the chapters that follow, beginning with an inquiry into the relationship between capitalism and democracy.

Summary

From the formative period of sociology in the 19th century to the 21st century, sociologists have been seeking to comprehend the character and the varied societal impacts of industrial society. They have done so with the realization that it has dramatically sped up the processes of social change and has exhibited a capacity to transform itself and its surrounding social and natural environment in profound ways. Although numerous 19th-century figures contributed to our initial understanding of industrialization and its consequences, none left as consequential a legacy as did Karl Marx. His analyses of capitalist industrial society were shaped by his engagement with crucial intellectual predecessors—philosophers, economists, and social theorists. Out of this, he produced his own novel interpretation of the inner dynamics and the potential future of capitalist industrial society. Contrary to Marx's predictions, or hopes, it is clear from the vantage of subsequent history that, as Luc Boltanski and Ève Chiapello (2005) put it, "The capitalist system has proved infinitely more robust than its detractors . . . thought" (p. 27). In turn, the 20th century scholars examined in the second half of this chapter—Joseph Schumpeter, Thorstein Veblen, C. Wright Mills, and Daniel Bell—engaged the legacy bequeathed by Marx and took up the crucial issues that had preoccupied him in their own efforts to assess changes that had occurred since Marx's time and to determine where industrial society might be heading in the future.

3

Democracy

From the Fall of the Bastille to the Fall of the Berlin Wall

Although democratic ideas have shaped Western thought for more than 2,500 years, with the ideal of the Greek city-state serving as a powerful model of the democratic polity, it is only the past two centuries that can appropriately be regarded as the "democratic age." During this time, democratic ideals took root, first among the new middle classes in the nation-states of Western Europe and North America. These ideals filtered throughout all segments of those societies, and over time they spread across the globe (Glassman, Swatos, and Kivisto 1993; Markoff 1996).

Two powerful symbols can serve to frame this period of history: the fall of the Bastille and the fall of the Berlin Wall. The former was the infamous prison that the Parisian masses stormed and destroyed on July 14, 1789. The Bastille represented the oppressive domination of the monarchy and nobility, and its destruction marked the beginning of the French Revolution and signaled the beginning of the end of the old regime. Together with the American Revolution, which can be viewed as the first successful anticolonial revolt, the French Revolution was a world historical event despite the fact that it did not manage to smoothly introduce democracy into French political life. Instead, the nation moved back and forth throughout the 19th century between democratic and nondemocratic political regimes. Nonetheless, it reflected the rise of democracy and the attendant values identified with it: liberty, equality, and fraternity.

If the Bastille symbolizes the beginning of an era, the fall of the Berlin Wall on November 9, 1989, has become a symbol of the end of an era (Figure 3.1). I visited Berlin on the first anniversary of that momentous event and vividly recall that while chiseling pieces of the wall to take home, I was amazed at how quickly and relatively peacefully the totalitarian regime that had been in power for nearly half a century had collapsed. To millions, this collapse signified the failure of the antidemocratic approach of communist regimes in the 20th century and the pervasiveness of the appeal of the democratic vision to nations with little or no direct experience with democracy. Linked to this, the fall of communism can also be seen as a repudiation of the antimarket approach of the former Soviet Union and its satellites.

These changes have led some scholars, such as Francis Fukuyama (1992), to argue that we have entered a new age in which old ideologies have lost their appeal and the battle over competing worldviews is over. In short, he contends that representative democracy and capitalism have emerged as the uncontested models for political and economic systems in the contemporary world.

Although this view depicts the triumph of democracy in the modern world, other contemporary theorists have presented more tempered views. Some political theorists, such as Samuel Huntington (1976), contend that an excess

Figure 3.1 The Opening of the Berlin Wall

SOURCE: Photograph copyright © 1998 Christopher Morris/Black Star. Used by permission.

of democracy leads to serious societal problems, whereas others question whether, over time, contemporary liberal democracies can maintain the level of legitimacy needed to sustain themselves. Still others, including Benjamin Barber (1984), have expressed concerns about the limited and anemic character of contemporary democracies and have argued for the need to find ways to expand citizen involvement. These debates reflect competing understandings about the core character of a democratic polity. Conservatives such as Huntington opt for an elite version of representative democracy, whereas liberals such as Barber seek the expansion of participatory democratic practices. Others on the political Left have sought to outline theoretical cases for more radical models, including the deliberative democratic theory of Jürgen Habermas (1984) and the communicative democratic theory of feminist philosopher Iris Marion Young (1997:60–74).

In this chapter, we address these and related issues first as they have been developed in the work of Max Weber, who both witnessed and participated in German politics in the early decades of the 20th century. His complex and subtle political thought is discussed in considerable detail and is contrasted to that of influential contemporary Robert Michels. We then turn to two American theorists: Talcott Parsons and Seymour Martin Lipset. As will be shown, Parsons was especially interested in the significance of citizenship, whereas Lipset devoted considerable energy to analyzing the nature of the relationship between capitalism and democracy. Finally, we turn to the work of the German theorist Jürgen Habermas. Deeply influenced by Marx, Weber, and Parsons, Habermas's thinking is nonetheless highly original and provocative and has proven to be highly relevant in studying contemporary politics.

Max Weber: Prophet, Pessimist, and Realist

Max Weber is deservedly viewed as not simply one of the most important classic figures in sociology but an intellectual giant, the relevance of whose ideas far transcended disciplinary boundaries and extended well beyond his times, continuing to help us make sense of contemporary social life in a new century (Sica 2003). His wife, Marianne Weber (1988), in a letter written six years after Weber's death, asserted, "In my judgment Weber's fame is only at its very beginning. People will be stupefied when they put their hands on his work. I live for his immortality on earth" (p. xvi). A few years later, the theologian Karl Jaspers (1964) said of Weber that he was "the greatest German of our age" (p. 189). In retrospect, it is clear that these assessments were not far from the mark. Weber's contribution, not simply to sociology but to contemporary ethical and political thought, has proven to be of singular importance.

A scholar of prodigious range and penetrating insight, Weber once confessed that politics was his first love. Given his family background, this is not especially surprising, but his actual forays into active political engagements were limited and met with only partial success. For example, during World War I he ran unsuccessfully for election to the Reichstag, and in 1919 he was selected to be part of a delegation that attended the peace settlement negotiations in Versailles (Honigsheim 1968; Mommsen 1984). The most significant contribution Weber made to politics, however, was not a result of these activities: rather, it was an intellectual contribution in which he wrestled with the most fundamental questions about the bases of political authority, leadership, and decision making; the relationship between politics and economics; and the ethical undergirding of political action.

In addressing these issues, Weber had much to say about the possibilities and the potential shortcomings of democracy. His resistance to romanticizing democracy—refusing, for example, to define it as the "best of all possible political systems"—was part of an attempt to realistically assess its strengths and weaknesses. It is difficult to summarize Weber's general attitude about democracy because to appreciate it one needs to know how his views are related to his understanding of the development of capitalism and the growth of bureaucracies. Before discussing these matters, however, we first consider the social milieu in which his ideas emerged and developed (Bendix 1960; Loewenstein 1966; Scaff 1989).

The Divided Soul of Max Weber

Karl Emil Maximilian Weber was born in Erfurt, Germany, on April 21, 1864, the first child of Max Weber, Sr., and Helene Fallenstein Weber. He was born into an economically comfortable and solidly bourgeois household. His father, who was trained as a lawyer, was a prominent member of the political establishment. He served in a leadership role in the National Liberal Party and was elected to the Reichstag. The senior Weber appears to have lacked any deep ideals or convictions. He was a pragmatist, familiar with and secure in the world of backroom wheeling and dealing. He was keenly interested in and knowledgeable about the inner workings of the political establishment in Germany. Because of these preoccupations, he has been depicted, perhaps somewhat unfairly, as a superficial and indulgent man, at home in the "well-fed, self-satisfied" world of politicians and bureaucrats (Mommsen 1984; Käsler 1988:2).

In stark contrast to the hedonism of his father, Weber's mother was an ascetic. She grew up in and absorbed the values of a family that placed a premium on intellectual pursuits, and Weber's ultimate choice of a scholarly career clearly revealed the imprint of his maternal upbringing. Weber's mother was also a deeply religious woman. An outgrowth of her religious beliefs led her to an interest in humanitarian social reform. Helene's strict Calvinist background, however, made her fearful of the possibility that she might not be saved, and this anxiety prompted her to lead a life of self-denial in which her concerns were more on otherworldly considerations than with the everyday pleasures pursued by her husband (Weber 1988:31–63).

Not surprisingly, the household was characterized by considerable tension between the parents, a tension that intensified over time, and Max Weber appears to have internalized those tensions. Early in his life, it appeared that he was going to follow in his father's footsteps, but as he matured, father and son became increasingly alienated from one another. Although over time Weber's sympathies were closer to his mother, he could not share her deeply religious nature. Indeed, he once described himself as "unmusical religiously." Although it is difficult to determine exactly what he meant by this (he did claim that he was "neither antireligious nor irreligious"), it is evident that he did not share his mother's piety (Weber 1988:324; Swatos and Kivisto 1991a). He did, however, share her interest in social reform.

The Formative Period of Weber's Thought

Despite the tension, Weber's family situation during his youth made possible the opportunity for him to meet many important political and academic figures because they were frequent guests in the Weber household. These included, in addition to leaders of the National Liberal Party, some of the most influential scholars of their time, such as the philosopher Wilhelm Dilthey and historians Heinrich von Treitschke and Theodor Mommsen. Weber and his younger brother Alfred, who also became a well-known sociologist, were permitted to listen in on their intellectually stimulating discussions (Weber 1988:39).

After a stint at the University of Heidelberg and a tour of military duty, Weber was awarded a doctorate of laws in 1889 from the University of Berlin, having written his dissertation on the history of trading companies in the Middle Ages. Two years later, he completed his "Habilitation" thesis with a study of the agrarian history of Rome. As these topics suggest, he was trained in economics and history. In his subsequent shift to the new discipline of sociology, these disciplines, far from being abandoned, were incorporated into and became an integral part of his contributions to sociology.

His rigorous and disciplined lifestyle—resembling his mother's rather than his father's—made him a formidable intellectual figure. The breadth and scope of his knowledge was nothing short of remarkable. Indeed, Weber was earmarked by some of his professors as one of the best and brightest of his generation. Mommsen identified Weber as the aging scholar's heir apparent, once informing his student, "When I come to die, there is no one better to whom I should like to say this: Son, the spear is too heavy for my hand, carry it on" (Coser 1971:237).

Soon after he completed his university work, Weber became engaged to and subsequently married his cousin Marianne Schnitger. Together they formed a remarkable intellectual couple, and their home became a meeting place for intellectuals holding widely divergent views. At approximately the same time he formed a friendship with Friedrich Naumann, the head of the Christian-Social Movement, and also became involved in the activities of the Evangelical-Social Congress, a Protestant reform association. Initially under the auspices of the Verein für Sozialpolitik and later in conjunction with the activities of members of the congress, and particularly in connection with an ethical tract written by his cousin Otto Baumgarten on the conditions of the working class, Weber commenced on his first major sociological investigation. This project involved a study of agricultural workers in the East Elbian region of Germany near the Polish border. The 900-page report, written in a year's time, was an early example of applied social research because it was intended to yield reform-oriented policies designed to remedy problems identified by the project (Bendix 1960:14–41; Käsler 1988:52–63; Swatos and Kivisto 1991b).

Although concerned primarily with economic issues, Weber's approach to the topic reflected what would characterize his subsequent work: an assumption that the economy and the political are intricately intertwined and that political considerations play a significant role in determining economic success or failure. In contrast to the rest of Germany, which had become a unified nation only in 1871, the region east of the Elbe River was characterized by a quasi-feudal agrarian system controlled by the great landowners, known as the Junkers, who possessed considerable political power. They had been the bulwark of the Prussian state, sharing that state's patriarchal, militaristic, and traditionalist worldview. Their economic position was threatened by imported grain, and in the face of this competitive threat they called on the government to impose tariffs on agricultural imports. At the same time, they began to replace German workers with impoverished immigrant workers from Poland and Russia.

Weber's response to this situation foreshadowed future concerns that would be developed in his writings on politics. One of the more unsavory aspects of his response was an ethnocentric hostility to migrant workers. This was a product of Weber's fervent German nationalism, an aspect of his political thought that has troubled many scholars influenced by his ideas

(Loewenstein 1966; Mommsen 1989; Scaff 1989). It remains clear, however, that throughout his life, Weber was concerned with the conditions necessary for the emergence of a powerful modern German state, one capable of competing against other European nations also in the process of industrializing. Weber believed that the economic crisis in East Elbian, Germany, could be resolved only when the power of the Junkers was undercut. He considered them to be the main impediment to the kinds of political and economic developments that were necessary for Germany to become simultaneously a successful industrial nation and a modern democracy (Giddens 1995b:15–56).

Clearly, Weber wanted to see Germany emerge as a powerful capitalist industrial nation. Somewhat less clear was his political vision, particularly his views on the efficacy and necessity of democracy. Two views, however, were clear early on in his political thinking: because of the links between the economy and the polity, the middle classes had to play a crucial role in German political life, and strong leaders were a necessity. These views were reinforced in his 1895 inaugural lecture at the University of Freiburg that was devoted to the topic of "The Nation State and Economic Policy." Indeed, in this address, with a tone of skepticism, pessimism, and resignation that would become hallmarks of Weber's subsequent writings, he made very clear the vantage point from which he made his judgments about Germany's political options. In no uncertain terms, Weber (1994) proclaimed, "I am a member of the bourgeois (*bürgerlich*) classes. I feel myself to be a bourgeois, and I have been brought up to share their views and ideals" (p. 23). After identifying himself with the worldview of his audience, Weber proceeded to criticize the German bourgeoisie for their lack of political maturity, reflected in their failure to rein in the political influence of such anachronistic elements as the Junkers (Loewenstein 1966; Mommsen 1987; Scaff 1989; Weber 1994:1–28).

Weber had quickly established himself as an intellectual figure of singular importance who was preoccupied with the fate of politics in the modern world (Lassman and Velody 1998). Moreover, it was clear that he sought to define himself as something more than a solitary scholar content to remain in his study. Rather, he wanted to be seen as a public intellectual, involved in the political affairs of his day: not merely a scholar, but a man of action.

Breakdown and Beyond

In 1896, Weber was appointed to a professorship of political science at the University of Heidelberg, and it appeared that from this position he was poised to become that man of action residing in the world of academia. Weber was a driven man who pushed himself hard, both physically and emotionally, attempting to fuse the dual vocations of the scholar and the public man. Unfortunately, tragedy struck, leaving his promising career in shambles.

The precipitating event occurred in 1897 when Weber's parents visited their son and daughter-in-law. During the stay, Weber got into a bitter argument with his father regarding the elder Weber's authoritarian treatment of his wife. As Marianne Weber (1988) described the scene, "The son was no longer able to contain his pent-up anger. The lava erupted and the monstrous thing happened: The son sat in judgment on his father" (p. 230). The argument ended with Weber demanding that his father leave his home. His father returned to Berlin and died shortly thereafter, without the two having achieved reconciliation.

Although he did not admit to feeling guilty about this event, Weber had a nervous breakdown several months afterward. For the next several years, he was effectively incapable of engaging in either scholarship or political activity. Weber had burned his candle at both ends, and he had internalized the contradictions between his mother's and father's respective worldviews. These factors, no doubt, were major contributors to his collapse (Mitzman 1970).

What exactly do we know about Weber's breakdown? Until recently, intellectual historians had to rely to a considerable extent on Marianne Weber's account of her husband's psychic suffering. Her biography has proven to be a problematic source for two reasons. First, our contemporary understanding of mental illness is quite different from that of Weber's era. The diagnostic language we use today makes it difficult to translate into the language from the early part of the 20th century. Consequently, if one asks today what exactly the illness that caused his psychic suffering was, it is quite true that "a precise answer to this question is no longer possible" (Radkau 2009:149). Second, Marianne did her part to prevent a clinically dispassionate assessment of Weber's psychological problems in order to protect her husband's intellectual legacy.

Elizabeth Kolbert (2004) is not off the mark in describing Marianne's biography of her husband as a "deeply odd book" (p. 157). It contributed to a widely held view that, due to their apparently unconsummated marriage, Weber remained a sexually repressed celibate throughout his life. As recent biographical evidence makes clear, this was not the case. There is abundant evidence to prove that he entered into two highly erotic extramarital relationships, with Else von Richthofen and Mina Tobler. We have recently learned a considerable amount about the depth of Weber's illness and his sexual proclivities from German historian Joachim Radkau's (2009) provocative biography. Unfortunately, in his attempt to turn our received understanding on its head by making the case that not only was Weber propelled by sexual drives heretofore unappreciated but that these drives somehow contributed to his intellectual virtuosity, Radkau has also produced a deeply odd book—one that fails to convincingly connect Weber's genuinely, deeply troubled psychological state to his intellectual contributions.

In addition to this psychological explanation, however, Weber's problems can be partially attributed to his bleak intellectual assessment of the prospects for German economic and political development (Portes 1986). While he never taught again, Weber did regain his intellectual powers, and between 1903 and his premature death due to pneumonia in 1920, he produced an enormous body of writings that today are considered to be far more important than anything that preceded the breakdown. Indeed, he resumed writing with what has become his best-known work, *The Protestant Ethic and the Spirit of Capitalism* ([1904/1905] 1958). This essay and a speech on "Politics as a Vocation" that he delivered to a student group in Munich the year before his death—in the aftermath of the nation's defeat in World War I—can be seen as framing his prophetic vision of the future, providing a starkly pessimistic account of Germany's economic and political prospects.

The Iron Cage: The Economic Undergirding of Modern Democratic Politics

Near the end of *The Protestant Ethic and the Spirit of Capitalism*, which is an excursion into the formative period of capitalism, Weber ([1904/1905] 1958) turned his attention to the future rather than the past, writing,

> This order is now bound to the technical and economic conditions of machine production which today determine the lives of all the individuals who are born into this mechanism, not only those directly concerned with economic acquisition, with irresistible force. Perhaps it will so determine them until the last ton of fossilized coal is burnt. . . . But fate has decreed that [the future will become] an iron cage. (p. 181)

The metaphor of the iron cage (rendered a "steel-hard casing" in Stephen Kalberg's translation [Weber 2002:123]) is a reflection of Weber's deep concern that the modern industrial world posed a threat to individuality and freedom and thus had negative implications for democracy. The capitalist economic order was so powerful that he saw no way out. In fact, he was highly critical of anyone who engaged in the kind of wishful thinking that suggested people could turn back the hands of time to return to an idyllic preindustrial world. He was also suspicious of socialists who thought that by abolishing capitalism, the problems of an industrial society would be overcome. In his view, socialism would not simply share with capitalism the problems inherent in industrial society but, in fact, would render them even more problematic.

On the 100th anniversary of the book's publication, Elizabeth Kolbert (2004) reflected on his argument, claiming that "the reason Weber's essay remains so compelling despite all the controversy is that it isn't really a work about the past; it's an allegory about the present" (p. 154). This, I would contend is not an accurate assessment. Rather, it's both, with the bulk of the work constituting an exploration into the cultural history of Western Europe.

The Protestant Ethic Thesis

What was it that Weber thought he had identified as inherent in capitalist industrial society that would progressively transform our world into the prison house suggested by the iron cage metaphor? To answer this question, we need to briefly consider his understanding of the "spirit" of capitalism. The capitalist mentality encouraged, in his view, a unique orientation toward economic activity. It contrasted sharply, for example, with economic traditionalists, who were content to work merely to get by, as well as with persons motivated solely by greed or by a desire for ostentatious displays of wealth. Weber found in Ben Franklin's writings a perfect instance of what he meant by the capitalist spirit. To claim, as Franklin did, that "time is money" and "a penny saved is a penny earned" is to define accumulation as the goal of economic activity, with self-discipline and rational calculation as desiderata. The capitalist should be seen as a rational miser—a person devoted to the task of creating wealth not to enjoy its fruits but to reinvest it to generate even more wealth.

Why would someone act in this way? This is the fundamental question addressed in the book, which Colin Campbell (2006) correctly reminds us is "essentially an examination of the role of motives in human action" (p. 205). Like a monk who gives up the pleasures of the world to devote himself to an otherworldly life of prayer and contemplation, the capitalist is an ascetic. Unlike the monk, however, the capitalist remains in the world and amasses wealth. Weber called this unique economic ethic "innerworldly asceticism" and argued that such a mentality could not be understood without linking it to the religious transformation brought about by the Protestant Reformation. Indeed, he contended that it was not by chance that capitalism arose in certain places in Western Europe where and when the Protestant Reformation took root (Marshall 1982; Poggi 1983).

Specifically, Weber attempted to illustrate how the emergence of inner-worldly asceticism revolved around two figures associated with the Reformation, Martin Luther and John Calvin. Luther's importance for the Protestant ethic thesis involved his rejection of the idea that the highest form of religious vocation, or "calling," demanded a retreat from the world to a monastery. In Luther's theology, all worldly occupations could be seen as religiously inspired callings. Mundane work acquired religious significance. This was an important step toward activity in the world, but according to Weber it was not sufficient to explain the ultimate impact of Protestantism on the emergence of capitalism.

Here, Calvin's contribution proved to be decisive. According to his doctrine of predestination, an omnipotent and omniscient God had determined, even before people were born, whether they were among the saved or the damned, chosen for eternal life in paradise or an eternity in hell. This created great anxiety and inner turmoil for believers who wanted to know something about the state of their eternal souls. According to Weber, the faithful searched for a sign that would give them some sense of their relationship to God, and they found it in economic success. In other words, believers viewed the acquisition of wealth to be an indication of God's grace. The result was that people were motivated to acquire wealth through disciplined work because by so doing they gained some assurance of their status as one of the elect (Weber [1904/1905] 1958; Poggi 1983:62–78).

This suggested that there was a connection between the ethics of Protestantism and the capitalist spirit. Contrary to a common misunderstanding of Weber's thesis, Protestantism was not to be seen, in any simple way, as the cause and the capitalist spirit as the effect. Weber was intent on challenging the economic determinism that he associated with contemporary Marxist theorists, but he did not offer the religious factor as a simple alternative to the causal role of economic forces (Cohen 2002). Rather, Weber characterized the connection as one of an "elective affinity." In other words, it was not by chance that capitalism emerged in precisely those lands where Protestantism had become the dominant form of Christianity. Weber did not mean that this was the whole story in understanding the rise of capitalism. In his view, however, it was an important part of the puzzle, one overlooked by those inspired by Marx's materialist theory of social change.

Subsequent comparative studies of the major world religions were designed to further our understanding of why the historical fate of Western civilization appeared to be so different from that of the rest of the world. In his studies of Hinduism, Buddhism, Confucianism, Taoism, and Islam, Weber attempted to identify the elements of their respective economic ethics that seemed to work against the development of the capitalist spirit (Weber [1904/1905] 1958, [1916] 1951; Käsler 1988:94–127; Huff and Schluchter 1999).

Bureaucratization of the World

Weber was the first scholar to analyze modern bureaucratic organizations, which he considered an essential component of capitalist industrial society. Indeed, he believed that bureaucracy is as central to the modern economy as is the machine, convinced, as Kolbert (2004) put it, that "only a well-ordered bureaucracy is capable of supporting a modern technological society" (p. 157). The reason for this is that to succeed in the competitive marketplace the capitalist had to make decisions based on efficiency, calculability, predictability, and control. Weber agreed with Marx that capitalism encouraged a rational, scientific worldview. Technology was harnessed to machine production in the interest of increasing productive capacity. Likewise, business organizations were also rationalized, the result being the novel form of bureaucratic organization, which was becoming so pervasive that it appeared appropriate to define the modern age as the age of bureaucracy (Mommsen 1974; Glassman et al. 1993).

Once in motion, industrial society no longer needed to rely on the Protestant ethic. Instead, a society dominated by machine production and bureaucratic organization developed its own internal dynamic. Weber agreed with Marx's general depiction of the class structure of capitalist society, and he saw the potential for considerable class conflict. He did not, however, share Marx's belief that class conflict could provide a way to resolve the central problems of industrial society. The egalitarian aspirations of socialism could not be realized because of the necessity of bureaucracy in any industrial society, and bureaucracy entails decision making in terms of a hierarchical chain of command. Likewise, freedom is jeopardized insofar as individuals are controlled and constrained in the interests of the effective functioning of bureaucratic organizations.

In describing bureaucracy, Weber often used the image of a machine. People become cogs in a machine, losing their sense of individuality, creativity, and freedom. Bureaucracy produces an alienated and dehumanized attitude that, in Weber's words, works at "eliminating from official business, love, hatred, and all purely personal, irrational, and emotional elements which escape calculation" (Weber [1921] 1968, vol. 3:975; see also Giddens 1971:217).

Mechanization and bureaucratization combine to create an extraordinarily productive economic system, creating a material abundance unthinkable in earlier epochs. At the same time, these two phenomena conspire to construct the iron cage. Moreover, this trend is not confined to the economic realm, but it increasingly pervades all facets of social life—and Weber was particularly concerned with the way bureaucracy came to define contemporary politics. He (as cited in Lyon 1994) was convinced that the single most significant threat to democracy was bureaucracy:

> Together with the machine, the bureaucratic organization is engaged in building the bondage houses of the future, in which perhaps men will be like peasants in the ancient Egyptian state, acquiescent and powerless, while a purely technical good, that is rational, official administration and provision becomes the sole final value, which sovereignty decides the direction of their affairs. (p. 31)

Democracy Versus Bureaucracy

The reason I have devoted so much attention to economics in a chapter on politics is that although Weber insisted on the relative autonomy of politics, his understanding of the prospects for democracy were defined in terms of its major challenger, bureaucracy, which has its origins in capitalist industrialization.

Before we can understand his views on the conflict between democracy and bureaucracy, we must first grasp what Weber meant by democracy. This is a difficult task because Weber's own political orientation toward democracy is difficult to summarize and has been the subject of considerable debate and controversy. At some junctures in his life, Weber seemed to have little sympathy for democracy, whereas at other points he appeared to advocate it as a necessity for the modern nation.

Wolfgang Mommsen, a long-time student of Weber's thought, reflects the difficulty involved in assessing Weber's perspective on democracy because Mommsen's views have changed throughout the years. In his earliest writings, Mommsen depicted Weber as a nationalist determined to promote the greatness of Germany and urging the emergence of a powerful charismatic leader who had both the will and the power to transform the nation. In short, Weber's views were seen as fundamentally antidemocratic and, in fact, as a precursor to fascist thought. Years later, Mommsen changed his mind and concluded that Weber was, in fact, a proponent of liberal democracy whose pessimism about the prospects for the future was so intense that he could most appropriately be described as a "liberal in despair" (Mommsen 1984, 1989; Scaff 1989:152–155).

Others have suggested that Weber viewed democracy only as a means to an end and not as an end in itself, and thus his support for democracy was always a tempered one: The best he could muster was an attitude that said, in effect, "two cheers for democracy." His fear, as Anthony Giddens (1994) noted, was that "democracy is a dreary business" lacking a heroic dimension and producing a leveling mediocrity (p. 105). It is quite clear, however, that Weber sought to encourage political developments in Germany that were intended to enhance, rather than undermine, democracy.

To sort out these divergent assessments, it is necessary to understand two features of Weber's thought on democracy: what he actually took democracy to be and, relatedly, how much democracy he thought one could realistically expect in the contemporary world of nation-states. Regarding Weber's definition of democracy, he contended that it referred to a political system in which the people were defined as participants in the polity rather than as passive subjects. Key to the notion of participation is an understanding of what it means to be a citizen. For Weber, to be a citizen meant that one was able to participate in decision making and policy formulation as well as to participate in choosing leaders (Weber 1978, 1994). Weber took it for granted that the process of democratization was one the central developmental trends of the modern world, seen, for example, in the suffrage movement, the demand for multiparty political systems, the call for fair elections, and the expanded role of elected legislative bodies.

Although Weber wrote about direct, participatory democracy—examining, for example, the significance of such techniques as ballot referenda and recall initiatives—he nonetheless thought that such direct approaches to decision making were of decidedly limited importance in the world of the modern nation-state. Democracy had its roots in the much smaller-scale enterprises of the Greek city-states, in which the active involvement of all citizens was a possibility (note, however, that a majority of the residents of these city-states, including women and slaves, were denied the right to become citizens). At the local level, direct democracy was a possibility, but according to Weber it is not possible in the large-scale nation-states characteristic of the contemporary world (Table 3.1).

Table 3.1 Balancing Bureaucracy and Democracy: Weber's "Constructive Oppositions"

Working parliament	versus	Government bureaucracy
Government bureaucracy	versus	Political leadership
Leadership by plebiscite	versus	Party bureaucracy leadership
Party bureaucracy leadership	versus	Emotionalized population

Instead, in such a context, the only viable form of democracy was representative democracy in which the citizens accorded considerable decision-making authority to elected officials. As a consequence, one of the major concerns of Weber regarded the matter of political leadership because the success or failure of democracy in any particular nation would be decided in no small part by the caliber of the nation's political leaders. Moreover, he sought to understand the proper relationship that needed to be established between leaders and the general citizenry.

Weber Contra Michels's "Iron Law of Oligarchy"

Weber's assessment of democratic prospects in Germany and elsewhere can be better appreciated by contrasting his views to those of his friend, Robert Michels, who in 1911 published *Political Parties*. Michels dedicated the book to Weber, although their views on politics differed appreciably. Michels underwent a profound political shift, moving from the Marxist Left to the far Right, where he ultimately embraced fascism. The conclusion he arrived at in this empirical study propelled him on this political odyssey: He claimed to have discovered what he provocatively called the iron law of oligarchy, and in so doing he proved the futility of attempting to establish democratic political systems.

What was this so-called law, and how did Michels think he had proven its existence? In its simplest formulation, the law states that "who says organization, says oligarchy" (Michels 1958:401). By this, Michels meant to indicate that democracy was impossible. He contended that even organizations dedicated to democratic principles would eventually and inevitably be transformed from democratic rule to oligarchic rule. Michels's evidence derived from research on the organizational transformations that had taken place in two branches of European socialism: political parties and leftist labor unions. In short, he selected to study organizations committed to democratic principles rather than those, such as a political party dedicated to something as fundamentally undemocratic as a monarchy, that made no such claims and thus would not be expected to operate democratically.

Michels claimed that over time, the socialist-inspired organizations moved from mass participation to a situation in which decisions were made by a small number of elites while the mass of the membership remained passive and uninvolved in defining goals and formulating plans to implement them. In other words, democracy gave way to oligarchy. This transformation occurred for several interrelated reasons. First (here, the imprint of Weber's thought is obvious), technical and administrative experts are needed to ensure the effective and rational functioning of the organization.

Thus, these experts must be granted considerable freedom to make decisions on their own rather than seeking to represent and reflect the will of the membership at large.

Second, operating with an elitist view of ordinary people, Michels claims that they exhibit a tendency to become dependent on those in positions of leadership. At the same time, leaders possess certain qualities that distinguish them from the masses and make them ideally suited to run the organization in accordance with their own judgment of how that should be done. In short, the gulf between the leaders and the led becomes increasingly more pronounced. When the experts and leaders are granted certain privileges or rewards because of the importance attached to their positions, this tendency is further exacerbated (Michels 1958; Roth 1963; Smelser and Warner 1976:237–253).

As a consequence of these conclusions, Michels contended that it was folly to advocate democracy. Instead, powerful charismatic leaders were needed to mobilize the masses in the pursuit of objectives formulated by the leaders and not the led. Although some commentators have suggested that Weber drew similar conclusions, such is not the case. He disagreed with Michels's overly restrictive definition of democracy, one that was unwilling to consider representative democracy as a genuine form of democracy. Because Weber disagreed, he did not think that the stark antithesis between democracy and oligarchy captured the range of alternative forms of governance that were actually possible.

Weber's Assessment of Socialism

Marxists tended to fuse democratic aspirations to a socialist transformation of the economy. Weber was sympathetic toward the desire of socialists to improve the conditions of the working class via the trade union movement, and he even urged electoral support for the moderate Social Democratic Party. Moreover, his openness to Marxist ideas is evident in the fact that one of the members of his inner circle of intellectual colleagues was Georg Lukács, arguably the most important Marxist theorist of revolution in the 20th century. Nonetheless, Weber could be scathing in his criticisms of thinkers on the far Left. Their utopian visions were, in his view, ill-conceived recipes for disaster. He once said of two important German Marxist theoreticians, "[Karl] Leibknecht belongs in the madhouse and Rosa Luxemburg in the zoological gardens" (as cited in Giddens 1995b:28).

The reason for this harsh assessment was that Weber was convinced that such Marxists failed to understand that a revolutionary transformation of society—one that destroyed capitalism and replaced it with socialism—would not resolve some of the central problems inherent in an industrialized and bureaucratized world. Replacing private ownership with public ownership would not mean much to most industrial workers. In an essay titled "Socialism," published during World War I, Weber (1978) made the following observation: "For the workers would very soon discover that the lot of the mine worker is not the slightest bit different whether the mine is privately or publicly owned" (pp. 254–255).

Weber thought that the socialist program, which he basically saw as a call for the creation of a welfare state, could only have practical significance if it were advanced within the parameters of capitalism, calling for political reforms that worked to the advantage of the most economically disadvantaged members of the society. To have any chance of achieving such goals, it was necessary for a multiparty democratic system to be in place. What was the role of political parties within the framework of the modern nation-state? We can better understand this only after becoming acquainted with the conceptual outline of Weber's formal political theory (Freund 1968; Eden 1984).

Herrschaft

Herrschaft is a key term in Weber's political sociology. It is usually translated as "authority" or "domination" and is connected to another key term, *macht*, or power. *Power* refers to the ability to accomplish a goal, despite resistance, and to get others to do what one wants them to do. *Authority* or *domination* refers to a situation in which individuals are perceived by the general population to be the rightful or legitimate bearers of power. In other words, whereas power alone implies a situation predicated on the ability to use force, authority contains the additional feature of consent. Weber considered herrschaft to be a bedrock, immutable feature of the world of politics. This applied to democratic and nondemocratic regimes. There was no way out of the fact that in the political realm, one would always confront struggles over power, over who would dominate whom, and on what basis that domination would occur (Weber [1921] 1968; Bendix 1960:285–416).

In *Economy and Society*, Weber ([1921] 1968) identified three ideal types of "legitimate domination": (a) traditional domination, which is based on appeals to custom and historical practice (e.g., monarchy); (b) charismatic domination, which involves allegiance and devotion to a leader based on that individual's presumed extraordinary character and abilities (e.g., Hitler or Gandhi); and (c) legal-rational domination, which places a premium on loyalty and obedience to the impersonal rule of the law (pp. 944–954). To say these are ideal types is to say that they are pure conceptual models. In the real world, they never appear in pure form but, rather, in various kinds of admixtures. To assess any particular political system, however, these ideal types are intended as benchmarks for comparative analysis.

In the contemporary world, legal-rational authority is the type associated with bureaucracy. It increasingly replaces traditional authority as the principal form of order. Weber was especially interested in determining the nature of the relationship in modern democracies between charismatic authority (which has the potential for disrupting the status quo) and legal-rational authority.

Politics as a Vocation

Democratic regimes, Weber was convinced, would of necessity entail large, specialized administrative staffs of members appointed to their positions on the basis of their expertise. In other words, inherent in modern democracies are powerful bureaucracies. Bureaucracies cannot be eliminated because they are necessary to ensure the rational functioning of large-scale organizations. Thus, the question arises as to whether and how it is possible to minimize the negative consequences of bureaucratic domination. Weber's proposed solution was to play democracy against bureaucracy in what Wolfgang Schluchter (1989) refers to as a situation of "constructive opposition" (p. 373).

Whether this could be accomplished revolved around the issue of political leadership and the role of political parties. On what basis would the citizenry select leaders to represent their interests? Would the leaders be able to control the bureaucrats, or would the latter—nonelected officials—ultimately dominate political decision making? What was the relationship of leaders to parties?

Weber believed that the only antidote to the stultifying effects of bureaucratic domination is a political system that he termed *plebiscitary democracy*. Such a system required charismatic leaders who would use their electoral appeal, at appropriate times, to initiate actions that challenged and deviated from existing bureaucratic procedures. To protect against the ascendance of antidemocratic demagogues, however, these leaders should operate within both political parties and a parliamentary system. Indeed, both parties and legislative bodies were important insofar as they would be training grounds for future leaders and check charismatic leaders from abandoning democracy.

When he delivered his valedictory speech, "Politics as a Vocation," Weber articulated the requirements of the person with a genuine call to political leadership. Delivered in the aftermath of Germany's humiliating defeat in World War I, he speculated on the nation's prospects for the immediate future. At the end of the address, he pondered whether political leaders with a true calling could be found anywhere on the German political landscape. His conclusion was disquieting for the primarily student audience. Weber (1978) could not point to any place where such leaders could be found, and thus he offered the following pessimistic prognosis: "It is not 'summer's front' which lies before us, but first of all a Polar night of icy darkness and severity, whichever group may outwardly be victorious at present" (pp. 224–225).

The problem, from his perspective, was that Germany lacked the requisites to create the proper balance between democracy and bureaucracy. Weber died without seeing the accuracy of his prognosis: the fracturing of German democracy, the intensification of conflict between the extreme Left and extreme Right, and ultimately the culmination of the destruction of German democracy with the ascension to power of the Nazis. Although he had focused on the democratic prospects of his native Germany, Weber's skepticism and his conviction that there were no easy political solutions to the problems he had identified give his work a contemporary poignancy. His pessimism about the logic of domination in the modern world made possible by the new modes of control parallels the perspectives of several recent social theorists, but perhaps nobody more than the late French social theorist Michel Foucault (1988; for a comparative analysis, see Szakolczai 1998). Jeffrey Alexander (2006) is quite right when he observes that in Foucault's writings "we come face to face with the dark side of modernity" (p. 19). His work on power/knowledge offers a forceful critique of new modes of authoritarian control and new forms of injustice, but there is a one-sided quality to his theorizing due to the fact that he fails to reckon with the Janus-faced character of modernity. Unlike Foucault, who does not attempt to link his work to the heritage bequeathed by Weber, a wide array of subsequent theorists concerned with the fate of democracy throughout the world have felt compelled to wrestle with Weber's penetrating assessments (Diggins 1996).

Talcott Parsons on the Democratic Prospect

In 1925, five years after Weber's death, a young Harvard graduate student spent a year studying in Weber's old hometown, Heidelberg. Talcott Parsons made this journey after spending a year at the London School of Economics (LSE), where, as at Harvard, he claimed that he had never heard Weber's name mentioned. This is curious given that one of the people he met at the LSE was R. H. Tawney ([1926] 1958), the author of *Religion and the Rise of Capitalism: A Historical Study*, a work that has often been compared to Weber's Protestant ethic essay. Once he arrived in Germany, Parsons soon fell under the spell of Weber's thought, and he had an opportunity to meet and study with a number of Weber's former associates. Marianne Weber invited the young student to the intellectual salon at her home that had continued after Weber's death. Parsons was so intrigued by the German scholar's ideas that in his dissertation he addressed Weber's theory of capitalism, comparing it with the views of Werner Sombart, one of Weber's contemporaries. In addition, Parsons translated *The Protestant Ethic and the Spirit of Capitalism* (Weber [1904/1905] 1958) into English. Thus began his career as a major expositor of Weberian thought in America (Parsons 1959; Hamilton 1983:31–34; Alexander 1987:22–35; Brick 1993).

Parsons, however, was far more than an exegete of the work of others. He would become, beginning with the publication of *The Structure of Social Action* (1937), the single most important sociological theorist, not simply in America but in the world (Wearne 1989). After World War II, Parsons played a singularly prominent role in shaping future generations of sociologists. His home institution, Harvard, became in effect the center of the sociological universe, and the best and brightest became his students. Many of these youthful academicians went on to become influential social thinkers in their own right, including two individuals discussed elsewhere in this book, Robert K. Merton and Robert Bellah (for a discussion of Merton on democracy, see Hollinger 1996:80–96).

Parsons's own theoretical contributions, known at various points in his career as functionalism, structural functionalism, and systems theory, began as an effort to distill from the writings of a number of classic figures in sociology—the four most important for his purposes being Max Weber, Émile Durkheim, Vilfredo Pareto, and the economist Alfred Marshall—a convergence that could become the basis for the creation of a grand theoretical synthesis. Parsons's career was devoted to articulating and advancing this synthesis (Parsons 1937; Alexander 1982/1983; Levine 1995; Ferraro 2001; Trevino 2001).

Parsonian Thought in the Context of His Times

The halcyon days of Parsonian thought were the two decades from the end of World War II until the period of widespread societal discontent that occurred during the 1960s. His sociological theory resonated with the times. This was a period of unprecedented prosperity in the United States, a time when many thought that public policies had been devised that could be used to avert anything similar to the economic disaster of the Depression. The welfare state erected during the New Deal was taken to be a part of the social landscape. At the same time, this was the height of the Cold War, and the United States was viewed by many as the embodiment of a political system dedicated to democratic principles. The Cold War pitted this bastion of the "Free World" against the repressive authoritarian regimes of the Communist bloc, dominated by the Soviet Union (Mills 1963; Parsons 1990).

In this context, Parsons's theory appeared to critics to express a remarkable naïveté about the actual state of American society and an unwarranted optimism about its ability to overcome various social problems without risk of significant conflict and unrest and without necessitating fundamental structural changes. During the last decade of his life, Parsons was witness to an unrelenting attack on his thought from sociologists caught up in the 1960s challenges to the legitimacy of American social institutions and values. Parsons was accused of being an apologist for the status quo, with his abstract theory, written in a difficult-to-penetrate prose, providing a gloss on the tensions and conflicts that were, when not overt, bubbling just beneath the surface. He was depicted as a conservative, papering over the cracks in the social contract, thus making America appear far more harmonious and orderly than the facts actually warranted (Gouldner 1970; Bourricauld 1981; Savage 1981; Buxton 1985; Apter 1987).

In the wake of the dramatic events of the 1960s, American society appeared far more fractured and fragmented than it did a decade earlier. Parsons's emphasis on wholeness, social integration, and the requisites of order seemed ill equipped to provide an adequate interpretive framework to account for societal crises. Thus, many sociologists rejected his approach to theory, with the result being that for contemporary social theory, in contrast to the 1950s and 1960s, no one theory can be seen as hegemonic. Instead of the unifying theory that Parsons sought to develop, sociology became a genuinely multiparadigm discipline, exhibiting considerable competition and contestation (Sciulli and Gernstein 1985).

Parsons as an Advocate of Social Reform

In recent years, a number of scholars have initiated a reevaluation and reappreciation of Parsons, and in the process they have presented a decidedly different picture than the one outlined previously (see, for example, Brick 2006:121–151). Quite correctly, this rethinking has concluded that throughout his long career, Parsons was never a conservative apologist for the status quo. Indeed, as a graduate student, Parsons was deeply influenced by democratic reformism and probably should be seen as a democratic socialist. During his undergraduate years at Amherst, he headed the campus chapter of the Student League for Industrial Democracy. During the 1930s, he aligned himself with the left wing of the Democratic Party, becoming an enthusiastic supporter of the New Deal. During the 1950s, he was a critic of

McCarthyism and, in fact, was placed under surveillance by the FBI (Keen 1993). He came to the defense of Robert Bellah, whose position at Harvard was threatened due to his past membership in the Communist Party (Bellah 2005). He supported the civil rights movement, opposed the war in Vietnam (expressing his willingness to serve as an adviser to antiwar candidate for president Eugene McCarthy), and voted for George McGovern. In other words, his politics were squarely located on the moderate Left, and from this vantage he was far more aware of societal crises and more critical of threats to democracy than had previously been realized (Parsons 1991; Alexander 1987; Camic 1989; Nielsen 1991; Brick 1993).

Democracy Under Attack

The formative period of Parsons's intellectual development was shaped by three significant world events: the Russian Revolution, which established the first communist state; the Depression that rocked economies throughout the world; and the rise of fascism in Germany and Italy. Both communism and fascism presented challenges to democracy, whereas the Depression called into question the ability of capitalism to work its way out of the economic crisis that began with the stock market crash in 1929. In this milieu, there was considerable speculation about whether the United States and other functioning democracies would follow the road to one or another form of totalitarianism: communism or fascism.

Parsons (1993, 1954) contributed to this discussion in several of his early writings, especially in a series of essays written during World War II on fascism as a social movement, on democracy in pre-Nazi Germany, and on the role of the authoritarian personality in German society. He agreed with the essentials of Weber's view that Germany lagged behind trends elsewhere because of the continued influence in Germany of premodern elements. Parsons (1954) described the difference between Germany and more established democracies as follows:

> It has thus long been clear to competent scholars that the German state differed markedly from its British or American counterparts. This difference may in the main be characterized in terms of its interdependent "feudal," militaristic, bureaucratic, and authoritarian features. The predominant impress of these elements came from Prussia, but the position of Prussia was sufficiently central to strongly color the whole of Germany. (p. 106)

With the German defeat in World War I and the punitive terms of the Treaty of Versailles, political factions on the extreme Left and the extreme Right jeopardized the democratic aspirations of the Weimar Republic. In explaining the meaning of the victory of the far Right with the rise to power of the Nazi Party, Parsons used Weber's typology of authority to describe how the Nazi state differed from Western democracies. Whereas in the latter, charisma was seen as being held in check by the more powerful legal-rational authority, in Germany charisma got the upper hand. Hitler's charismatic authority, fueled by a reactionary "blood and soil" nationalism, unleashed powerful irrational forces. This meant that rationality, in the form of getting the trains to run on time and in creating a highly efficient machinery of death in the assault on European Jewry, ended up in the service of the irrationality of charisma.

In a lengthy memorandum prepared for the Council for Democracy, Parsons (1993) scrutinized factors in American society that could be perceived to threaten democracy. Although he identified areas of concern, he was nonetheless confident that the demise of democracy in Germany was not a portent of things to come in America. The reasons he pointed to had mainly to do with deeply implanted cultural values that served to reinforce and solidify democratic institutions. Central among these values were (a) a "rational-critical spirit," which both facilitated scientific and technological learning and held in check the anti-intellectualism that was intrinsic to the Nazi appeal; (b) a respect for the law, which served as a break on any attempt by leaders to place themselves above the law; (c) the constitutional provision of civil liberties, which curbs authorities from acting in an arbitrary and capricious manner that infringes on the rights of individuals; and (d) an inclusive sense of what it means to be a citizen.

Citizenship in a Democracy

Whereas Weber concerned himself with the requisites for leadership in creating and sustaining a democratic polity, Parsons was particularly interested in the phenomenon of citizenship. This is nowhere more evident in his work than in his writings on race and ethnicity. For example, in an influential article on the civil rights movement, Parsons (1967) attempted to employ his general theoretical framework to assess the prospects for "full citizenship" for African Americans.

Relevance of T. H. Marshall on Citizenship

Parsons's views on citizenship were influenced by the work of T. H. Marshall (1964). Marshall argued that citizenship in democratic regimes grows over time so that ultimately it involves three distinct dimensions, which he termed the civil, the political, and the social. He considered this to be an evolutionary process, and this view of sequential development meshed with Parsons's own evolutionary view of social change. According to Marshall, civil rights were the first to be established. These included free speech, the right to fair trials, and equal access to the legal system. Political rights followed these civil rights and included the rights to vote, to run for elective office, to be involved in political parties, and to participate in various ways in the legislative process. The third dimension arose with the advent of the modern welfare state. Although Marshall had in mind the British welfare state, which took shape during the reign of the Labour Party in the 1920s, Parsons's primary focus was the impact of Roosevelt's New Deal in advancing this dimension. Social rights were those things that were defined as entitlements, such as Social Security, unemployment benefits, health benefits such as Medicare and Medicaid, and educational benefits.

Full Citizenship for African Americans?

Using the general theoretical explanation of the expansion of what it means to be a citizen in a modern democratic state, Parsons (1967) turned to the case of African Americans during the height of the civil rights movement. He addressed two interrelated topics: the historical factors that denied African Americans full citizenship and the forces at play that could be seen as promoting their inclusion as full citizens. Regarding the first topic, he asked the following: What has prevented blacks from enjoying the fruits of full citizenship? Why have they been relegated to the status of "second-class citizens"? What explanation can be offered to account for the fact that for several centuries this group has been systematically denied the benefits of full incorporation into what Parsons refers to as the "societal community"?

Because Parsons, more so than his mentor, Weber, accorded a priority to the role of ideas in encouraging or inhibiting change, his answer hinged on the matter of cultural values and in so doing ignored such explanations relying on distinctly economic or political factors. Essentially, he argued that blacks have been excluded because, like Jews and Catholics in the past, their values were seen as antithetical to core American values, and thus they were defined as not being capable of incorporation into American society. The fact that until the 20th century most blacks lived in the South was an important part of the reason they had been excluded for so long, because in Parsons's view, the South was a regionally isolated place where archaic values survived. Most important, southern values were at odds with the general societal thrust for a more inclusive vision of citizenship. Over time, these anachronistic values would weaken to a point at which they could no longer impede the full inclusion of black Americans into the ranks of American citizens.

Citizenship and Solidarity

The singular importance Parsons attached to citizenship was due to the fact that he thought that in genuinely modern societies, citizenship becomes the central criterion for national solidarity. In the past, differences based on religion, ethnicity, or territory were sufficiently powerful to be used as a basis for determining who would be included and who would be excluded from general societal membership. In a fully modern society such as the United States, however, "the common status of citizenship provides a sufficient foundation for national solidarity" (Parsons 1971:22).

What this meant for Parsons was that the pluralistic character of American society posed no intrinsic problem to the forging of a common national identity and purpose. Ethnic, religious, and regional differences could be accommodated by the larger, overarching national identity, and conflicts arising because of these differences were capable of resolution without the fear that they would tear the society apart or result in a bloody civil war. Giuseppe Sciortino (2005) has observed that Parsons "was among the first theorists to stress the optional elements of contemporary ethnic identity and group membership" (p. 122). In *The System of Modern Societies,* Parsons (1971) discusses these issues in terms of the societal community. The concept was the focus of *American Society: A Theory of the Societal Community*, a manuscript that he left unfinished when he died, but has recent been published as a result of the editorial efforts of Sciortino (Parsons 2007). The societal community refers to a sphere of society distinct from the economy, the polity, religious institutions, and the family. As such it can be seen as his distinctive take on civil society, a sphere that he thinks promotes both social solidarity and inclusion.

In stark contrast to Weber, whose deep pessimism clearly colored his views on the prospects for democracy in Germany, Parsons's remarkable optimism shaped his sunny conclusions about democracy in America. Moreover, because Parsons tended to see the United States as a model of modernity, his thinking would lead one to conclude that democracy was secure in other advanced industrial nations and that a democratic wave would sweep over the globe transforming the political systems in previously undemocratic nations poised on the road to modernity (Parsons 1967, 1993; Spinner 1994; Faist 1995). Given that in Parsons's work society and the nation-state are synonymous, however, the idea of conceiving citizenship as a global phenomenon that was capable of transcending state boundaries remained underdeveloped. This has led, as will be discussed in Chapter 6, to the recent call for an unbounded theory of citizenship reflecting the impact of globalization (Kivisto 2002:24; Kivisto and Faist 2007:102–129).

Capitalism Versus Democracy? Lipset and Beyond

It has often been noted that all existing democratic nations have capitalist economies but not all capitalist economies exist in democratic polities (Glassman et al. 1993; Lipset 1994). This suggests the possibility that democracy needs a capitalist market economy, whereas the reverse is not necessarily true. Is there, to use Weber's phrase, an "elective affinity" between capitalism and democracy? If there is, how should we understand the nature of the relationship?

This is a question that political sociologist Seymour Martin Lipset has wrestled with during the course of his career, evident from his early empirical investigations into *Agrarian Socialism* and *Union Democracy* to his presidential address to the American Sociological Association (Lipset 1950, 1994; Lipset, Trow, and Coleman 1956). It was in *Political Man*, however, that he most clearly articulated the central argument of his understanding of the relationship between capitalism and democracy (Lipset 1963a).

Whereas Weber was preoccupied with the uniqueness of the German case and Parsons with the American case, Lipset has explicitly and consistently concerned himself with cross-national comparisons. His thinking on the subject crystallized as the Soviet bloc nations—the Second World—rejected market economies in favor of state-centered "command" economies, whereas former European colonies in what became known as the Third World obtained independence and began the process of nation building and economic development (Lipset 1963b). Lipset sought to find clues that would help ascertain the likelihood that democratic forces might emerge in the Soviet bloc to challenge communism. At the same time he sought to determine the extent to which a democratic impulse would infuse the new postcolonial nations. In other words, he was interested in identifying those factors that served to either advance or retard the cause of democracy. In this regard, he deemed socialism as a means of advancing democracy to be a failure. In his study with Gary Marks on the factors that contributed to the failure of socialism in the United States, the final chapter claims that the exceptionalism of the American case has ended as other liberal democracies have increasingly come to look more like the American model, rather than the other way around (Lipset and Marks 2000:261–294).

From Alcove No. 1 to the Hoover Institution

Lipset was part of a remarkable generation of New York intellectuals who cut their political teeth on socialism during the 1930s as undergraduates at New York's City College. His confreres included Daniel Bell (discussed in Chapter 2) and a number of others who would go on to make their names as important figures in American sociology, including Morroe Berger, Nathan Glazer, Alvin Gouldner, Peter Rossi, and Philip Selznick. Lipset's father was a trade unionist and socialist, and Lipset took this political perspective to heart by joining, like Bell, the Young People's Socialist League. When he entered City College, Lipset became a participant in the heated debates that transpired in Alcove No. 1 of the college's dining hall—the place where the anti-Stalinist leftists (many of whom saw themselves as Trotskyites) congregated (Lipset 1964; Jacoby 1987).

Disillusioned by the antidemocratic political system erected in the Soviet Union and concerned about the threat of fascism, Lipset wanted to discover in what circumstances socialism and democracy were possible. He became a sociologist to probe this abiding concern. Thus, his landmark studies on Canada's agrarian socialist party, the Cooperative Commonwealth Federation, and on the International Typographical Union in the United States were efforts to revisit Michels's iron law of oligarchy. In both case studies, Lipset concluded that, contrary to Michels's prediction, the organizations functioned democratically. Without denying that many democratic organizations were transformed into oligarchic ones, Lipset disagreed with Michels's conclusions and sought to determine which factors served to promote or enhance democracy and which ones worked against it (Lipset 1950; Lipset et al. 1956).

Lipset became a major figure in the development of political sociology in the second half of the 20th century, teaching at a number of prominent institutions, including Harvard and Berkeley. Over time, his political views moved further to the Right because he concluded that the utopian vision of his socialist youth could not be realized, and he sought to discover what was necessary to realistically preserve democracy. Ultimately, Lipset was defined by many (although not all) as a neo-conservative, and for a time he settled into the Hoover Institution on War, Revolution and Peace, a conservative think tank located on the campus of Stanford University.

Economic Development and Democracy

In his move across the political spectrum, Lipset became convinced that a crucial requisite for a thriving democracy is a flourishing economy, one in which the vast majority of the population is in a position to live relatively comfortably and to maintain a conviction that the economy is fundamentally stable. In other words, he thought that the economic well-being of the citizenry is important as well as their faith that their economic status is not going to erode or otherwise be threatened by economic upheaval.

Lipset (1963a) identified the level of economic development of a nation as the most critical factor in establishing the precondition for democracy. He described the relationship as follows: "All the various aspects of economic development—industrialization, urbanization, wealth, and education—are so closely interrelated as to form one major factor which has the political correlate of democracy" (p. 41). Simply stated, the greater the economic affluence of a nation, the better the prospects for democracy.

This being the case, if nonmarket economies such as that in the Soviet Union could generate economic prosperity, it would appear that one need not have a capitalist economy to ensure a democratic polity. If such economies failed to create general affluence, however, they would offer infertile ground for democracy to flower.

Class Structure of Democratic Polities

Like Weber (but unlike Parsons), Lipset was especially interested in identifying the particular class configuration that was most conducive to democracy. In the beginning of *Political Man*, he quoted approvingly from a passage in Aristotle's *Politics*, in which the Greek philosopher made the case that the most stable form of democracy is achieved only when the middle class is sufficiently large to ensure that neither the wealthy elites at the top nor the poor at the bottom come to control political life. Instead of a class structure that can be visually depicted as a triangle with a large base, the classes in a democracy can be portrayed as a diamond (Lipset 1963a:51; Figure 3.2).

Lipset treated economic development resulting in a sizable, stable, and content middle class as a necessary, but not sufficient, condition for democracy. A number of other factors are also crucially important, including (here the influence of Parsons can be seen) an important role for cultural values. Democracy relies on a culture that promotes values emphasizing egalitarian ideals, tolerance, a recognition of political opposition and dissent, a belief in freedom of speech and assembly, and a respect for the rule of the law and for fundamental human rights. Democracy requires a high caliber of political leadership, vibrant political parties, an informed citizenry, and effective political institutions. In short, given these many requisites, it appears that democracy is not easily achieved, and citizens must work unceasingly to sustain the conditions that ensure its survival.

Figure 3.2 Lipset on Class Structure and Democracy

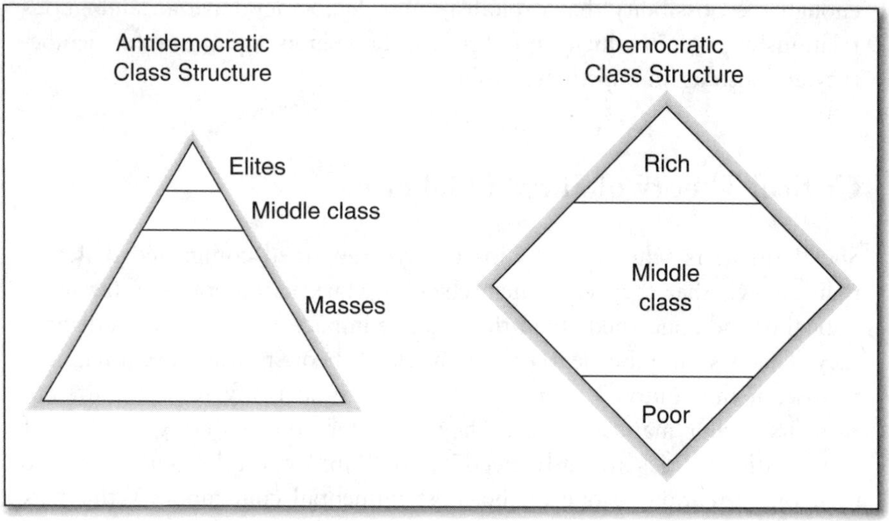

Critics have pointed out that, from Lipset's perspective, the role of the middle class in promoting democracy is overwhelmingly positive. It is this class that has abandoned the revolutionary ideologies of the past in favor of a rational assessment of what is politically feasible, and thus it advances the cause of a "vital center" committed to democracy (Lipset 1963a; Diggins 1988:247–248). The threats to democracy come from the fringes, from the extremes on the political Left and Right (Lipset 1970; Lipset and Schaflander 1971).

In making this case, the former socialist seemed to have little regard for the role played by the working class in advancing democracy. Indeed, he was inclined to depict the working class, in contrast to the middle class, as susceptible to the appeals of right-wing authoritarianism. This view has been challenged by those sociologists who suggest that the middle class has promoted democracy when challenging powerful upper classes but has also sought to limit the expansion of democracy when members of the working class attempted to become full participants in the political system (Korpi 1982; Rueschemeyer, Stephens, and Stephens 1992).

In addition, perhaps because Lipset, like Parsons and Weber, thought that democracy in modern societies meant a representative form that required an informed but essentially passive citizenry, his work does not address in any sustained way the topic of citizen participation. This means that he does not examine the possible weakening of democracy because of the influence of such factors as the mass media (particularly television), the role of money in the political process (elections, lobbying, etc.), and the withdrawal of citizens from public involvement. In other words, Lipset does not consider seriously enough the possibility that capitalism and democracy have an ambiguous relationship, one in which capitalism can be seen as a requisite for democracy and also as an impediment to it.

Critical Theory of Jürgen Habermas

Social theorists who, unlike Lipset, have remained committed to leftist politics—whether they view themselves as Marxists or not—are far more critical of and concerned about the negative impact of capitalism on democracy. This is seen quite clearly in the work of theorists who have attempted to discern the contours of a capitalism that is in many respects different from its earlier manifestations. They are intent on analyzing the fate of democratic politics in "advanced" and "late" capitalist societies. We turn our attention to one of the most influential contemporary theorists who continues to embrace, as did Marx, the goals of freedom, equality, and just and humane communities: Jürgen Habermas.

The most important German intellectual of his generation, Habermas has had a profound impact on social thought in his native land and throughout the world. As an indication of his stature, when he turned 80 on June 18, 2009, it made front-page coverage in major German newspapers. In a message posted on the website of German embassies, a statement published by Federal Foreign Minister Frank-Walter Steinmeier read in part, "Mr. Habermas, you were and still are the European voice of reason. We are lucky that this voice emanates from Germany and is heard throughout Europe and around the entire world" ("Habermas, Germany's Greatest Living Philosopher," 2009). Although his thinking has shifted in various directions over time, in part as a reaction to a wide array of predecessors and contemporaries whose ideas have proven crucial in formulating his own positions, the common thread connecting his work is his abiding concern for creating a critical theory that can assist in constructing a society that is rational and that facilitates the expansion of social equality and human freedom (Habermas 1970, 1971, 1989a).

Born into a middle-class family in 1929, Habermas's formative years took place during Nazi rule, and he came of age politically in the wake of the regime's demise. Alan Ryan (2003) writes that

> he is thus a member of the so-called "skeptical generation," the young people who were not implicated in Nazism, but who were old enough in the immediate postwar years to develop anxieties about the continuities between Nazi Germany and the Federal Republic [that followed Nazi rule]. (p. 43)

His eyes were opened to the horror of the era by the Nuremberg tribunal, and he was dismayed to discover that so many Germans refused to recognize the barbarism that had been unleashed by the Nazis. When he began his career as a university student, he was further disturbed by the fact that the de-Nazification of Germany had not gone far enough. For example, he encountered professors who had either enthusiastically embraced fascism or passively acquiesced in its perversion of German higher education (Alway 1995:100).

At the same time, as Steven Seidman (1994) noted, "Habermas reached adulthood during the democratic reconstruction of postwar Germany and in the context of postwar Western economic progress" (p. 174). This ambiguous situation is reflected in Habermas's thinking as he critiques the failure of Germany (and other capitalist industrial nations) to realize the promise of Enlightenment ideals of equality, freedom, justice, and democracy while at the same time seeing in these societies considerable positive potential.

During this period of intellectual ferment, Habermas turned to Marxism, but a Marxism quite at odds with its orthodox version. For example, Habermas does not think that a revolutionary transformation of society will be brought about by a class-conscious proletariat. Rather, he thinks Marx had mistakenly reduced the public realm, including the arena of politics, to an economic base. Although he believes that economic factors have a profound impact on the rest of society, this does not mean that politics and culture are simply the effects of economic factors; rather, they must be seen as maintaining a certain autonomy from the economic realm. Put another way, in contrast to both Marx and many subsequent Marxists, Habermas has exhibited an enduring concern with the fate of democracy, analyzing threats to it while looking for ways to shore it up.

Habermas found ideas that were kindred to his early reflections on philosophy and politics in the writings of members of the Institute for Social Research, commonly known as the Frankfurt School. The most important members of this school, including Max Horkheimer, Theodor W. Adorno, and Herbert Marcuse, had been political exiles in the United States during World War II. Whereas Marcuse stayed, becoming a mentor to the American New Left in the 1960s, both Horkheimer and Adorno returned to Germany after the war and revived the school.

Habermas would study with them during the late 1950s, serving as a research assistant to Adorno. Habermas eventually became the most illustrious representative of the "second generation" of the Frankfurt School and the inheritor of a vision of politics and philosophy that has frequently been described as neo-Marxist (Jay 1973; Tar 1977; Wiggershaus 1994). This label, however, fails to do justice to the multiple influences on Habermas. Of the scholars discussed herein, for example, he has been deeply influenced by Weber and Parsons. The result is a creative and original theoretical synthesis in which Habermas has attempted to steer a path between the optimism of Marx and Parsons and the pessimism of Weber and his Frankfurt School mentors—as noted earlier, the spokespersons for what has been called the "melancholy Left."

Democracy and the Public Sphere

Habermas's reflections on democracy emerged out of his experience of the reconstitution of democratic politics in postwar Germany and amount to a critical appreciation of actually existing democracies. For Habermas, democracy must be seen first and foremost as a process that results when a certain kind of social interaction prevails. Specifically, democracy should be seen as a particular way by which citizens make collective and rational decisions, "a way that [such decisions] can be made dependent on a consensus arrived at through discussion free from domination" (Habermas 1970:10). This is Habermas's vehicle by which citizens discover in the process of undistorted communication a conception of moral universalism, a quest that links him to the Enlightenment philosophy of Kant and to the recent theory of justice articulated by John Rawls.

Much of Habermas's theoretical efforts, from his first major work, *The Structural Transformation of the Public Sphere*, which first appeared in Germany in the early 1960s, to what some consider to be his magnum opus, *The Theory of Communicative Action*, have been devoted to explicating the historical and social structural factors that have served to inhibit or advance his vision of democracy (1984, 1987, 1989a).

Although Habermas found much of value in Marx's work, he thought that a major shortcoming led to Marx's less than satisfactory understanding of democracy. Habermas criticized Marx for attempting to reduce social life to the realm of work and to see labor as the singularly most fundamental and overarching theoretical concept. Nonetheless, viewing Marxism as a critical theory of society, Habermas sought not to abandon it but to revise and reformulate it. His attempt at a "reconstruction of historical materialism" begins by complementing labor with the idea of interaction and, relatedly, with the notion of communicative practices (Habermas 1971, 1973, 1979; Holub 1991).

At the same time, Habermas is responding to Weber, who, he thinks, employed an overly restrictive definition of rationality that inevitably led to his pessimistic assessment about the future's iron cage. Habermas distinguishes two types of rational action: purposive-rational action, which is dictated by the observance of technical rules, and communicative action, in which consensual norms arise out of an intersubjectively shared common language. Whereas the former is the rational action guiding economic and technological forces, the latter is the type of rationality that should guide citizen decision making (Habermas 1970, 1984).

If democracy is about free and open dialogue, where does such discussion take place and under what conditions? Where is the space in which democracy is nurtured? Habermas (1989a), in response to these queries, has referred to this space as the *public sphere*, a term that resembles another concept that is currently receiving considerable attention: civil society (Calhoun 1993; Kumar 1993; Edwards 2004; Alexander 2006). Civil society is a contested term, but in general it has come to refer to a realm of social life distinct from both the state and the market where participation in public life occurs with a spirit of cooperation and a norm of reciprocity. Seen in this light, Habermas construes the public sphere as a space within civil society where citizens participate in reasoned debates about the public good. In concrete terms, he was especially intent on indicating the significance of the coffeehouses and salons found in urban centers in 18th century Europe, for he thought that in such public places "the emerging middle classes debated plans for democracy in a straightforward, rational manner" (Alexander 2006:71). By claiming that a prerequisite of a democratic polity is an autonomous public sphere, Habermas can be seen as building on the work of Weber and Lipset in attempting to identify the most important social structural conditions underpinning democratic societies.

What Habermas refers to as the "bourgeois public sphere" came into its own in the 19th century, most fully in Britain, as a result of the triumph of capitalism and the establishment of a laissez-faire state. In contrast to the feudal era, in which the economy and polity were intimately linked, this linkage was uncoupled in the earliest phase of the capitalist era. The public sphere can be visualized as being carved out between the economy and the state. This means that the public sphere is both separate and distinct from the economy and the state. It is an arena that is accessible to all citizens on the basis of equality and thus is not dominated or controlled by powerful economic actors or by state officials.

Nancy Fraser (1992) succinctly describes Habermas's sense of the public sphere when she writes, "It designates a theater in modern societies in which political participation is enacted through the medium of talk. It is the space in which citizens deliberate about their common affairs, and hence an institutionalized arena of discursive interaction" (p. 110).

The public sphere requires the existence of independent voluntary associations of citizens and an institutionalized apparatus that permits the unrestricted dissemination of information and ideas. Thus, the panoply of organizations—ranging from local parent-teacher associations and neighborhood clubs to labor unions, human rights organizations, environmental organizations, and so on—is part and parcel of the public sphere. In addition, so are media committed to ensuring that citizens are informed about the vital issues of the day and to providing outlets for articulating an array of stances on issues and forums for debate and dissent.

Critics of Habermas contend that he tends to romanticize the public sphere during its earlier years, confusing his ideal vision about how it should have functioned with the reality of the historical situation, which involved from its inception persistent intrusions of powerful economic interests and the repressive tactics of the state. The result was that the public sphere never managed to be as autonomous as he seems to think. This may be a somewhat unfair characterization of Habermas's assessment because he provides ample evidence of being aware of the limitations of actual existing public spheres in the past. He does seem to think, however, that public spheres in the past exhibited greater autonomy than their contemporary versions for reasons discussed in the following section (Lowenthal 1976; Fraser 1992).

At the same time, Habermas has left himself open to charges of utopian thinking when, especially deriving from the recent stages of his thought, he has developed the ideal of a state of undistorted communication, free from coercion and restraint (Habermas 1979, 1984). In Habermas's view, democratic decisions arise dialogically. In an ideal speech situation, people talk to others to come to an understanding of which ideas and values are best, not to manipulate others to get one's way. In other words, he assumes a willingness on the part of citizens to freely embrace the better argument (Habermas 1996).

There are examples of situations in which this ideal seems to have been more or less realized, such as old New England town meetings and Quaker meetings. The participants in these examples can be fairly depicted as being cooperative, tolerant, critical, self-reflective, and rational, whereas the differences among them in terms of both economic status and levels of human capital (e.g., amount of education) are not great. In short, like Lipset, Habermas thinks that high levels of social inequality are detrimental to democracy (Habermas 1979, 1984, 1987; Ingram 1987).

Whereas, in Lipset's work, it appears that the levels of inequality in contemporary liberal democracies are not deemed to be especially problematic, Habermas is more critical of existing realities. He is cognizant of the difficulties inherent in overcoming disparities in, to use the terminology of the French social theorist Pierre Bourdieu (1986; see also Bourdieu and Wacquant 1992), economic capital (material property), social capital (social networks), and cultural capital (status). Bourdieu, who until his death in

2002 held the prestigious chair at the Collège de France that had first been occupied by Durkheim, devoted considerable energy to indicating the ways that these and other modes of capital, singularly or in combination, function to perpetuate inequalities in life circumstances and chances. Bourdieu points to the structural impediments to achieving greater levels of equality. Habermas appears to think that the rule of law in democratic societies can provide a basis for overcoming some of these disparities, permitting people who have been marginalized and discriminated against to be included in the political order, in which they can become participants in the ongoing process of "democratic self-determination" (Habermas 2002:139).

Another issue that has been voiced, particularly by feminist theorists, is that Habermas has not been as attentive as he might have been to both the distinction and the relationship between the private and public spheres. They point out that liberal democracies have historically defined this divide in ways that contribute to the oppression of women by restricting their activities to the private realm (Benhabib 1992). Finally, another concern has been raised by scholars such as Joan Alway (1995) about the tendency in Habermas's writing to assume an overly rationalistic and overly civilized view of humans, thereby failing to adequately account for the irrational, emotional, playful, erotic, and selfish aspects of human beings.

The Fate of the Public Sphere in Late Capitalism

Changes in capitalism since its initial laissez-faire stage have produced a variety of what Habermas (1975) refers to as "crisis tendencies" in the ensuing advanced and late stages of capitalism. The former refers to the period in which modern welfare states emerged. The outgrowth of economic distress, the modern welfare state resulted in an alliance between economic elites and political leaders, thereby linking or integrating the economy and the polity in a way quite at odds with the separation between the two in the earlier period. This move, Habermas argues, signals a distinct threat to the public sphere. He uses the rather opaque notion of the "refeudalization" of the public sphere to describe this shift. What he is defining resembles in its essentials the process Mills described in *The Power Elite* (1956).

Given his focus on communication, it is not surprising that Habermas is especially concerned about the concentration of media power in the hands of political and economic elites. Large media conglomerates have arisen to choke dissident voices out of the market, and these corporations, far from being independent of political power, serve as apologists for it. The result is that genuine public debate has given way to propaganda and increasingly sophisticated public relations. What we are left with is a "faked version" of public debate in an increasingly "manufactured public sphere" (Habermas 1989a:195, 217). Frank Webster (1995) concludes, I think quite accurately, that

> reading Jürgen Habermas on the history of the public sphere, it becomes impossible to avoid the conclusion that its future is precarious. His account of its more recent development is gloomy: Capitalism is victorious, the capacity for critical thought is minimal, there is no real space for the public sphere in an era of transnational media conglomerates and a pervasive culture of advertising. (p. 104)

At the same time, unlike theorists who seemed to think that capitalism had managed to overcome its crisis tendencies—and one could include Mills, Parsons, and Lipset in this group—Habermas continued to agree with Marx's thesis of the inherent crisis tendencies of capitalism. In the recent phase of capitalism—late capitalism—in addition to the potential for economic crisis is the threat posed to the social system by three additional crisis tendencies, which he refers to as crises of rationality, legitimation, and motivation (Habermas 1975:45–50; see also Dandaneau, 1998).

Deepening Democracy: The Colonization of the Life World and the New Social Movements

The complex integration of the economic and political subsystems threatens the public sphere and increasingly penetrates and attempts to mold and control all aspects of everyday life, penetrating into family relations, friendships, and community life (Table 3.2; Habermas 1975, 1987, 1989b). Instrumental rationality (here, Habermas's fusion of Marx and Weber and the influence of Max Horkheimer is clear) seeks to supplant communicative

Table 3.2 Crisis Tendencies in Late Capitalism

	Crisis	
Origin	System	Identity
Economic system	Economic	—
Political system	Rationality	Legitimation
Sociocultural system	—	Motivation

SOURCE: Habermas (1975:45).

rationality. Rather than the two coexisting, albeit in a state of perpetual tension, the colonization of the life world refers to the process by which instrumental rationality comes to dominate societal decision making at the expense of communicative rationality.

Far from resulting in a smooth and seamless bureaucratic and technocratic capitalism, the contradiction between instrumental and communicative rationality results in a serious threat to the stability of the social system. The threat is seen as the various crisis tendencies surface: (a) The welfare state is necessary to address various negative economic side effects, but it produces a fiscal crisis for the state insofar as citizens resist higher tax rates that make the welfare state possible; (b) governmental policies designed to ensure the vitality of the economy as a whole get pitted against the competing self-interests of different sectors of the capitalist class; (c) discouraged from active participation in political decision making, people increasingly refuse to legitimate the political subsystem; and (d) this refusal is linked to an erosion of the psychological dispositions needed to ensure that people will be motivated to act in ways designed to ensure the functional stability of the society as a whole.

The challenges to the logic of late capitalism have arisen in a variety of what are collectively known as the "new social movements," which include the environmental, antinuclear, peace, feminist, and gay rights movements. During the 1960s, Habermas (1970) was opposed to the far Left's desire for revolutionary change and willingness to employ violence. For this reason, he is supportive of the new social movements because they are radical reformist rather than revolutionary, and they are committed to nonviolence. He would concur with Alain Touraine's (2000) contention that these movements "have democratic aspirations" and seek "to give voice to those who have no voice" (p. 117). They seek to preserve and build on the positive elements of existing society. These movements seek to effect change through communication, and for this reason they are vitally important because they have the potential for revitalizing the public sphere in nations with late capitalist economies. At the same time that Habermas has speculated on the revitalization of democracy in Western nations, his ideas have been used by others to explore the chances for democracy in the former communist nations of Eastern Europe, nations in which the former regimes had systematically attempted to eliminate a public sphere.

Underlying Habermas's tempered hope about the prospects for resisting the erosion of the public sphere and the colonization of the life world is a particular understanding of human nature. It presupposes that people are by nature political and thus concerned about and willing to participate in issues related to the well-being of society as a whole. To better evaluate this presupposition, Chapter 4 discusses the sociological efforts directed at understanding the shifting character of the relationship between the individual and the larger society in the modern world.

The Civil Sphere: Solidarity and Justice

Jeffrey Alexander, Professor of Sociology and Director of the Center for Cultural Sociology at Yale, is the author of *The Civil Sphere* (2006), which constitutes a profound effort to rethink a two-century-long discourse on civil society. The imprint of a number of prominent theorists is evident in his work, though none more significant than Parsons and Habermas. The early part of his career was shaped by his ongoing engagement with the work of Parsons, reflected in his efforts to forge a neo-functionalist theory that both builds on and revises Parsonian social theory. Of particular salience for the discussion in this chapter, Alexander (1998) has been intent even after leaving the neo-functionalist quest behind with attempting to articulate an empirically rich theoretical account of the social space wherein solidarity and justice are pursued—an effort that preoccupied Parsons until his death. That Alexander calls this space the civil sphere is an indication of his perceived debt to Habermas, for his term represents a merger of the terms *civil society* and *public sphere*.

Like Habermas, Alexander defines the civil sphere as occupying a more delimited social space than one finds is the case of many civil society theorists who are inclined to see civil society as constituting everything outside of the state and the economy. Alexander excludes not only family but also religion and community organizations. He is particularly leery of including those voluntary associations like sports clubs and fraternal organizations whose raison d'être does not entail the promotion of an expansion of solidarity or the pursuit of justice. This would place outside the civil sphere such organizations as the fanciful list that I conjured up elsewhere, however worthwhile for other purposes they might be: "model airplane clubs, ultimate Frisbee leagues, wine tasting gatherings, and the United States Bowling Congress" (Kivisto 2007:114). Put in other terms, Alexander does not include organizations that do not, in his view, constitute genuine spaces where people come together as a public. In this regard, he quotes approvingly Habermas's statement in *The Structural Transformation of the Public Sphere* about "the sphere where private people come together as a public," going on to note that as such it combines a commitment to individualism, including the idea of individual rights, with a simultaneous commitment to communal solidarity (Habermas 1989a:271; Alexander 2006:44).

Democracy is an ongoing and never-ending achievement, a project based on the recognition that real, existing democracies fall short of the ideal, and, insofar as they do, efforts must be expended to not simply protect or defend the status quo but to deepen, expand, and enrich democratic practice. In exploring how that is done, Alexander pays far more attention than Habermas to the role of progressive social movements (while, it should be noted, ignoring their reactionary counterparts). His views on these "new social movements" have been explicitly shaped by Touraine's work with its stress on their reformist rather than revolutionary character. The model of such a social movement for Alexander was the American civil rights movement, which he depicts as a prime example of mobilized collective action with the goal of effecting "civil repair" (Alexander 2006:193–209). By this he means that it sought to accomplish two interrelated objectives. First, it sought to promote justice by freeing African Americans from the oppressive system of Jim Crow, which was a racial formation that perpetuated black oppression and exploitation. It did so by demanding equal rights for blacks, both formally and substantively. Second, it sought to overcome the other feature of Jim Crow, which was that it prevented blacks from being included as full members in the solidarity community of the larger society. As such, the movement also demanded inclusion, and in so doing, it sought to make the nation's civic values more universal.

As such, the civil rights movement was only in part a struggle over material resources and power. It was also a "discursive struggle" (Alexander 2006:233). The success of the movement in dismantling Jim Crow was to no small extent due to the fact that it succeeded in linking the movement's aspirations to the larger society's values and ideals. Alexander is especially attentive to the role of the mass media in this discursive struggle, for it was its ability to win the battle over public opinion that proved to be crucial, paving the way for the civil transformation that produced the new racial formation that we now inhabit.

While some would accuse Alexander, like Parsons, of looking at American race relations through rose-tinted glasses, a closer examination of his work will reveal that this assessment is mistaken. To say that the civil rights movement succeeded did not mean that it created a color-blind society in which race no longer played a role in shaping life opportunities or in structuring patterns of inequality. Rather, it is simply to claim that one particularly odious racial formation—Jim Crow—came to an end. Much has changed since the civil rights movement wound down in the late 1960s. Some of the changes have been positive (e.g., the black middle class has grown), some negative (e.g., inner-city neighborhoods have become poorer and more dangerous), while the significance of yet other changes are somewhat difficult to decipher (e.g., the impact of the new immigration). A recent prognostication by Richard Alba (2009), a leading scholar of race and ethnicity in America, about where race relations may be headed in the 21st century offers grounds for cautious optimism. Whether or not the particulars of his assessment would likely be endorsed by Alexander is not known. What is certain is that, for Alexander, the capacity of the nation to redress the racial inequities that shape the racial formation of the post-civil rights era will be dependent on a vibrant civil sphere. It is here that "hopes for civil repair" will be articulated, and insofar as this transpires, there are reasonable grounds to "hope for a democratic life" (Alexander 2006:553).

Summary

Social theorists consider democracy to be a human achievement that needs to be continually re-created. Max Weber's contribution to the dialogue concerning the viability of democracy in the contemporary world continues to have relevance, even though it was shaped by the historical contingencies of his own experience: He lived through the formative phase of the modern German state and was deeply concerned about the impediments that liberal democracy had to confront. His realism about the prospects for democracy in Germany and the challenges it faced were tinged with pessimism but not despair. He was concerned about the conflictual relationship between bureaucracy and democracy but sought to indicate that this tension did not necessarily signal the impossibility of democracy in modern societies. Perhaps reflecting their American roots, both Parsons and Lipset are considerably more optimistic about the democratic prospect than Weber, although in both cases attention is given to those elements of the social structure that serve either to promote or to impede democratic practice: For Parsons, of key concern is the expansion of citizenship, whereas for Lipset, it is the existence of a large and comfortable middle class. Habermas, influenced by Weber, Marx, and Parsons, offers a cautionary rejoinder to their optimism by pointing to the threat to the public sphere caused by the inequalities and the concentration of power generated by advanced capitalism. As the preceding discussion of Alexander indicates, contemporary discussions about these and related themes concerning the future of democracy are embedded in a discourse shaped in significant ways by these seminal thinkers.

4

Individualism

The Tension Between Me and Us

This chapter explores the distinctive character of individualism in contemporary social life. To do so, I raise questions about the interconnections between individualism and community. They are treated in tandem because neither concept can be adequately comprehended without an appreciation for the meaning of the other. At the outset, I point out that the two terms at first appear to differ in one important way: They tend to be assessed somewhat differently. Whereas individualism is frequently depicted as a potential problem, community is usually construed as a desideratum.

Individualism, as will be shown, is a term that was coined in the 19th century, which is a reflection of the novelty of the phenomenon. Since then, it has been evaluated in widely divergent ways. On the one hand, it tends to be portrayed in a positive light when it is associated with freedom from social constraints and from oppressive conditions. On the other hand, individualism is sometimes viewed in negative terms, when it is seen as leading to separation from others and to an absence of a sense of reciprocal obligations.

In contrast, the word community has been part of the English language since at least the 14th century, referring since that time to a sense of a people's common and shared identity and to feelings of mutuality and belonging. British cultural theorist Raymond Williams (1976) observed that, unlike the dual-edged character of individualism, the word community "seems never to be used unfavorably" (p. 66). Although this is a bit of an overstatement, in fact, the term often does seem to have a halo over it, despite the fact that people often leave particular communities, including small towns, monasteries, and religious sects, because they are experienced as being too restrictive and parochial. As George Hillary (1955) pointed out more than half a century ago, there is considerable conceptual confusion about what community means. Indeed, he identified 94 different uses of the term. For our purposes, the definition proposed by Steven Brint (2001) offers a useful clarification insofar as it serves as a corrective to the overly instrumental and rationalistic biases of most contemporary sociological approaches. In Brint's view, communities are "aggregates of people who share common activities and/or beliefs and who are bound together principally by relations of affect, loyalty, common values, and/or personal concern (i.e., interest in the personalities and life events of another)" (p. 1).

It is generally agreed that individualism is one of the signature characteristics of the modern world because people have managed to free themselves from the constraints imposed by traditional societies, and it is also generally assumed that insofar as individualism takes root in the culture and the social psychology of a society, new bases of moral order become necessary. None of the early figures in sociology devoted more attention to new modalities of social solidarity and their attendant impact on the moral order than the founder of academic sociology in France, Émile Durkheim. We focus on his contribution to this topic in this chapter.

Durkheim's fruitful encounter with these ideas was shaped by a wide and diverse array of influences, ranging from progenitors of modern social thought, including Jean-Jacques Rousseau, Montesquieu, Henri Saint-Simon, and Auguste Comte, to conservative thinkers repelled by modernism, such as Joseph de Maistre and Louis de Bonald. For our purposes, however, it will suffice to explore the way in which Durkheim was both influenced by and responded to two thinkers who are crucial to the development of the two concepts we seek to explore: Alexis de Tocqueville on individualism and Ferdinand Toennies on community. These two figures are singled out because each is, perhaps more than any other social theorist, identified with each of these respective concepts. Durkheim's understanding of the problematic relationship between these two terms is in no small part an outcome of his engagement with, and critical evaluation of, their writings.

Durkheim has had a profound influence on American sociology. With his ideas in mind, we discuss in the latter part of the chapter four highly influential and original American sociologists who, in different ways, owe him an intellectual debt: Robert K. Merton, David Riesman, Robert Bellah, and Erving Goffman. We first discuss Tocqueville and Toennies.

Alexis de Tocqueville on Individualism

On May 11, 1831, Alexis de Tocqueville, a 26-year-old Frenchman from the ranks of the nobility, along with his close friend Gustave de Beaumont, began a 9-month sojourn in America. Their rather circuitous journey took them to major cities along the eastern seaboard, including New York, Boston, Philadelphia, and Washington, D.C. They traveled westward to such relatively new cities as Buffalo, Cincinnati, Detroit, Green Bay, and Memphis, as well as to the older city of New Orleans in the Deep South (Jardin 1989; Lerner 1994). The purported reason for the trip, which was to study the penal system of the United States, has almost been forgotten—it was overshadowed by the profound analysis of the social and cultural conditions of this new nation that is contained in Tocqueville's classic *Democracy in America* ([1853] 1969).

Tocqueville's analysis of the United States and his later interpretation of the causes and consequences of the French Revolution, which was published as *The Old Regime and the French Revolution* three years prior to his death in 1859, laid the basis for viewing him as one of the founders of comparative historical sociology (Tocqueville [1856] 1955; Birnbaum 1970). Recently, Jon Elster (2009) has gone so far as to refer to him as the "first social scientist." He is also rightly seen as a political theorist who continues to speak to our age, whether we characterize it as democratic or, as political theorist Sheldon Wolin (2001, 2008) does, postdemocratic.

Both a genuine inquisitiveness and pragmatic considerations motivated Tocqueville's trip to America. In the wake of the French Revolution, which abolished the monarchy and assaulted the privileges of the aristocracy, an extended period of political turmoil and uncertainty characterized French social and political life. Although he was born after the revolution, Tocqueville intimately understood something of the human toll produced by revolutionary upheaval because some of his relatives had been sent to the guillotine. Tocqueville undertook his investigations, quite simply, because he felt compelled to understand the new world that was emerging before his eyes. The pragmatic part of the equation had to do with Tocqueville's desire to figure out what he needed to do to succeed in this new social milieu. He was a realist who understood what conservative romantics of his era, such as Joseph de Maistre and Louis de Bonald, could not accept: Namely, that there was no possibility of returning to the past. Thus, he was intent on carving out a niche for himself in France's new social order.

This is not to suggest that he was not critical of many features of the new era. His aristocratic background profoundly shaped his perspective on the new postaristocratic era, producing what one commentator describes as a version of "aristocratic liberalism" (Kahan 2001). His recent biographer, Hugh Brogan (2008), reinforces this assessment as he offers abundant evidence to support the view that Tocqueville's aristocratic sense of self prevented him from knowing how to relate easily to members of the middle class. He was clearly anxious about the implications of democratic politics, particularly the expanded role it granted to the middle classes and the poor. He was also concerned about what he referred to as the materialization, or what in contemporary parlance might better be described as the commercialization, of life in such societies (Welch 2001; Mitchell 2002).

Alan Ryan (2007) quite rightly contends that "Tocqueville is venerated by almost all his commentators" (p. 53). While his work is sufficiently supple to support varied interpretations, he has become particularly canonized by right-wing thinkers such as Harvey Mansfield and Michael Ledeen. Few have questioned whether or not he "got" America right. One who has is Garry Wills (2004), arguing that Tocqueville had a tendency to intuit rather than carefully observe America. Moreover, he thought that the French traveler relied too much on the opinions of a handful of Federalists on the East Coast whose worldview most closely resembled his own. The result was that he tended to accept their views on matters such as race, public opinion, and populist politics uncritically; their particular prejudices found their way into his writing. Elster's (2009) overall positive assessment of Tocqueville's contribution is tempered somewhat by his appreciation of the fact that his writing is frequently characterized by "ambiguity, vagueness of language, a tendency to speculative flights of fancy, and self-contradiction" (p. 2).

Yet despite these criticisms about both his skills of observation and analysis and his frequent lack of expressive clarity, Tocqueville has consistently exerted a profound impact on efforts intended to understand the American character and the nation's democratic temperament and related institutional structure.

America as a Model of Europe's Future

Personal ambition does not fully explain why he believed he had to cross the Atlantic to adequately appreciate the dawning age of democracy, with its attendant advocacy of egalitarian ideals. Although we cannot discount the sheer quest for adventure on the part of the 26-year-old, it is also the case that it was Tocqueville's conviction that in the frontierlike character of a "historyless" nation one could find the potential and the problems of democracy in their most pristine form. Although he had a keen appreciation of the similarities and differences among societies, he did not think that democracy in America was qualitatively unique. Instead, Tocqueville was convinced that America represented the contours of things to come for France and, indeed, the rest of Europe. Thus, he wrote in the introduction to *Democracy* ([1853] 1969),

> I admit that I saw in America more than America; it was the shape of democracy itself which I sought, its inclinations, character, prejudices, and passions; I wanted to understand it so as at least to know what we have to fear or hope therefrom. (p. 19)

Not the least of the "inclinations" he addressed was individualism. In a remarkable, albeit somewhat cryptic, passage in Volume 2 of *Democracy*, Tocqueville ([1853] 1969) set out to describe the nature of social relations in democratic societies. To do so, he made use of the term individualism, which he described as "a word recently coined to express a new idea" (p. 506). This neologism was minted in the 19th century because of the need to depict and identify something that existed neither in European feudal society nor elsewhere in the world (Dumont 1977). The linkages that connected all people in the hierarchical feudal or aristocratic world were severed by democracy.

Tocqueville clearly understood that people in premodern societies did not always act in ways that advanced the interests of the community. He did not romanticize the premodern relationship between society and the individual. Despite the fact that people's identities were far more meshed with a collective identity, much could go wrong in the way people related to and connected with their society. The linkages could be undercut. Tocqueville referred to a situation in which people disengage, withdraw, or overtly challenge larger societal interests as egoism, which he juxtaposed to individualism in an attempt to illustrate how this latter term is the historically specific outgrowth of the age of democracy. To clarify the significance of individualism, the following shows how Tocqueville ([1853] 1969) distinguished the two terms:

> Egoism is a passionate and exaggerated love of self, which leads a man to think of all things in terms of himself and to prefer himself to all. Individualism is a calm and considered feeling which disposes each citizen to isolate himself from the mass of his fellows and withdraw into the circle of family and friends; with this little society formed to his taste, he gladly leaves the greater society to look after itself. (p. 506)

Thus, individualism does not appear to be a social state that leaves the individual alone. It is not about alienation, or what Philip Slater (1970) referred to as the "pursuit of loneliness." Indeed, in a state of individualism the individual is in a position to develop and nurture intimate affective bonds with loved ones. The concern that Tocqueville expressed here is that in so doing, people turn their backs on the larger society, refusing to embrace the duties of the citizen, whose obligations extend beyond the realm of intimates to people they do not know and to that more abstract entity, the nation.

Destructive Individualism

As Tocqueville's discussion proceeded, it took a more ominous turn. First, he emphasized the destructiveness of egoism, which he said "sterilizes the seeds of every virtue" (Tocqueville [1853] 1969). The problem is that individualism, which is likely to grow in democratic societies, moves beyond its initial challenge to "public virtues," and "it attacks and destroys all the others too and finally merges into egoism" (p. 507). Lost is a connection to the past—to tradition—and to the world of one's contemporaries. The danger of individualism, then, is that "each man is forever thrown back on himself alone, and there is danger that he may be shut up in the solitude of his own heart" (p. 508).

Tocqueville's pessimism was somewhat tempered later in the volume when he wrote about how Americans attempt to combat the corrosive implications of excessive individualism through what he referred to as "self-interest rightly understood." Although this phrase remains somewhat opaque, it is clear that Tocqueville thought that there were ways to mitigate, although not eliminate, the problems created by individualism.

Tocqueville certainly did not share the cheery understanding of individualism embraced by perhaps the greatest American literary figure of the 19th century, Ralph Waldo Emerson (1875), in his essay "Self-Reliance." In Emerson's view, self-reliance was a virtue: Independence and autonomy are desirable. For him, the problem was not individualism but society, which thwarts the pursuit of self-reliance, forcing people into patterns of conformity and dependency. Thus, he argued, individualism requires nonconformism and resists the temptation to imitate others. It grants to the individual alone the authority to make assessments about good and bad and right and wrong. It does not care about public opinion or seek its accolades. Accordingly, in Emerson's view, the genuinely self-reliant individual is one "who in the midst of the crowd keeps with perfect sweetness the independence of solitude" (p. 245).

The contrast between Emerson and Tocqueville could not be starker. Whereas Emerson found his expression of the notion of individualism in self-reliance—something positive that was to be pursued—Tocqueville saw something that was inevitable in the democratic age, but he was convinced that its deleterious consequences had to be minimized. Interestingly, Emerson thought that individualism was threatened by the social conditions of 19th-century America, whereas Tocqueville believed that it was precisely on American soil that individualism would flourish more rapidly than elsewhere. It was, as we shall see, Tocqueville's, and not Emerson's, concerns that would inform the work of Durkheim. And it was Tocqueville's ghost hovering over the shoulders of mass society theorists during the 1950s, including David Riesman, discussed later in this chapter.

Ferdinand Toennies on Community

Among the familiar typologies constructed by the early pioneers of sociology in their respective efforts to capture the character of the modern industrial epoch by distinguishing it from the preceding era—Herbert Spencer's military-industrial, Henry Sumner Maine's status-contract, and Durkheim's mechanical-organic—none is as familiar as Ferdinand Toennies's *Gemeinschaft und Gesellschaft* ([1887] 1957), which is usually translated as "community and society." Indeed, it is fair to say that Toennies's subsequent reputation rests largely with this work, which was his first book, published when he was 32 years old.

This work filtered into American sociology during the first half of the 20th century, disseminated by the efforts of the likes of Edward Alsworth Ross, Pitirim Sorokin, Robert McIver, and Toennies's son-in-law Rudolph Heberle, who settled and taught in the United States. As Werner Cahnman (1995) observed, however, "The most far-reaching influence of Toennies on American sociology was mediated by Robert E. Park and his students at the University of Chicago" (p. 131). The influence is evident, for example, in Chicago school sociologist Louis Wirth's classic article on "Urbanism as a Way of Life" and in the obvious parallel between Toennies's typology and the folk-urban continuum formulated by anthropologist Robert Redfield (the son-in-law of Park).

Despite the frequent references to the conceptual distinction Toennies formulated, it is not always clear in what ways his typology differed from or was essentially the same as those of the others noted previously. Sorokin, for instance, viewed Toennies and Durkheim as employing terms that were essentially interchangeable, whereas Cahnman (1995:87–88), quite correctly I think, takes issue with this assessment. Part of the exegetical difficulty lies with the fact that it is not always clear whether Toennies was speaking in terms of a formal sociology of pure concepts or in evolutionary terms wherein gemeinschaft, exemplified by the powerful bonds of kinship and tradition, was seen as gradually disappearing and being replaced by gesellschaft, characterized by the weaker social ties of associations established to a considerable extent on the basis of self-interest (Freund 1978:152–157; Mazlish 1989:168–178; Sztompka 1993:105–106).

What is clear is that, behind the formal exterior of Toennies's presentational style, we can detect a certain disdain for gesellschaft and a yearning for the increasingly lost world of gemeinschaft. His sociology was infused with, if not quite a cultural despair, certainly a criticism of things to come. As Robert Nisbet (1976) noted, Toennies's thought bears a family resemblance to that of 19th-century conservative social critics such as Thomas Carlyle and Matthew Arnold. He shared with them, in Robert Nisbet's words, an appreciation of the "rust of progress":

> Like a great many artists and philosophers of his day he declares that the achievement of progress, as commonly defined in terms of industry, democracy, technology, individualism, and equality, has carried with it dislodgements of status, rents in the social fabric, and transformations of identity which have in turn led to a proliferation of moral, social, and psychological problems. (p. 121)

Toennies's Ideas in the Context of His Life

Toennies's biography partially explains his romantic longing for community. He grew up in relatively comfortable circumstances on a farm in Schleswig-Holstein, and he retained throughout his life a deep affection for the organic wholeness of that world. He viewed with regret the inroads of modernization that began to transform the province after Prussia gained control of the area due to its victory in the War of 1866 (Mitzman 1973:91–92). Toennies, however, did not remain in this idyllic rural world, moving instead into the cosmopolitan world of German intellectuals. After transferring from several universities, he finally completed his doctorate at the University of Berlin. Due to his father's largesse, he was unencumbered by financial concerns and thus was able to devote himself to independent scholarship during much of his life. Along with the likes of Max Weber, Georg Simmel, and Werner Sombart, he was one of the founders of academic sociology in Germany, and as an indication of his place of prominence in this circle, he was president of the German Sociological Society from 1909 to 1933.

To his credit, he disbanded the society after the Nazis ascended to power, when he became aware of their intention to transform the discipline into an ideological tool of the regime. This act of courage, for which he was dismissed from his position by the government, was a reflection of his general political orientation, which was remarkably progressive for someone with such a negative assessment of gesellschaft (Heberle 1968:99). He was a complex person who was temperamentally conservative while at the same time involved in a variety of liberal reform activities. For example, he was an advocate for trade unions, consumer cooperatives, and other progressive political movements. He joined the Social Democratic Party in response to the threat of the German Right (Liebersohn 1988:11–39).

Toennies appreciated Marx's critique of the alienating character of capitalism but shared none of Marx's zeal for revolutionary upheaval. He had a romantic attachment to a German past that was disappearing, but he shared none of reactionary romanticism's perverse glorification of the *Volk* (the people), with its attendant anti-Semitism.

Gemeinschaft and Gesellschaft

With the previous biographical background, we can perhaps better appreciate the significance of Toennies's distinction between *gemeinschaft* and *gesellschaft* and, with this typology, the related distinction he made between two types of will, *wesenwille* and *kurwille*. According to Toennies, the social world is *willed*, by which he meant that it is created by the intentionalities of people acting in concert with others. What he sought to draw attention to in making the distinction between the two types of will was that different kinds of society will arise depending on which will is predominant at any particular time. Wesenwille is defined as natural will. Actions based on this type of will are less consciously chosen, predicated instead on tradition, habit, or emotion. Although not devoid of a rational element, this type of will differs from kurwille, which is a type of will akin to Max Weber's purposive, instrumental (means-ends) rationality (Heberle 1968:100).

The different wills are directly related to the two ideal typical social formations, gemeinschaft and gesellschaft (Table 4.1). The former is the result of wills based on habit, tradition, shared beliefs, and affective bonds, whereas the latter is based on purposive rationality. The kinds of social groupings that are closest to the gemeinschaft model include the family, the peer group, the neighborhood, the social club, and the religious sect. Note that these are the sorts of bonds that Brint (2001) had in mind in his definition of community discussed previously. The impersonal gesellschaft model is evident in the realm of the modern business corporation based on contractual relationships, the city, mass political parties, and the nation. Toennies ([1887] 1957) contended that gemeinschaft referred to the private realm, whereas gesellschaft referred to the public world. He noted that in

Table 4.1 Gemeinschaft Versus Gesellschaft

Characteristic	Gemeinschaft	Gesellschaft
View of the individual	Collective, tied to the group or community	Autonomous, individualism
Social relations	Familiar, intimate	Impersonal
Social differentiation	Low	High
Key institutions	Family	State and economy
Geographic locale	Village	City
Social control	Custom, religion	Law, contract

the former, one is bound to it over time, whereas one "goes into gesellschaft as one goes into a strange country" (p. 35). Moreover, he asserted that "gemeinschaft should be understood as a living organism, gesellschaft as a mechanical aggregate and artifact" (p. 35).

From the perspective of Toennies's formal sociology, one could conclude that social entities of both types coexist at any particular point in time. Although this is true, Toennies also held an evolutionary perspective on social changes that viewed the modern industrial world as moving progressively from organizational forms that were predominantly gemeinschaft oriented to primarily gesellschaft types brought about, he thought, by economic, political, and scientific changes. The commercialization of economic transactions, the impersonalization of politics, and the rationality associated with scientific thought served to erode the bases of communities.

As a consequence, a wide range of pathologies could be attributed to the loss of community-like attachments. Many of Toennies's empirical studies were concerned with understanding the impact of these changes on social relations. He paid particular attention to a variety of social problems, such as crime, suicide, mental illness, and illegitimacy (Oberschall 1965:51–63). Gesellschaft created problems that needed to be overcome. Toennies did not think it possible to return to the past, but he hoped, at least during the later years of his life, that in the future it might be possible to create a novel social order that would reproduce the positive elements of gemeinschaft, making possible the creation of what Marshall McLuhan (1964) decades later dubbed the "global village." In the meantime, the impersonality of contemporary society would mean that alienation is one of its endemic features.

Émile Durkheim and the Quest for Community

Émile Durkheim shared the concerns voiced by both Tocqueville and Toennies. Although he also agreed partially with their particular diagnoses of the contemporary threat to community, he offered his own related, but nevertheless distinctive, assessment while at the same time formulating his own prescription for overcoming the maladies of modern industrial society.

Durkheim was the person singularly most influential in establishing sociology as a legitimate academic discipline in France. Indeed, his professional life was devoted to this cause. After being appointed in 1902 to a position at the Sorbonne, France's elite university, Durkheim succeeded in having his position redefined from professor of the science of education to professor of the science of education and sociology, thus becoming the nation's first academic sociologist. He founded France's first sociological journal, *L'Année Sociologique,* and attracted a brilliant cadre of students to pursue studies in sociology (Lukes 1972; Tiryakian 1978). Although often insecure about his status and always fearful of the possibility of failure, Durkheim became such a powerful presence at the Sorbonne that his critics, complaining about his power, frequently castigated him as playing the role of a "secular pope" (Lukes 1972:375). His impact continued to be felt long after his death, though his influence has not always been explicitly articulated or acknowledged. Charles Lemert (2006), for example, has made a convincing case about the intellectual debts to Durkheim owed by such later luminaries in French intellectual life during the latter half of the 20th century as Claude Levi-Strauss, Michel Foucault, Pierre Bourdieu, and Jacques Derrida. More recently, his intellectual presence is tangible in efforts to advance cultural sociology (Alexander and Smith 2005).

Durkheim's major works include *The Division of Labor in Society* ([1893] 1964), *Suicide* ([1897] 1951), *The Rules of Sociological Method* (1938), and what some believe to be his magnum opus, *The Elementary Forms of the Religious Life* ([1912] 1965). Although these titles seem to suggest a person with far-ranging and diffuse interests, in fact, Durkheim's entire intellectual career amounts to a remarkably coherent and persistent attempt to accomplish two intertwined goals. First, he wanted to establish sociology as a rigorous science of society, one that staked out its independence from other sciences, such as psychology, by defining the realm of "social facts" as the appropriate and legitimate subject matter of the discipline. Second, he was intent on employing this science in explicating the new bases for social solidarity made necessary by industrialization, thereby playing a vital role in rearticulating the moral bases of the new social order.

Given these goals, it is fair to conclude that he was at once a sociologist and a moralist (Jones 1986; Mestrovíc 1988; Turner 1993).

Bases of Solidarity

Durkheim's lifelong concern with the moral or social bases of solidarity is in part a reflection of the perceived threat to solidarity that was an ever-present possibility in France during his lifetime. Robert Alun Jones (1986:11–23) noted that Durkheim's life was framed by two wars. Born in 1858 in Épinal, in the Lorraine region bordering Germany, he was only 12 years old when, on a flimsy pretext and with inadequate preparation, the French ruler Napoléon III declared war on Prussia. The French were isolated from other nations in the region and suffered a humiliating defeat. The terms of the treaty called for the transfer of Alsace and part of Lorraine to Germany. This territorial loss was a bitter one, and one of the reactions of the 12-year-old Durkheim's neighbors was to engage in anti-Semitic scapegoating, blaming local Jews for the plight of France (Lukes 1972:41).

The war and its immediate aftermath highlighted the profound divisions within French society, which pitted republicans against monarchists, radicals against reactionaries, and Roman Catholics against anticlericalists and secularists. Civil war broke out in 1871. It ended when the republicans taking part in the Paris Commune were defeated. Out of this crisis, however, emerged the Third Republic, to which Durkheim was committed. Although the republic actually survived throughout his lifetime, its future was often uncertain.

At the other end of Durkheim's life was another war, longer and far more destructive than the first—World War I—that once again pitted Germany against France, but this time it also involved other European powers and the United States. Although France emerged a victor in this war, the victory was somewhat pyrrhic given the war's human toll. Certainly for Durkheim, who was a patriotic defender of the French war effort, the personal consequences of the war were tragic. Not only did a number of his most promising students lose their lives in battle, he also lost his beloved son, André. He tried to combat his own despair brought about by this death, plunging even deeper into his work. The result, however, was that his own health declined. Durkheim suffered a stroke and several months later died at the relatively young age of 59 (Jones 1986:23).

Although it is this historical context that serves to locate Durkheim's sociological career, his contribution to the discipline transcends the particularities of France in the late 19th and early 20th centuries. Durkheim was intent on understanding French society and any other particular society in terms of processes of change that were operating at a larger, civilizational level, which entailed a broad sociological vision that sought to locate the distinctive features of specific societies in terms of civilizational complexes and intercivilizational encounters (Durkheim and Mauss 1971; Nelson 1973).

The Distinctiveness of Durkheim's Ideas

Multiple forces shaped Durkheim's social thought (Lukes 1972; Poggi 2000), including such biographical features as the impact of his Jewish roots (both his father and grandfather had been rabbis) and his subsequent concerns about the challenges confronting Jews in France (Strenski 1997). They also include such diverse intellectual influences beyond developments in French social science as philosophers from Spinoza to Kant (Nielsen 1999), French socialist and republican thought (Stedman Jones 2001), and German social science (Jones 1999). In his attempt to understand society, he differed little from many of his contemporaries. Indeed, many commentators have found similarities between his work and that of such figures as Spencer and Toennies. What this trio and others shared was a conviction that Western civilization stood at the crossroads. Their world was viewed as a transitional epoch in which the new had not yet borne fruit, whereas the old had not completely withered on the vine. As noted previously, one of the ways these pioneer sociologists sought to capture the transition was via the familiar typologies mentioned previously.

Despite the surface similarities, however, there were significant differences that serve to contrast their respective writings. Durkheim, in fact, was quite intent on differentiating his views from those of both Spencer and Toennies. This was first evident in a review he wrote about Toennies's ([1887] 1957) *Gemeinschaft und Gesellschaft,* in which he said that he agreed with the author about the fact that there are two major types of society and he agreed in general with Toennies's characterization of the first of these types. He parted company with Toennies regarding the depiction of gesellschaft, as he (Durkheim 1972) made clear in the following passage:

> If I have properly understood his thought, gesellschaft is supposed to be characterized by a progressive development of individualism, the dispersive effects of which can only be prevented for a time, and by artificial means, by the action of the state. It is seen essentially as a mechanical aggregate. (p. 146)

In other words, Durkheim believed that Toennies saw individualism as working against a moral order. In such a social universe, people become, in effect, isolated atoms floating in space, unattached to one another. This, Durkheim contended, is a view that Toennies shared with such utilitarian philosophers as Jeremy Bentham. In such a state of affairs, Toennies seemed to suggest, the only thing that held people together and that prevented the fracturing of social relations and the relationship of the individual to society was the imposition of order and coherence by the state. Durkheim, in signaling his point of departure from Toennies, asserted that "the life of large social agglomerations is just as natural as that of small groupings. It is no less organic and no less internal" (Durkheim 1972:146).

This organic metaphor is carried over into Durkheim's ([1893] 1964) first major sociological work, his book on the division of labor. This work constituted his first systematic formulation, both of the differences between preindustrial and industrial societies and of the bases for social solidarity in industrial societies. Contrary to Marx, who sought to comprehend the underlying dynamics of capitalism, Durkheim paid scant attention to capitalism per se, writing instead about industrial society in general. This is evident insofar as the divisions he wrote about in *The Division of Labor in Society* ([1893] 1964) bore little resemblance to the social classes described by Marx. Instead, he focused on the divisions into various specialized occupations and with this the rise of professions that were becoming so characteristic of contemporary industrial society.

Durkheim's typology for preindustrial and industrial societies is, as noted previously, posed in terms of two differing kinds of social solidarity: mechanical and organic. His use of these metaphors is intentional because by depicting preindustrial societies as mechanical and industrial societies as organic, he was standing Toennies on his head (Durkheim [1893] 1964:37–38). There is something peculiar about his metaphors. After all, because premodern peoples are generally seen as being bonded to the collectivity and at one with their natural world, shouldn't this be described as organic? In the machine age, however, when people have been forced off the land and out of tradition-based communities by the dictates of the impersonal marketplace and forced into the artificiality of cities where their social relations are defined increasingly in terms of a world of strangers, this would hardly appear to be organic. Indeed, because industrialization and mechanization are closely related words, isn't it appropriate to characterize the machine age as one in which mechanical solidarity prevails? The question that needs to be addressed is why Durkheim would switch these terms in this way.

The Division of Labor

In *The Division of Labor in Society* (Durkheim [1893] 1964), the answer hinged on the impact of structural changes, resulting from the expansion of the division of labor, on social solidarity. In brief, Durkheim noted that in mechanical societies there is a relatively simple social structure with a minimal amount of labor division. For example, as anthropologists have subsequently shown, in early human communities, such as those of hunters and gatherers, the major societal division is made across gender lines, within the confines of kinship relations. Clans, tribes, villages, and other forms of what Durkheim referred to as "segmented societies" did not rely, or relied minimally, on external social organizations, instead functioning as small networks for the provision of life's basic necessities. Segmented societies were not economically interdependent in any significant way. The solidarity that bound their members together was related to the sameness of their lives. In other words, people were bound together by commonly held values or what Durkheim ([1893] 1964), borrowing from Rousseau, referred to as the "collective conscience."

Modern industrial societies are defined by their increasingly complex social structures and by an ever more refined division of labor. Industrial societies necessitate the specialization and compartmentalization of work, and with this arises a growing interdependency. The new reciprocity characteristic of social relations is precisely the quality of industrial societies that establishes the basis for organic solidarity. The differences in the functions performed by a society's members produce individual differences, thereby serving as a stimulus to individualism. In other words, although the bonds of mechanical solidarity were based on "a more or less organized totality of beliefs and sentiments common to all the members of the group," this gave way in industrial society to potent new forces that were characterized by heightened complexity and differentiation, an increased dependence on society, and, seemingly paradoxically at first glance, a growing level of individual autonomy (Durkheim [1893] 1964:129).

From his earliest writings to his last, Durkheim was concerned about the social problems that were endemic to industrial societies. At the same time, he sought to distinguish those problems from the ones resulting from the dislocations arising out of the transition period between epochs, when a moral vacuum was created due to the demise of mechanical solidarity prior to the foundation of binding organic moral constraints (Durkheim 1958a, 1961, [1893] 1964, 1972, [1924] 1974). Anthony Giddens (1971) correctly points out that "the notions developed in *The Division of Labor* constitute the foundations of Durkheim's sociology, and the bulk of Durkheim's subsequent writings represent elaborations of themes originally set out in that work" (p. 82).

Suicide

Giddens's (1971) observation is certainly evident in Durkheim's second important book, *Suicide* ([1897] 1951). This book has been hailed as a landmark work in empirical sociology, as a model of what sociologist Robert K. Merton referred to as middle range theory, and as a powerful manifesto on behalf of sociology. It has also been criticized for conceptual confusion, lapses in logic, problematic uses of data, and some questionable interpretations of data (Johnson 1965; Douglas 1967; Pope 1976; Lehmann 1995).

There are several reasons Durkheim chose to write about suicide. At the personal level, the suicide of Victor Hommay, a very close friend, may have contributed to his interest in the subject. Beyond this, however, because suicide was seen as a serious moral or social problem, and because Durkheim was interested in the ways in which sociology could play a significant role in addressing social problems and informing moral understanding, the subject could be construed as an ideal research site. This was particularly so because he was intent on indicating how sociology's object domain differed from that of psychology. Especially given the fact that suicide seemed to readily lend itself to psychological analysis, if he could illustrate how sociology could shed light on this phenomenon in a way that psychology could not, he would have advanced the cause of the discipline. In other words, he wanted to establish the scientific status of sociology by showing how it could provide a compelling account of the power of society in influencing this seemingly most individual of acts (Lukes 1972:191–95; Thompson 1982:109).

The study of suicide afforded Durkheim the opportunity to explore the dangers of contemporary individualism and an opportunity to develop a theoretical account of particular pathological social conditions that prove incapable of providing people, as Steven Lukes (1972) stated, "with the requisite sources of attachment and/or regulation, at the appropriate level of intensity" (p. 217). When this occurs, those psychologically vulnerable people who could be considered suicide prone are more likely to respond by committing suicide.

Durkheim ([1897] 1951:44) defined suicide as any direct or indirect act that the individual commits with the knowledge that it will result in death. In attempting to make his case that suicides are responsive to changing social conditions, he focused on suicide rates, beginning with the assumption that a certain number of suicides can be expected to occur in any society, with different societies varying in terms of their particular aptitudes for suicide (Nisbet 1974; Jones 1986). From this perspective, suicide rates are an example of social facts. Thus, the focus of his investigations was on the differing influences of different social environments, and insofar as this was the case, he was not concerned with individual motives, which were properly seen as falling under the purview of psychology.

The data amassed from a number of European countries revealed persistent differences in suicide rates depending on such factors as religious affiliation and marital status. They also revealed the impact on suicide rates of particular changes in the social environment, such as those produced by economic crises (Durkheim [1897] 1951).

In providing a theoretical framework for the interpretation of these findings, Durkheim began with the view that social cohesion in any society or among any category of people could be either normal or pathological (Figure 4.1). He then proceeded to identify four pathological states that could account for heightened suicide rates. Whitney Pope (1976) said bluntly that these suicide types referred to "states of groups or social conditions causing people to kill themselves" (p. 12).

Underpinning this typology is Durkheim's view of human nature, which he depicted as Homo duplex, creatures divided between a social and an asocial side. Human beings are driven by insatiable drives that need to be limited and contained by society. Durkheim thought that there was a delicate balancing act to be accomplished to achieve a relative harmony between fulfilling individual needs and desires and meeting the obligations and responsibilities demanded by society. Any harmony to be achieved between the individual and society must be derived from external social forces, specifically from a

Figure 4.1 Durkheim's Theory of Suicide

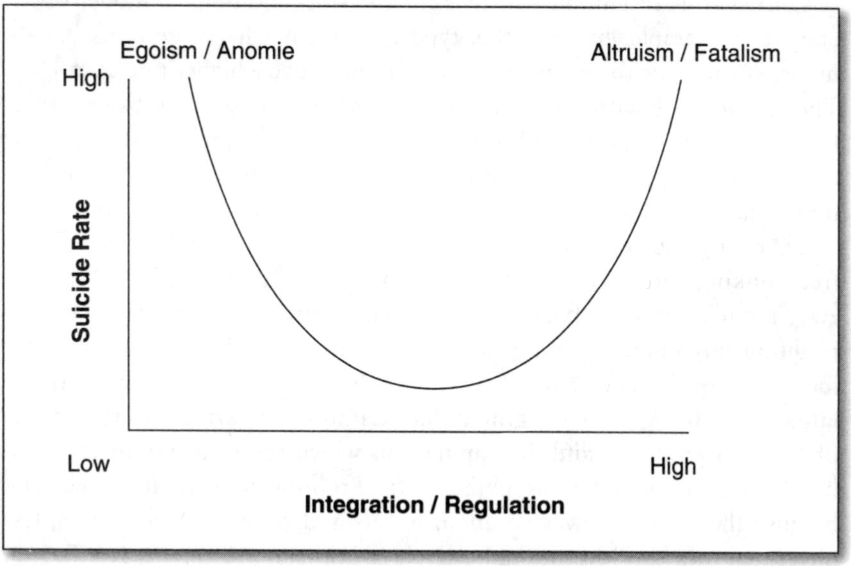

SOURCE: Pope (1976:57).

morality shaped by particular societies that inculcate values that are perceived to be both desirable and obligatory (Durkheim [1897] 1951, 1961, [1924] 1974).

The four types of suicide Durkheim identified are egoistic, altruistic, anomic, and fatalistic. These should be seen as polar pairs related to integration and regulation. Regarding integration, egoism and altruism refer to the ways that individuals are connected to or bonded with others and the extent to which they identify with and see themselves as a part of their society. Jack Douglas (1967) succinctly describes what Durkheim had in mind when writing about integration, suggesting that it refers to "the strength of the individual's ties to his society or to the stability and durability of social relationships within populations" (p. 36).

Egoism and Altruism

In the case of egoism, the balance between the individual and society is upset because an individual's activities and beliefs take precedence over collective bonds. In this situation, the level of integration is too low. Altruism, however, refers to situations in which individuals are not sufficiently individuated from the collectivity and the obligations it imposes on them. People do not have sufficient autonomy. In this case, the balance is upset in favor of society because the level of integration is too high (Durkheim [1897] 1951:152–240; Douglas 1967; Pope 1976).

Durkheim found ample evidence for egoistic conditions in modern societies. For example, he used this type to explain why Protestants have a higher suicide rate than Catholics, who in turn have a higher rate than Jews. The reason rests with the differing belief systems and institutional structures of these religious traditions. Protestants are more egoistic because (a) their theology encourages a direct relationship to God on the part of individual believers, whereas the other traditions see this relationship as mediated by the religious community; and (b) Protestantism encourages free thinking and, as with Luther's notion of the "priesthood of all believers," a willingness to challenge church authorities, whereas the other two traditions discourage such attitudes. The result is that Protestants are more inclined to be detached from their society than Catholics and Jews, with the latter group being more integrated than Catholics in part due to the impact of external prejudice and discrimination, which serves to reinforce social bonds within the religious community. Protestants were more egoistic because they shared fewer common beliefs and rituals and thus were less integrated into the institutional church (Durkheim [1897] 1951:157–160; Jones 1986:92).

Similarly, in referring to the family, Durkheim understood the fact that unmarried people commit suicide more frequently than married people to be an example of egoistic suicide because unmarried people are more detached from their society and thereby less integrated than their married counterparts. The same logic was used to explain why people in smaller families have a higher suicide rate than people in larger families. In parallel fashion, he argued that during periods of political crisis brought on, for example, by wars and revolutions, integration is strengthened, and during such periods the suicide rate is reduced, if only for the moment.

Whitney Pope (1976) succinctly summarizes Durkheim's argument regarding egoistic suicide as follows:

> The lower the rate of social interaction, the weaker collective sentiments; the weaker collective sentiments, the weaker social integration; the weaker social integration, the less individuals act in service of social interests; the less individuals act in service of social interests, the less meaning they find in life and the higher the social suicide rate. (p. 23)

When Durkheim turned to egoism's conceptual antithesis, altruistic suicide, the empirical evidence he mustered was of a rather different order than that employed in his discussion of egoism. Much of his evidence came from ethnographic accounts of such preindustrial societies as traditional Japan and India. When he did turn to European societies, he focused on military systems because in such systems individuals are required to abandon or limit their own interests in deference to the interests of the group. Altruistic suicides occur when the individual is sacrificed in the interests of the group; suicide in such situations is seen as a matter of duty (Durkheim [1897] 1951:228–240; Lukes 1972:207). It is precisely this exaggerated sense of obligation to the organization and the social relationships it engenders that results in overintegration. The fact that Durkheim contrasted life in the military to civilian life reflects his sense that altruistic suicide is atypical of everyday contemporary life in modern industrial societies.

Anomie and Fatalism

Regarding regulation, Durkheim understood this to be the ability of society to control and channel human actions and aspirations. Without effective regulation, the insatiable nature of human wants and desires proves to be a threat both to the well-being of the individual and to the interests of society. Thus, although regulation is essential, like integration it can be either too strong or too weak. When either of these states occurs, the two opposing types of suicide related to regulation increase. These two types are anomic suicide, in which regulation is too low, and fatalistic suicide, in which it is excessive (Pope 1976:25–27; Thompson 1982:111–114; Graeff and Mehlkop 2007).

Anomie is a term that is difficult to translate, but it has frequently been treated as essentially meaning "rulelessness" or "normlessness." Some commentators view the term as being akin to alienation. According to Stjepan G. Mestrovíc and Helene M. Brown (1985), Durkheim used it as a synonym for the French word *dérèglement*, which they translate as "derangement." However subtle the differences are among these definitions, they all imply that anomie should be regarded as a painful condition for society and for individuals.

Two empirical examples were used in *Suicide* (Durkheim [1897] 1951) to illustrate instances of anomic suicide: One derived from the economic sphere and the other from the family. In the former case, Durkheim contended that during periods of economic upheaval, anomie can arise. This is the case not only during recessions or depressions in that business cycle but also during boom periods. The reason for this, according to Durkheim, is that in both boom and bust periods people can become disoriented in an atmosphere in which it appears that anything goes and that ordinary constraints on conduct lose their efficacy. Individuals who no longer know what to expect or how to contain their drives and passions become candidates for anomic suicide. Similarly, people who experience divorce find themselves in a situation in which the regulative function of matrimony is lost, and they are therefore more likely than people who remain married to commit suicide. Because both economic cycles and divorce are part of the fabric of modern societies, anomic suicide is depicted, along with egoistic suicide, as particularly prevalent (Durkheim [1897] 1951:241–276; Besnard 1993; Lehmann 1995).

In stark contrast, fatalistic suicide would appear to be an inconsequential phenomenon. Durkheim discussed this type of suicide very briefly—in fact, in a single footnote located at the end of the chapter on anomie. This type of suicide derives from a situation of excessive regulation. Although Durkheim cited two examples that can occur in industrial societies—that of very young husbands and of childless women—he did not analyze these, and his assertions are open to question (Lehmann 1993, 1995). The other example he cited, that of slaves, reflected his assumption that fatalistic suicides are of little contemporary relevance, and this can account for the fact that his discussion of this type is so cursory.

During the century since *Suicide* (Durkheim [1897] 1951) was published, it has been pointed to as a model of research informed by a compelling theoretical model and, as such, has been seen as playing a singularly important role in establishing sociology as a science. At the same time, as noted previously, critics have taken aim at the book, questioning or criticizing its use and interpretation of data and raising concerns about its conceptual adequacy (Douglas 1967; Pope 1976; Jones 1986; Pearce 1989; Besnard 1993; Lehmann 1995).

These matters need not concern us here. Instead, we are interested in understanding Durkheim's contribution to the discussion of the role of individualism in the modern world and the attendant vicissitudes of community. What is clear in this study is that two of the types of suicide he identified are reflective of the modern condition: egoistic and anomic. Both arise due to an excess of individualism. Because it was Durkheim's intention in this work to highlight the social dangers of individualism, it might be suggested that he, like Toennies and Tocqueville, had a negative assessment of individualism, seeing it as undermining community ties.

Such a view, however, would constitute a serious misreading of Durkheim because although he saw some of the problems engendered by modern individualism, he also saw its positive side. He was definitely not a reactionary or conservative intellectual intent on returning to the past, when the individual had not fully emerged from the group. Although he was concerned about conditions that prompted the weakening of emotional ties between people, alienation, and the erosion of a sense of the common good, he was also convinced that (a) individualism was a constituent part of modern society and (b) individualism could, when properly channeled, serve to enhance organic solidarity (Giddens 1971; Mestrovíc 1988:134–140; Kateb 1989).

The Dreyfus Affair and Individualism

Nowhere are Durkheim's views on individualism more evident than in an article he wrote in 1898, one year after the publication of *Suicide* ([1897] 1951). "Individualism and the Intellectuals" (Durkheim [1898] 1969) was written in the midst of the Dreyfus Affair. This episode served to reveal the intellectual and moral fault lines in French society, pitting secularists, liberals, and socialist intellectuals on one side and reactionary Catholics, monarchists, anti-Semites, and right-wing nationalists on the other side. In a subsequent essay, Durkheim ([1899] 2008) located this episode in terms of what he called an "acute social crisis" (see also the commentary by Goldberg 2008).

The affair began in 1894, when Alfred Dreyfus, a Jewish officer in the French military, was arrested and convicted of spying for Germany. Two years later, a member of the French general staff unearthed documents that clearly exonerated Dreyfus. Instead of freeing an innocent man, however, high-ranking military officials engaged in an elaborate plot to conceal the evidence. When this conspiracy was revealed to the public, a major conflict ensued between defenders of Dreyfus and supporters of the military command. Supporters of Dreyfus came largely from the political and cultural Left, whereas those on the Right opposed granting Dreyfus a new trial or release from prison.

Although Durkheim thought that intellectuals should generally refrain from active engagement in political matters, and he generally stood clear of political involvement, this cause proved to be an exception. Although not the stirring appeal contained in Émile Zola's "J'accuse," Durkheim's essay was a more nuanced manifesto on behalf of the embattled Dreyfus and of liberalism in general. For our purposes, its importance rests with the way Durkheim made his case because he did so by providing not simply an account of modern individualism but, rather, a defense of it.

According to Durkheim, individualism is the product of society—the result of certain features of modern industrial societies stemming ultimately from the growth in the division of labor. Individualism, however, is not simply the individualism of the utilitarian philosophers, who viewed people as egoists motivated solely by self-interest. On the contrary, another kind of individualism is integral and essential to the promotion of organic solidarity. This individualism takes on a religious cast because the individual is invested with sacred meaning. Durkheim ([1898] 1969) stated that the individual

> is conceived as being invested with that mysterious property which creates an empty space around holy objects . . . and it is exactly this feature which induces the respect of which it is the object. Whoever makes an attempt on a man's life, on a man's liberty, on a man's honour inspires us with a feeling of horror in every way analogous to that which the believer experiences when he sees his idol profaned. . . . It is a religion of which man is, at the same time, both believer and God. (pp. 21–22)

Durkheim ([1893] 1964:407) elsewhere referred to this as the "cult of the individual," which implied not a narcissistic love of self but, rather, a respect for the integrity of all individuals. In other words, this deification of the individual resulted in a respect for and endorsement of human rights, a "sympathy for all that is human, a wider pity for all sufferings, for all human miseries, a more ardent desire to combat and alleviate them, a great thirst for justice" (p. 24). In terms of the Dreyfus case, Durkheim was arguing in favor of a position that valued the rights of the individual rather than a blind allegiance to the state.

In a more general sense, Durkheim was arguing that the social structural changes brought about by the expansion in the division of labor were not, in and of themselves, sufficient to ground a new basis of social solidarity. What was also needed was a new basis for morality, and he found it in what Lise Ann Tole (1993) called his "model of enlightened individualism" (p. 21). This model would replace the older, outlived morality that was incapable of accounting for individualism, while at the same time serving as a check on the negative potential of an unbridled egoistic individualism. Moreover, in his view, the political implications of such a basis for organic solidarity included support for liberal democratic rule and sympathy toward a non-Marxist, reformist version of socialism (Durkheim 1958b; Seidman 1983:152–178; Mestrovíc 1988:69–70; Gane 1992; Stedman Jones 2001).

Durkheim in America

Durkheim was familiar to his American contemporaries, the generation of early sociologists who pioneered the discipline in America: Albion Small, Edward Alsworth Ross, Charles Horton Cooley, William Graham Sumner, F. Lester Ward, and others. His work had an especially pronounced impact on the Chicago school of sociology, and its leaders ensured that Durkheim would become familiar to American sociologists by translating many of his writings in the department's influential publication, *The American Journal of Sociology.*

Nonetheless, his ideas have come to be associated most closely with the school of sociology known as functionalism, especially as Talcott Parsons and Robert K. Merton developed it. His ideas, however, have had a more general influence, as seen, for instance, in the attempts of sociologists during the post-World War II era to grapple with matters related to individualism and community in what came to be known as "mass society." Durkheim's ideas are at least implicitly present in perhaps the most influential of the books to come out of that period, David Riesman's *The Lonely Crowd* (Riesman, with Glazer and Denney [1950] 1989). Durkheim had a more direct bearing on the idea of "civil religion" as articulated by Robert Bellah (1970:168–190), a former student of Parsons and a key interpreter of Durkheim's work in America. In a somewhat different, although related, way, Durkheim's imprint is to be found in the work of Erving Goffman. We discuss these varied appropriations of Durkheim as they relate to the topic of the individual and community.

Merton's Elaboration of Durkheimian Themes

Robert K. Merton was a student of Talcott Parsons at Harvard who went on to become one of the key exponents of functionalist sociology and one of the most important sociologists in the world. His life can be construed as an American success story: Born in 1910, a son of poor Jewish immigrants in a Philadelphia slum, Meyer R. Schkolnick would transform himself from the ethnic and class outsider into the consummate sociological insider known to the world as Robert K. Merton (a slight variation on his 14-year-old magician's stage name, Robert K. Merlin). His long career at Columbia University has won him accolades and honors within and outside the discipline. Given his move from the bottom up and from the margins to the center of the world of intellectuals, Merton was in a particularly advantageous position to understand the differing social psychologies of people depending on their particular locations in the social structure (Page 1982; Crothers 1987:24–26; Merton 1994).

Merton's thought tends to parallel, or at times to amplify, Durkheim's social thought. Like Durkheim, Merton saw both the negative and the positive sides to modern individualism, and he sought to analyze its Janus-faced character. The negative aspects of individualism are contained in Merton's work on deviance, framed in terms of his understanding of social strain. The positive aspects can be seen in his articulation of his theory of role-set (Coser 1975:237–263; Sumner 1994:120–121).

In developing a theory of social strain, Merton (1938, 1968) sought to build on Durkheim's work on anomie, expanding this into a more general theory of deviance. Thus, he picked up on that part of Durkheim's work that focused on the downside of modern individualism. He differs from Durkheim insofar as Merton is essentially interested in this microsociologically, whereas Durkheim always had macrosociological concerns in the forefront of his work. In other words, Merton is primarily concerned with the realm of social psychology (Sztompka 1986; Besnard 1987:250–266).

Merton's argument, in essence, is that any society defines as part of its value system goals to which individuals should aspire and acceptable means by which those goals can be realized. Strain occurs when individuals embrace the goals but find that their opportunities to reach them by legitimate, socially sanctioned means are stymied. When there is a disparity between goals and means, the individual can be said to inhabit an anomic state (Merton 1968:185–248; Besnard 1987).

Merton constructed five ideal types based on varying responses to goals and means (Table 4.2). One, the conformist, depicts an individual for whom there is no strain between the two. Such an individual might, for example, approve of the goal of upward social mobility and also accept such a prescribed means as pursuing higher education to achieve the goal. This person is not experiencing the consequences of an anomic state.

Table 4.2 Merton's Social Strain Theory

Individual Response	Cultural Goals	Socially Approved Means
Conformity	Accept	Accept
Innovation	Accept	Reject
Ritualism	Reject	Accept
Retreatism	Reject	Reject
Rebellion	Reject-substitute	Reject-substitute

In contrast, the other four types, which are all seen as deviant, are evidence of anomie. These include the innovator, who accepts the goals but employs negatively defined means such as criminal activity in the interest of achieving monetary success and thus upward mobility. A ritualist continues to respect the means but becomes indifferent to the ends. Such a person can look like a conformist in terms of outward behavior but has lost any connection with an ultimate purpose for engaging in conformist actions. A retreatist, as the word implies, responds to social strain by abandoning and withdrawing legitimacy from both the goals and the means—the response, for example, of a hermit who simply withdraws from social life. Like the retreatist, the rebel rejects goals and means, but unlike the retreatist, the rebel advocates alternatives to both. Thus, someone who rejects the idea of upward mobility because it promotes inequality and the means for mobility, which encourages competition, might join a commune in which equality is valued and cooperation is seen as replacing competition as the primary everyday mode of social interaction (Merton 1968:230–246; Crothers 1987:119–126).

Although Merton's treatment of anomie remains at the microsociological level, it is a sociological and not a psychological theory. That is, he sees the source of strain in the social system and not in the individuals who are experiencing anomie. Alvin Gouldner (1970:426) went so far as to suggest that underpinning Merton's social strain theory of anomie is a radical critique of the internal contradictions of a capitalist system, which encourages acquisitive conduct while being incapable of meeting the aspirations of everyone. Merton may or may not agree with this assessment of his work. He is characteristically silent about whether behind the facade of objectivity lurks a social critic (Merton 1976, 1994).

What is clear is that, building on Durkheim's writings on the division of labor, Merton also saw another side to individualism. Whereas Durkheim discussed the impact of differentiation among people brought about by industrial society, Merton (1968:422–440) stressed the significance of an internal differentiation in which people are compelled to perform multiple roles. Rose Laub Coser (1975) argued that Merton's theory of the role-set "offers tools for developing a theory of individual autonomy in modern society" (p. 239).

The theory begins with the commonplace observation that people play a number of different roles in everyday life. For example, it is routine for a person to be expected to be a parent, friend, employee, citizen, customer, and lover within the course of a single day. Although these role expectations can sometimes be neatly synchronized, this is not always the case, and the potential for conflicts and incompatibility are relatively great. This makes conscious decision making on the part of the individual necessary, and from of the choices people make, roles are articulated and coordinated.

Although social structure continues to shape role definitions, individual choices appear to have greater say in Merton's thought than they do for Durkheim. Indeed, Coser (1975) writes,

> Merton has stood Durkheim on his head; rather than having the individual confronted with ready-made social norms that are external, coming down in toto, so to speak, for Merton individuals have to find their own orientations among multiple, incompatible, and contradictory norms. (p. 239)

In other words, for Merton individualism appears to be a given part of the human condition in the modern world, and far from bemoaning this fact, he—at least implicitly—appears to appreciate individualism's virtues. Cognizant of its pitfalls, Merton nonetheless does not feel compelled to speak out about individualism's excesses. Nor does he share the conviction of some of his contemporaries that individualism is actually being threatened by bureaucratization in what has become known as mass society. Although Merton eschewed the role of social critic, we now turn our attention to some of his contemporaries in sociology who did not.

The Lonely Crowd in Mass Society

During the period approximately between the end of World War II and the advent of the Vietnam War, a number of sociologists attempted to play the role of public intellectual by writing books intended for an audience beyond the confines of the discipline. They wrote for an educated lay audience concerned with little understood changes in American society in the aftermath of the horrors of fascism. This period was framed by both the

Cold War, which pitted America against the Soviet Union, and unprecedented economic prosperity in the United States. Their thinking was profoundly shaped by the specters of both Hitler's and Stalin's versions of mass society.

These sociologists shared a desire to engage in social criticism in a way that a number of other intellectuals of the period did, including Dwight Macdonald, Lionel Trilling, Irving Howe, Philip Rahv, and Paul Goodman, as well as Vance Packard, whose writings were more popular or middlebrow (Jacoby 1987; Horowitz 1994; McClay 1994). What differentiated the sociologists from a number of these figures was, quite simply, that they attempted to employ the findings of sociological research to inform their social criticism. Some of the works of this particular genre were community studies, which had a long and venerable tradition in American sociology, ranging from the Chicago school to such classics as Robert and Helen Lynd's *Middletown* (1929) and *Middletown in Transition* (1937) and Lloyd Warner and Paul Lunt's (1941) study of Yankee City.

Among the important books to emerge in the 1950s were William H. Whyte, Jr.'s study of the planned community of Park Forest, Illinois, *The Organization Man* (1956); John Seeley, Alexander Sim, and Elizabeth Loosley's study of an affluent East Coast suburb known to us as *Crestwood Heights* (1956); and Arthur J. Vidich and Joseph Bensman's study of upstate New York's *Small Town in Mass Society* (1958). Although each of these studies addressed somewhat different sociological questions, they had a common concern: Mass society, with its large-scale centralization and bureaucratic character, was inimical to both the well-being of communities and individualism. Their work evoked a concern with the problem of the "eclipse of community" (Stein 1960) and with the demands for social conformism that threatened individualism.

The intellectual historian H. Stuart Hughes (1975) described what the critique of mass society entailed for these and other intellectuals at midcentury, when Americans entered a period of "national soul-searching," as follows:

> What they saw about them was a situation at once uniform and fluid—a state of social "nakedness" in which the notion of community seemed to be slipping away and the individual lacked a cushion of intermediate groups to protect him against direct and overwhelming pressure from the wielders of political and economic power. (pp. 134–135)

Although each of the books noted previously—and many others as well—found large and receptive audiences, none had the impact of *The Lonely Crowd* (Riesman et al. [1950] 1989). As an indication of the impact of this book, Riesman appeared on the September 27, 1954, cover of *Time* magazine (Figure 4.2). The cover contained a portrait of a bespectacled, professorial Riesman. Behind him was a sea of humanity—the mass society. Rising above the mass, on two beams of light directed in opposite directions, were two men, each moving upward along one of the beams. The man located in the bottom beam was dressed in Victorian attire and had strapped to his back a gyroscope. The man in the other beam wore a 1950s executive-style suit. Unlike the other man, this one's left hand was outstretched, and he appeared

Figure 4.2 Time Magazine's Cover Portrait of David Riesman

SOURCE: Copyright © 1954 by Time Inc. Reprinted by permission.

to be looking outward. Strapped to his back was a radar dish. These, Riesman thought, are the emblematic types that make up the American social character that is portrayed in its many dimensions in *The Lonely Crowd* (Riesman et al. [1950] 1989; McClay 1993).

Riesman contended that during the postwar period, the country was undergoing a profound change in which an older type of social character that had been the predominant type earlier in the nation's history—at least among the middle class—was giving way to a qualitatively different type. The older type he called the "inner-directed" person, whereas the new type was referred to as the "other-directed" person. By social character, Riesman et al. ([1950] 1989) meant the "more or less permanent socially and historically conditioned organization of an individual's drives and satisfactions; the kind of 'set' with which he approaches the world and people . . . [and] which is shared among significant social groups" (p. 4).

Although the focus of the book is on two types of social character, four types are actually sketched out by Riesman. One of these, the "tradition-directed" person, is seen as a vestige of the preindustrial past, a type characteristic of agrarian societies and thus not applicable to modern industrial societies. The other, which Riesman called the "autonomous" individual, is a social type that he hoped to see emerge in the future to rectify the problems that inhere in both the inner-directed and other-directed types. It is less a reality than an ideal that the author would like to see realized.

The *Time* cover becomes comprehensible with an appreciation of Riesman's definitions of inner direction and other direction. The former is characterized by the internalization of values and goals instilled early in life by parents and other close authority figures. Once internalized, they become guiding principles by which a person can make his or her way in the world. For the inner directed, their own consciences are the repositories of their values, and from this they derive their sense of appropriate goals. They possess a highly individualized character, and when they get off course because of unconscious urges or external influences, they feel guilt because their actions do not fit their internal behavioral requirements. In other words, the inner directed possess what Riesman called a "psychic gyroscope" that serves them by helping to keep them focused and on course (Riesman et al. [1950] 1989:24).

Riesman's biography can be seen as a paradigmatic instance of an inner-directed person. Trained as a lawyer, he clerked for Supreme Court Justice Louis Brandeis and then resisted an offer to work for the Securities and Exchange Commission, choosing to work for a small Boston law firm instead. He left this position to teach in the law school at the University of Buffalo, to the consternation of several friends who said they would try to find an appointment for him at Harvard, darkly suggesting that going to

Buffalo would be a disastrous career choice. When the school shut down during World War II, he first became deputy district attorney for New York County and then took a position in the legal department at the Sperry Gyroscope Company. Riesman again went his own way, resisting overtures to serve as the president of Sarah Lawrence and Reed colleges, choosing instead to teach at the University of Chicago as an assistant professor in its social science department—without the credentials of a PhD (Riesman 1990; Turner and Turner 1990; McClay 1993).

Resisting offers for positions in large bureaucratic governmental agencies or administrative positions in higher education can be viewed as Riesman's own resistance to larger societal trends that were viewed as undermining the possibility of inner direction, being indicative of the expansion of the other-directed personality. The other directed are shaped less by their families than by their peers. Moreover, families are not as separate from or as independent of the larger social environment as they once were. The result is a personality type that seeks constantly to be in tune to external social surroundings, to fit in, and to respond in ways that are seen as socially approved. To be accepted, the person absorbs signals and adapts accordingly, learning how to read the nuances and subtleties of the messages he or she receives. The reaction to situations in which such acceptance is uncertain leads not to guilt but to anxiety. To allay anxiety, the other-directed person needs to be constantly receiving and processing signals from the social environment. For such a person, Riesman et al. ([1950] 1989) writes, the "control equipment, instead of being like a gyroscope, is like a radar" (p. 25).

Riesman's explanation for this shift in social character is not particularly convincing, relying as it does on a rather convoluted demographic argument about the changes wrought in societies characterized, respectively, by "high growth potential" (traditional), "transitional growth" (inner directed), and "incipient population decline" (other directed). It would be more appropriate to treat the traditional type as characteristic of preindustrial society and the inner directed as appropriate for a period of capitalist expansionism, with its emphasis on entrepreneurial initiative and risk taking demanded of a competitive market. But as Howard Brick (2006) has noted, Riesman "examined society without economy" (p. 172). That being said, there is an obvious family resemblance between Riesman's inner-direction and Weber's "inner-worldly asceticism" that informs the "Protestant ethic."

In contrast, the other-directed person is best suited for the highly bureaucratic and administered world of advanced capitalism, in which the emphasis is on cooperation rather than competition and on conformism rather than individuality. Thus, the shift from inner-direction to other-direction signaled a threat to individualism (Riesman et al. [1950] 1989). Riesman, in an essay titled "Individualism Reconsidered" (1954), contended that there was little to fear from an "unbridled" individualism—the excessive individualism of Durkheim—in America at midcentury. Of far greater concern was the enforced conformism of a mass society. Writing during the Cold War, Riesman and the other critics of mass society were, clearly, thinking of the possibility that the collectivist "groupthink" of the Soviet Union might find its counterpart in the United States.

Habits of a New Generation's Heart

A generation later, discussions of mass society had all but disappeared. A new reconsideration of individualism commenced in an era shaped by the disillusionment of the Vietnam War, the aftershocks of the youth counterculture of the 1960s, and the speculative economics of the Reagan presidency. Individualism seemed to be alive and well, with some hailing its salutary impact and others, such as Philip Slater in *The Pursuit of Loneliness* (1970), bemoaning what they saw as the alienating character of contemporary life. Those who assessed the new face of individualism in a negative light have attributed to it a corrosive role in the erosion of a sense of community (McClay 1994:287–295).

The book from this era with an impact comparable to that of *The Lonely Crowd* (Reisman et al. [1950] 1989) was *Habits of the Heart* (1985), by senior author Robert Bellah and junior colleagues Richard Madsen, William Sullivan, Ann Swidler, and Steven Tipton (all from the baby boomer generation). The intellectual heritage of this book is intriguing. First, it was written more than 100 years after the publication of Tocqueville's *Democracy in America* ([1853] 1969) and in fact derived its title from a phrase contained in that classic. Bellah et al. (1985) were rather self-consciously revisiting the themes and concerns first articulated by the distinguished French traveler. Second, Bellah, in his work on the sociology of religion, has proven himself to be one of the most important exponents of Durkheimian sociology. Bellah's discussions of civil religion, for example, emerged out of his encounters with Durkheim. Finally, Riesman served as a member of the advisory board assembled by Bellah.

The main perspective of the book suggests a sea change from the concerns of Riesman and associates. To wit, Bellah and associates (1985) write that they are concerned that "individualism may have grown cancerous—that it may be destroying those social integuments that Tocqueville saw as moderating its more destructive potentialities" (p. xlii).

They believe that the potential for a destructive form of individualism is rooted deeply in American culture, in a view of freedom that in essence demands that people be left alone by others, with the result being that they "leave the individual suspended in glorious, but terrifying, isolation" (Bellah et al. 1985:6).

Two types of individualism are identified as being of particular consequence at the current time: utilitarian individualism and expressive individualism. Utilitarian individualism has particular resonance in the economic sphere of a capitalist market economy, in which people act in a fashion intended to maximize their own self-interests. This type has an obvious relationship with Riesman's understanding of the inner-directed person. Expressive individualism is seen as arising in response to utilitarian individualism. It has its roots in 19th-century romanticism and in the 20th century is connected to the therapeutic culture of modern psychology (Rieff 1966; Campbell 1987). This type of individualism treats the person as a unique being to be actualized through a process of self-discovery. Life is seen as a quest for the realization of one's true essence. For example, the role of drugs in the 1960s counterculture was a manifestation of expressive individualism, as is the dramatic proliferation of self-help support groups in recent years. Both these examples reveal an interesting aspect of expressive individualism: It simultaneously pursues self-fulfillment and engages in a quest for a revitalization of community (Wuthnow 1994).

Bellah and colleagues (1985) do not think that either or both of these forms of individualism are inherently destructive of attachments to the larger community. Indeed, they spend considerable time in the book exploring the forces that have served as powerful antidotes to excessive forms of individualism, paying particular attention to the unifying force of both the biblical notion of an American covenant and the republican ideals of the proper role of the citizen.

Like Durkheim, however, they think that the fine balance that needs to be maintained between the individual and community has been upset, with the result being that individualism is growing too powerful, to the detriment of community. This is not to suggest that people are thoroughly isolated and detached from their communities. Far from it: They note that Americans continue to be more involved in voluntary civic organizations than their counterparts in other industrialized countries. The problem is that this involvement is eroding, as can be seen, in their view, by the fact that Americans are beginning to lose a shared language to describe their commitments to community (Putnam 1995; Bellah et al. 1996).

In case studies of people involved in a variety of civic activities, the authors observed that the subjects they spoke with were hard-pressed to provide a rationale for community involvement save that of expressive individualism, appealing to the sense of personal satisfaction or meaning such involvement provided. In other words, civic activity is described in terms of private rather than public purposes. Similarly, in the realm of religion, the authors depict the increasing privatization of religious beliefs. This is seen most vividly in the case of someone they call Sheila Larson, who says that religion is very important to her, although she has no involvement in any religious institutions. Most revealing, when asked to describe the character of her faith, she called it "Sheilaism," which she defined by saying, "It's just try to love yourself and be gentle with yourself. You know, I guess, take care of each other. I think He would want us to take care of each other" (Bellah et al. 1985:221).

Community is at risk when people lack a shared language of commitment and purpose. The privatization of discourse is a signal that individualism is at the moment eroding the public bases for civic incorporation and commitment. Bellah and associates (1985), however, are not unduly pessimistic about the future. As physicians to American society, they do not think that a cancerous individualism is necessarily a terminal condition. In fact, they wrote *The Good Society* (1991) as a follow-up to *Habits of the Heart* (1985). In this sequel, they attempted to encourage discussions about Americans' shared understandings of the common good. Bellah is also one of a number of prominent intellectuals—including fellow sociologist Amitai Etzioni, the philosopher Alasdair MacIntyre, political philosopher and feminist Jean Bethke Elshtain, and theologian Stanley Hauerwas—who are identified with an intellectual and political movement known as communitarianism (Etzioni 1993). The objective of this movement is to begin the process of finding a new equilibrium between the individual and the community, counterposing, for example, to the liberal individualist concern with rights a new sense of obligation and responsibility. Although critics have argued that communitarians are advocating a modified form of conservatism, I think it is far more appropriate to view them as liberals concerned with remedying problematic tendencies arising from liberal individualism.

One of the silences in their assessment of the causal factors contributing to the decline of community is the potential role played by a capitalist market economy in transforming both public and private life. A similar silence is also evident in Robert Putnam's influential and controversial best seller, *Bowling Alone* (2000), for which, perhaps reflecting public concerns about the presumed erosion of community, he received a $1 million advance from his publisher. Although not necessarily associated with the communitarian movement, Putnam shares their concerns.

The core argument Putnam advances is that social capital has declined in the United States in recent decades, a trend he and colleagues contend has its parallel in other advanced industrial nations (Putnam 2002). His definition of social capital is ambiguous and inflated, going considerably beyond the understanding of Bourdieu or rational choice theorist James Coleman, both of whom define social capital as the social networks that serve as resources for individuals. In this perspective, social capital is parallel to financial capital and cultural capital insofar as all three are resources that individuals can use in particular contexts to enhance their respective positions. Putnam differs by viewing social capital not primarily as a resource differentially available to individuals but, rather, as a factor that contributes to cooperation and trust, both prerequisites for civic participation. Although he does not totally dismiss the idea of social capital as a private good, his emphasis is clearly on the public good. It is seen as a critical variable shaping various levels of community involvement.

Putnam identifies the decline in social capital as a major causal variable in contributing to the withdrawal from public involvement—political, religious, and civic—on the part of growing sectors of the population. Leaving aside the empirical question of whether his data actually support his case, the question of why people have retreated from public involvement leads him to examine a wide range of possible culprits. Weighing a variety of possibilities, he places particular blame on the individualistic values of the baby boomer generation in contrast to their civic-minded parents and on the privatizing impact of television. Missing from his account is a willingness to seriously consider the impact of macrostructural factors associated with socioeconomic inequalities and power differences. In this regard, Putnam's analysis is part of a line of liberal social criticism concerned with the erosion of public life that, as radical critics argue, tends to conflate intermediate and causal variables.

Goffman on the Sacred Character of the Individual

Erving Goffman's concerns appear to be quite removed from the political reformism of Bellah and communitarian comrades. Indeed, commentators on Goffman's contributions to sociology have generally been reluctant to attempt to draw out the political implications of his thinking. At the same time, since his untimely death his reputation has grown, and sometimes effusive praise has been heaped on him. For example, he has been described by one well-placed observer of the sociological scene as "the greatest sociologist of the latter half of the twentieth century" (Collins 1988:41). Unlike that of many of his peers, his influence extended well beyond sociology, although unlike Bellah and others, he appeared to eschew any attempt to be a public intellectual. He generally refrained from commenting directly on the political and social issues of the day or engaging in critiques of existing social conditions. For this reason, his sociological vision also seemed quite removed from the critical theories of figures such as Marx and Habermas.

Instead, Goffman is known for his keen and discerning examinations of the workings of everyday life, depicting them as dramas of individual enactments and reenactments (Goffman 1959, 1961a, 1963, 1967, 1974). He is widely read outside of sociology in part because of the literary style of his work, which differed considerably from that of most professional sociologists. His style contains an implicit critique of the post–World War II sociological orthodoxy that sought through quantitative methodologies to construct a rigorous predictive empirical science. In this regard, he can be viewed as a transitional figure in the discipline, one embracing the legacy of such Chicago school luminaries as Robert Park and Everett Hughes, in contrast to the positivist trend in sociology at large (Fine and Manning 2000:465). He has often been seen as akin to a 20th-century Balzac, commenting acerbically on the "human comedy." Indeed, many—within and outside of sociology—view Goffman as a particularly astute and often cynical observer of contemporary middle-class America (Burns 1992).

Thus, in his early work *The Presentation of Self in Everyday Life*, Goffman (1959) used the metaphor of theatrical performance to describe the "fronts" that people select to perform, exploring in their enactments such features as "expressive control," "misrepresentation," "mystification," and "contrivance." The use of such language implied to many readers a portrait of contemporary America as a nation of manipulators and hustlers. Goffman's focus on interaction meant that he exhibited little interest in the inner workings of the self (Manning 2005:92).

Careful readers, however, have also found in his writings a kind of hard-boiled humanism (Lyman 1973; Lofland 1980; Collins 1988; Manning 1992). For example, Goffman's classic work, *Asylums* (1961b), based on ethnographic research at St. Elizabeth's Hospital in Washington, D.C., can be interpreted as a critique of mental hospitals—and by extension other "total institutions," such as prisons, military bases, boarding schools, and convalescent hospitals—on their assaults on the integrity of their inmates' identities. Thus, he wrote about the initiation of new arrivals into the mental hospital as a "degradation ceremony" in which the person is "stripped of one's identity kit" (Goffman 1961b:21, 139).

In a similar vein, in exploring the impact of stigmatization on a wide variety of socially marginalized people, ranging from the physically handicapped to ex-convicts, prostitutes, homosexuals, former mental patients, and the unemployed, Goffman aptly described the difficulties encountered by such people, who have to cope with identities that are in some fashion "spoiled." He did so in a manner that was sensitive to the dilemmas that stigmatized individuals confront in their daily lives without ever being patronizing or viewing them merely as victims (Goffman 1963).

In a sense, Goffman may have identified with such social outsiders, although this is not immediately evident. The Canadian-born Goffman's academic career was, on the surface, a conventional one. After obtaining an undergraduate degree in Toronto, he entered the graduate program in sociology at the University of Chicago, where he obtained his doctorate with a dissertation based on his research on interactional patterns on a remote island off the coast of Scotland, doing the actual writing in Paris during the heyday of existentialist philosophy (Manning 1992:3–4). Teaching positions at Berkeley, Harvard, and, finally, Pennsylvania (where he became one of the highest paid sociologists in the country) are indications of professional success; unlike Merton, however, Goffman never became a true insider. Indeed, he came to have a reputation as someone who purposefully stood at arm's length from sociology. In many ways, he refused to play by the rules of the game. Thus, when he was elected to the presidency of the American Sociological Association, it was a vote on the part of members for a perceived iconoclast, a deviant of his own making.

His work took as a given that individuals are thrust into the world and must make their way in it as best they can. The social structure is accorded a determinative primacy, within which transpire the presentation of self in everyday life, the interaction rituals, the impression management, and the other ways in which people navigate through the thicket of the public world. It is these aspects of the microlevel that constituted the focus of his sociological gaze (Goffman 1959, 1967, 1971). The purpose of such inquiry, according to Goffman, was not to change the world but simply to describe what one sees with as much acuity as one can muster.

As one perceptive commentator, Stanford M. Lyman (1973), noted, however, Goffman's work does more than describe, and this can account for its appeal to a large reading public: "For Goffman's sociology, without admitting such, seems to turn on the sacred character of the person and the rituals and rules which guard it" (p. 362). In this, Goffman expressed a remarkable affinity with Durkheim's notion of the cult of the individual, although Goffman expanded on it by seeing the sense of sacredness attached not simply to the idea of the individual in general but to particular individuals (Chriss 1993; Wiley 1994:108–109).

His focus on everyday rituals of civility is indicative of his conviction that identities are forged in interaction with others; he contended that, as with Cooley's "looking glass self," one cannot create and sustain a sense of individual identity without the support—overt and tacit—of others (see Scheff 2006 for the claim that Goffman was a symbolic interactionist working within the tradition that can be traced back to Cooley; see Collins 2005 for a recent account of the centrality of ritual; Cooley 1962). Thus, far from being inconsequential, such mundane interactions as those that occur in everyday, ordinary polite behavior are vitally important in helping people to affirm their identities (Collins 1988:46–50). In this sense, Goffman's sociology is a sociology primarily concerned with the quest for human dignity in social circumstances far removed from Toennies's preindustrial communities. Left unanswered by Goffman are questions concerning the macrolevel supports for and impediments to this quest in advanced industrial societies.

Such themes missing in Goffman's work can be found in that of another sociologist known for his literary style: Richard Sennett. In *The Corrosion of Character* (1998), he traces the implications of white-collar work in the era of the new capitalism, in which a premium is placed on fluid workplaces and flexible workers. Sennett questions the impact of this new economic order on human character, particularly on the possibility of creating and sustaining an integral self linked to the capacity to trust and to enter into relationships predicated on loyalty. He develops this line of analysis further in his book *Respect in a World of Inequality* (2003). Here, he examines the lives of those who fail to make it economically by not managing to enter into the ranks of the professional white-collar class. Of particular concern to him are the barriers they thereby encounter in the quest to obtain social respect and the implications this has for a sense of self. In *The Culture of the New Capitalism* (2006), he addresses what he calls "the specter of uselessness" (pp. 83–130).

For his part, Goffman steered clear of this type of critical sociology, with its albeit careful but nevertheless tangible critique of existing economic condition. As shown in Chapter 5, however, his appreciation of the fluid, complex, fragile, and transitory character of individual identity is one that has particular relevance to discussions about the impact of modern (or postmodern) culture on the fragmentation of the self.

Summary

Émile Durkheim's French predecessor, Alexis de Tocqueville, introduced into sociological discourse the idea that individualism was a hallmark of the modern age. Durkheim's German contemporary, Ferdinand Toennies, provided one of the most influential analyses of the concept of community. It was Durkheim, however, who most insightfully and productively explored the relationship between individualism and community. It was also Durkheim who focused on the social problems that can emerge when social forces threaten the healthy balance between the needs of the community and those of the individual that is necessary for a stable social order. As the discussions of Robert Merton, David Riesman, Robert Bellah, and Erving Goffman amply testify, his thought has had a profound influence on subsequent efforts to further our understanding of the dynamic and shifting relationship between community and individual. Merton pointed to the implications of social strain on this relationship. Riesman called attention to the threat to individualism in the middle of the past century brought about by the advent of mass society, whereas a quarter of a century later Bellah and associates saw reason to conclude that individualism had become sufficiently problematic that it was undermining community. Goffman worked hard to avoid appearing to be a social critic in the mold of intellectuals such as Riesman and Bellah. Rather, he articulated in his own signature fashion a perspective on the individual that, like Durkheim's, treats social structure as a given that individuals for better or worse must seek to negotiate in the process of achieving a sense of individual identity.

5

Modernity

From the Promise of Modern Society to Postmodern Suspicions

What does it mean to be modern? When did the modern age begin? Are we modern? What should we make of the claim made by Bruno Latour (1993), a French sociologist of science, that "we have never been modern"? Or what did Peter Wagner (2008) have in mind when he asserted, "But modernity today is not what it used to be" (p. 1)? Further along these lines, how should we respond to those—a growing chorus in recent years—who assert that, although we did until recently, we no longer live in modern society? Instead, they claim, we have entered a distinctly new "postmodern" world (Lyotard 1979; Harvey 1989; Jameson 1991). Finally, how do we unpack Charles Lemert's (2005) intentions in claiming that "postmodernism is not what you think"?

These and related questions preoccupy many contemporary sociologists, and appropriately so, given that sociology emerged as an effort to comprehend the form and content of modern society. The classic founders of the discipline who were discussed in Chapters 2 through 4—Marx, Weber, and Durkheim—are all theorists of modernity. Their insights into the nature of modern society have proven to be invaluable in making sense of the social world we inhabit. Moreover, the topics of the preceding three chapters address important facets of the modern condition. Modern society is made possible by industrialization and by advances in science and technology.

Democratic ideals and aspirations are intimately connected to modernity. Modernity reconfigures the relationship of individuals to other people and to their society by promoting individualism. Thus, modernity constitutes a synthesis of what we have been discussing; moreover, any of the trio of classic theorists could have appropriately been selected to introduce a discussion on this topic.

In recent years, however, it has become increasingly clear among scholars concerned with the history of sociology that one figure stands out as singularly important in helping us to comprehend modern culture and the varied ways it is experienced by individuals: the German sociologist Georg Simmel. His work is the focus of this chapter. David Frisby (1984) argued that "Simmel is the first sociologist of modernity. . . . [The reason for this assertion was that] no sociologist before him had sought to capture the modes of experiencing modern life" (p. 40). At the same time, while recognizing him as the sociologist par excellence of modernity, a case has also been made for viewing Simmel as a precursor to, or the first exponent of, a postmodern sociological vision (Bauman 1992; Weinstein and Weinstein 1993).

After providing some provisional definitions of key concepts and a discussion of Simmel, we discuss the work of his former student and leading figure of what became known as the Chicago School of Sociology, the American sociologist Robert E. Park. This leads us to an analysis of the controversial concept of postmodernity, in which the French social theorist Jean Baudrillard is the focus of attention. Following a brief examination of the work of Zygmunt Bauman, we conclude the chapter by exploring the idea of the "late modern age" as it has been developed by Britain's most important contemporary social theorist, Anthony Giddens.

Modernity and Postmodernity: Provisional Definitions

If we are to make sense of these theorists' claims, we need to have some idea of what kinds of culture we are talking about when we refer to both modern culture and postmodern culture. Thus, before we discuss Simmel, some definitional comments are in order. One thing is certain: Both modernity and postmodernity are notoriously difficult terms to define.

Modernity has often been viewed as being in opposition to and representing a break from tradition (Lyon 1994:19–21; Touraine 1995). If tradition looked to the past, modernity presumably turned its eye to the future. Modern culture is frequently associated, as Swedish social theorist Göran Therborn (1995) notes, "with words like progress, advance, development, emancipation, liberation, growth, accumulation, enlightenment, embetterment, [and] avant-garde" (p. 4). One might add to this the idea that modernism is often depicted as an expansive, and thus global, phenomenon. The association with these terms suggests that modern culture possesses an optimistic orientation about our ability to collectively resolve problems, to remedy human suffering, and to enrich social life. It presupposes our ability to acquire knowledge of both the natural and the social worlds and to use this knowledge to beneficially control and mold these worlds. As Wagner (2008) sees it, until recently, "modernity was associated with the open horizon of the future, with unending progress towards a better human condition brought about by a radically novel and unique institutional arrangement" (p. 1).

Postmodernism is a term of relatively recent vintage. As the term implies, it refers to a cultural sensibility that occurs in response to, and chronologically after, modernism (Lyotard 1979; Smart 1992; Touraine 1995). Insofar as it signals a move from one culture to another, it is a parallel term to postindustrialism. Postmodernism, however, differs from postindustrialism because whereas postindustrialism is seen as an outgrowth of industrial society, postmodernism indicates an exhaustion of modernism. Although some postmodernist theorists dispute this claim, I fully agree with Robert Antonio and Douglas Kellner (1994), who wrote that "postmodernists provide a pessimistic vision of the current era" (p. 127).

Thus, the move from modernity to postmodernity is in many ways a shift from optimism to pessimism. This can be seen in the (I presume rather tongue-in-cheek) suggestion by Charles Jencks (as cited in Harvey 1989:39) that postmodernity began at 3:32 p.m. on July 15, 1972—the moment when St. Louis's Pruitt-Igoe public housing project was dynamited into rubble (Figure 5.1). Built in the 1950s, this architectural award-winning project, designed by a disciple of the famous modernist architect Le Corbusier, was seen as far more than housing. It was construed to be a site where the problems of ghetto poverty could be solved and a place that would facilitate the sustenance of strong families, a vibrant community, active citizens, and economically productive employees. In short, the construction of Pruitt-Igoe was inspired by a modernist vision and hope.

In less than two decades, the project was primarily occupied by female-headed households mired in endemic poverty and dependent on welfare. It acquired a reputation as a dangerous, drug-infested, and crime-ridden place where residents moved out as soon as they could. Pruitt-Igoe came to be seen as part of the problem rather than part of the solution to inner-city poverty. Unable to envision any viable way to turn the project around, the local housing authority finally concluded that it had to be demolished (or, to use a term employed in other contexts by postmodernist theorists, "deconstructed").

Figure 5.1 The Demolition of the Pruitt-Igoe Housing Project in St. Louis

SOURCE: Photograph by Michael J. Baldridge. Copyright © 1972 by *St. Louis Post-Dispatch*. Reproduced by permission.

Thus, the fate of Pruitt-Igoe came to be seen as a sign of the failure of the modernist project and, as such, the beginning of the postmodern age.

With these admittedly abbreviated contrasting definitions, we now turn our attention to the theorist par excellence of the modern condition and possibly of the postmodern era as well: Georg Simmel.

The Ambiguous Legacy of Georg Simmel

Simmel's place in sociology's pantheon of founding figures is far less secure than that of Marx, Weber, and Durkheim. He is less widely known than this trio among sociologists, is less frequently read, and has contemporary critics who refuse to see his work as being of equal value to the discipline of Marx, Weber, and Durkheim. He did not create a school of thought that could be inherited by subsequent generations of sociologists. Thus, there is no Simmelian sociology in the same way that there is a Marxist sociology, a Weberian sociology, and a Durkheimian sociology. When Talcott Parsons wrote the draft for his monumental *Structure of Social Action* (1937), he included a chapter on Simmel, but before the manuscript appeared in print he had second thoughts about Simmel's importance and deleted that part of the manuscript (Jaworski 1997:45–60). Parsons, according to Donald Levine (2000), failed to appreciate the convergence of theoretical interests in Weber and Simmel and also failed to realize that Simmel had much to contribute to his own critique of utilitarian social action theory. Given the fact that this book played a significant role in defining the sociological canon, the omission of Simmel contributed for several decades to the relative devaluation of his work.

Simmel, however, was held in very high regard by many of his contemporaries. Weber, in particular, was impressed by the fecundity of Simmel's thought, and he intervened in efforts to advance Simmel's career. Durkheim and Toennies, although critical of aspects of Simmel's work, took him seriously. Simmel was highly esteemed by many influential American sociologists of the era, particularly those associated with the Chicago School of Sociology. Indeed, he served as an advisory editor of the school's influential *American Journal of Sociology*, and a substantial number of his essays appeared in translation in this publication. Although not a Marxist, he significantly influenced avant-garde leftist theorists such as Georg Lukács and Ernst Bloch (Leck 2000).

Academic Marginality

Part of the reason for the ambiguous reception of Simmel's work can be deciphered from the circumstances of his life. Born in 1858, he was the son of a prosperous Jewish businessman, a partner in a highly successful confectionery company. His father, who, like Marx's father, had converted to Christianity, died when Georg was a young boy. His relationship with his mother appears to have been strained and distant. He was raised by Julius Friedlander, a friend of the family and a prominent music publisher. The result of this upbringing was that although Simmel would remain financially secure throughout his life, he suffered, according to Lewis Coser (1971), from "a sense of marginality and insecurity" (p. 194).

His career choice parallels that of Weber and other sons who, in the words of Lawrence A. Scaff (2000), "fled the comfortable confines of . . . the wealthy upper middle class, for the speculative fields of science—a flight made possible in part by inherited wealth" (p. 252). Although he studied with some of Germany's most prominent academics and was seen by many as brilliant, his career was stymied. Unable to obtain a professorship, he had to content himself with remaining for years a *Privatdozent*, which meant that he was a lecturer who derived his salary from fees assessed to students entering his lecture hall.

It is difficult to unravel all the reasons for this situation. Part of the problem may have been Simmel's willingness to question and challenge his professors, something they were simply not used to encountering from their students. Part of the problem may have been due to what was perceived to be the quixotic nature of his interests. For example, in 1880 he produced a dissertation titled "Psychological and Ethnographic Studies on Music." Part of this study took up the topic of yodeling. Perhaps as a result of what was considered by his professors to be an unusual interest, his dissertation was rejected, and he was forced to write on another topic.

Among the most oft-cited reasons for his failure to advance in the German academic system, however, is anti-Semitism. Indeed, as Poggi (1993) has observed, "German universities and other academic institutions . . . systematically placed obstacles on Jewish scholars' roads to academic success" (p. 42). Indeed, there is ample evidence that Simmel's Jewish ancestry (he was not a religiously observant Jew; indeed, he had been confirmed as a Lutheran) was held up as a rationale for denying him various academic appointments that he appeared eminently qualified to receive (Morris-Reich 2008). Simmel was also involved, at least for a time, in socialist circles, and these political sympathies may have contributed to his career problems.

Further compounding his problems may have been the fact that professors became jealous of his success on the lecture platform. He was a gifted lecturer, attracting large numbers of students. Furthermore, he challenged the status quo by permitting female students to attend lectures prior to the time when they were allowed to enter Prussian universities as full-time students. Moreover, the types of students he attracted were not pleasing to conservative German academicians because they included political dissidents, cultural modernists, and Eastern Europeans, who were seen as ethnically inferior (Frisby 1984:27).

The result was that until near the end of his life, Simmel remained in Berlin, the cultural and political center of Germany and a dynamic and rapidly growing metropolis. At age 56, when he finally obtained an academic chair at Strasbourg University, he left Berlin reluctantly. His move to Strasbourg coincided with the beginning of World War I, and from his new locale, Simmel became—to the surprise of many—an ardent German nationalist. He became increasingly disillusioned with the war as it progressed, which increased his sense of marginalization from his new academic home. Simmel described his life in Strasbourg as being akin to life in a monastery because he lived a "cloistered" life—remaining the academic outsider until his death in 1918 (Frisby 1981:32).

Simmel on the Culture of Modernity

Simmel can be regarded as the preeminent figure from sociology's formative era responsible for promoting cultural sociology, which Steven Connor (2000) describes as scholarship focusing on "art, literature, and aesthetic and cultural life more generally, seeking to explain these phenomena not on their own terms, but in terms of their wider significance in social life as a whole" (p. 352). Because he was a sociologist of modern culture, Simmel's thinking often appeared to be a reflection of what he took to be a central defining trait of modernity—namely, its fragmentary character. Known primarily as an essayist, Simmel, in his writings, provided finely textured descriptions, or snapshots, of various social types, such as the stranger, the miser, and the adventurer, as well as various types of social interaction, including exchange, conflict, and sociability. Suzanne Vromen (1990) points out that Simmel "stands alone [among the classic figures] as the one who explicitly questioned the future of women in modern society" (p. 319). He addressed topics usually not deemed to be sociological, such as what happens to the aesthetic value of a vase when a handle, which has a utilitarian character, is added to it.

Simmel's style was that of a detached observer (in this regard, there is a definite stylistic affinity between Simmel and Goffman). Unlike Marx or Durkheim, he did not appear to be interested in finding ways to change the world. Although he spoke about the tragedy of modern culture, his tone, while critical, was by and large devoid of the pessimism of his contemporary, Weber. Not surprisingly, he has been described as a sociological impressionist and a flâneur, given to acute descriptions of the passing scene but lacking an overarching view of the social totality (Frisby 1981:68–101; Weinstein and Weinstein 1993; Levine 1995; Axelrod 1977).

There is a growing appreciation among commentators on Simmel, however, of the fact that, underlying these shards, the bits and pieces of contemporary social life that he scrutinized, was a well-articulated and coherent theoretical framework. To illustrate this fact, I single out for attention two important foci in Simmel's writings. The first is money because Simmel considered modern culture to be undergirded by an economic system based on money. The second is the city because Simmel considered the modern metropolis to be the site where contemporary culture revealed itself in its most pristine and stark form.

Philosophy of Money

Although Simmel was not a systematic theorist, his magisterial and complex book, *The Philosophy of Money* ([1907] 1991), contains his most sustained and coherent assessment of the form and content of modern culture and would serve as a framework for subsequent writings. In an advertisement that he took out to promote his new book (a common practice at the time), Simmel defined his intention as providing a complement to historical materialism. Rather than being concerned, as Marx was, with the material conditions—the economic factors—that led to the emergence of a money economy, he was primarily interested in discerning the varied ways in which a society predicated on a money economy transforms culture and in turn the individual's relations with others (Poggi 1993:62–68). Simmel sought to delineate the social psychology characteristic of a money economy, describing the varied ways that it structures our "internal and external lives" (Kracauer 1995:250).

Money, Simmel ([1907] 1991) pointed out, possesses no value in itself but functions as a tool to facilitate the exchange of goods and services. Money is instrumental, abstract, and impersonal. To cite one example of what he had in mind, in one widely cited passage of the book, Simmel observes that the monetary exchange between prostitute and client reinforces the fundamental character of prostitution, which entails "a wholly transitory connection, leaving no trace behind itself" (quoted in Poggi 1993:140). To borrow a term from Eva Illouz (2007), such encounters can be aptly described as "cold intimacies."

Objectively, it is no more than a means to an end. Thus, money promotes a rational orientation toward the world, and here Simmel's discussion bears a distinct resemblance to both Marx and Weber. Simmel goes on to note, however, that this rationality can become distorted for some individuals who treat money irrationally as an end in itself. The miser, for instance, is a social type who "finds bliss in the sheer possession of money, without proceeding to the acquisition and enjoyment of particular objects" (Simmel 1971:179). For the spendthrift, however, "the attraction of the instant overshadows the rational evaluation either of money or of commodities" (p. 182).

Money, by removing emotional involvements from economic transactions, makes it possible to expand considerably the range of one's trading partners. It expands individual freedom by severing the all-encompassing ties to a primary group (e.g., the family or the tribe) and in so doing promotes an individualistic worldview. Money encourages the individual to be future oriented—to look at the world in terms of novelty and transitoriness—and thus it serves to undermine a respect for and an attachment to tradition.

Although all this is liberating, Simmel also sees a negative side to money. Money places a barrier between people and tends to become an absolute value in and of itself. More pointedly, he wrote, "The whole heartlessness of money mirrors itself in the culture of society, which it determines" (Simmel [1907] 1991:344).

The world was thus conceived to function in a cold, instrumental manner, with an underlying assumption that it is possible to regulate the social world and to give it order without considering the values, beliefs, and emotional orientations of the people who constitute the society. Simmel ([1907] 1991) succinctly captured this rationalistic character of social life in the following passage:

> By and large, one may characterize the intellectual functions that are used at present in coping with the world and in regulating both individual and social relations as *calculative* functions. Their cognitive ideal is to conceive of the world as a huge arithmetical problem, to conceive of events and the qualitative distinction of things as a system of numbers. (pp. 443–444)

The consequence of this situation is that the modern world is characterized by a disjunction between objective (material) culture and subjective (individual) culture (Rowe 2005). At the individual level, this means that identity and the development of self can occur only by a process of distancing subjectivity from objective culture. In a manner that clearly parallels Marx, he refers to this distancing as alienation (Poggi 1993:202–203). At the collective level, Simmel viewed contemporary social movements, such as socialism and feminism, as well as aesthetic and quasi-religious movements, as responses to the alienating features of a money culture.

Social Differentiation in the Metropolis

Like Durkheim, Simmel was interested in the phenomenon of social differentiation; unlike Durkheim, who focused on the division of labor, Simmel was more interested in the ways social differentiation permeated all facets of everyday social relations. He observed that in primitive societies, individuals derived their identities from the group, and insofar as this was the case, there was considerable homogeneity among members. This changed in medieval Europe due to the existence of mediating institutions, such as professional guilds, that served as a buffer between the individual and the society at large. Nonetheless, although this made for greater heterogeneity in terms of the types of individuals in society, the individual's sense of identity was still largely determined by particular group identities.

The modern world changed this connection decisively. Simmel was fond of using geometric metaphors to describe social life, and in this connection, he spoke frequently about group affiliations as social circles. Unlike the premodern world, modern society is inherently pluralistic, which means that people live at the intersection of numerous social circles. Each of these various circles occupies part of the time, energy, and commitment of the individual, with various kinds of affiliations being more or less compatible with other affiliations. In this milieu, the individual is accorded considerable autonomy and flexibility in negotiating the varied demands for allegiance by the social circles in which he or she voluntarily chooses to participate (Simmel [1908] 1955).

One of the significant changes that occurs as a result of the complex "web of group affiliations" that enmeshes the individual is that there are parts of the life of the individual that are hidden from the members of the differing groups in which the person is involved. The result is not simply that the distinction between the public and private realms becomes more pronounced but that the individual's inner world can contain secrets that are not revealed even to one's closest acquaintances and intimates.

Simmel was interested in the space where modern life was played out, and for this reason he was particularly interested in the city because modern society took form originally and evolved most deeply and completely in the metropolis. Although others among his contemporaries, such as Weber and the French scholar Fustel de Coulanges, had written perceptively on the city, Simmel was the first sociologist of modern city life. Biographically, this should not be entirely surprising because Simmel spent his early years in the center of Berlin at a commercial intersection—the corner of Friedrichstrasse and Leipzigerstrasse, which has been compared to New York's Times Square—and in fact he remained in this rapidly growing and dynamic city for all but the last four years of his life (Coser 1971:194; Frisby 1992:99).

Because the money economy was crucial in shaping modern culture, and because it was in the metropolis that the money economy developed to its fullest, it was therefore in the city that one could expect to find modern culture most fully revealed. In an essay titled "The Metropolis and Mental Life" ([1903] 1971:324–339), published four years before *The Philosophy of Money* (Simmel [1907] 1991), Simmel provided an assessment of the impact of modern culture on the social psychology of urbanites.

In the essay, the reader will hear echoes of themes developed by both Durkheim and Weber. For example, Simmel raised the Durkheimian theme of the growth of interdependency in society. Although he agreed with Durkheim that this was due, in no small part, to the acceleration in the rate of occupational specialization, he thought that the need for intricate kinds of coordination was also brought about by the sheer density and complexity of metropolitan life. Simmel (1971:328) speculated on the kind of chaos that would bring commercial life in Berlin to a standstill if, even for an hour, all the watches in the city went wrong in different directions.

Likewise, the following introductory sentence of the essay (Simmel 1971) shares with Weber's writings—although without using such pessimistic imagery as that of the iron cage—a concern for the fate of the individual in the face of the progressive rationalization of the world:

> The deepest problems of modern life flow from the attempt of the individual to maintain the independence and individuality of his existence against the sovereign powers of society, against the weight of the historical heritage and the external culture and technique of life. (p. 324)

Like Weber, he saw the demands for punctuality, calculability, and exactness as arising out of forces of the modern world. He said that in the city, one finds a greater emphasis on intellectuality because reason replaces tradition and habitual action as a primary factor in shaping the conduct of everyday life. Paralleling Weber, Simmel evidenced a concern for the threat that modern culture, with its emphasis on instrumental rationality, posed for individual autonomy. Simmel, however, harbored no romantic longing to return to the organic wholeness of traditional societies, because he understood that, ironically, modern society both made possible individualism and served to undermine it.

He was keenly interested in exploring ways that people acted to ensure that they would not be overwhelmed by modern life. For instance, Simmel explained the characteristic reserve of urbanites—their blasé attitude—as a response to the flooding of the psyche by such a wide array of ever-changing stimuli that to do otherwise the individual would simply become overwhelmed (Simmel 1971:325–329). What some took to be the coldness or apathy of city dwellers, he saw as a necessary safeguard against the threat to individuality.

Tragedy of Culture

Simmel ([1892] 1977) understood the tension between the individual and the social structure through the lens of a philosophical position shaped by the German philosopher Immanuel Kant, which depicted human existence in terms of a dualistic tension that pitted life against form. Life was seen as an unbounded force of creativity, whereas forms become the containers that constrain and harness life. Thus, all of human existence is an unremitting struggle by life to overcome form, but as life liberates itself from one form it inevitably confronts—indeed, creates—a new form. The logic of cultural production entails acts of creation and destruction. It is the necessity of the destructive character of this process that leads Simmel to speak about the "tragedy of culture" (Nedelmann 1991).

Simmel understood this in part in an ahistorical manner (Simmel 1950; Weingartner 1960). There was no possibility that this conflict could ever be resolved or overcome. Quite simply, it was part of the human condition. Marxists, such as his former student Georg Lukács, criticized him for his tendency to treat culture in a timeless manner. More in line with what Lukács would want, however, Simmel, in his special fascination with the particular types of conflict found in modern culture, also appreciated the historically conditioned character of the dialectical process.

Although he seemed to agree in no small part with Weber's assessment of the oppressive character of bureaucratic rationalization, the social structural form giving shape to modern culture, his chosen focus was different because he was principally interested in examining the ways that people responded to the constraints imposed by modernity (Simmel 1971, 1984; Halton 1995).

Toward a Sociology of Leisure

Simmel was the first sociologist to turn his gaze toward the world of leisure and consumerism. This is evident, for instance, in an intriguing essay titled "Fashion" ([1903] 1971:294–323), in which he inquired into the reasons that changes in fashion—be it sartorial, culinary, artistic, architectural, musical, or other—occur so frequently in modern culture. The main reason for this, he claimed, was that the modern world is a "more nervous age" because it offers, in contrast to the past, such a wide array of consumer choices that make it possible for individuals to differentiate themselves from others. In other words, people will be attracted to new and different fashions at an accelerated rate as they seek to forge what they take to be a distinctive personal identity.

Fashion, however, is not simply a matter of individual choices. Rather, these choices are structured by class divisions and by social mobility. Simmel identified an antithesis between the desire for individual differentiation—for the desire to stand apart and to be unique—and the tendency toward social equalization—the willingness of all people, regardless of class position, to embrace reigning fashions—as being both a part of the motivation behind fashion choices and a reason for the unstable and generally short-lived career of any particular fashion (Simmel 1971:296; Nedelmann 1990; Lipovetsky 1994).

Simmel (1971) proceeded to make the following astute observation:

> The very character of fashion demands that it should be exercised at one time only by a portion of the given group, the great majority being merely on the road to adopting it. As soon as an example has been universally adopted, that is, as soon as anything that was originally done by a few has really come to be practiced by all . . . we no longer speak of fashion. As fashion spreads, it gradually goes to its doom. (p. 302)

Simmel (1971:313–314) believed, perhaps somewhat paradoxically, that fashion is one way that individuals seek to preserve their "inner freedom." Being willing to be dictated to and dependent on the external determinants of current fashions reflects a willingness to give up one's autonomy, but this, he thought, pertains only to "the externals of life." This willingness permits the individual to concentrate on preserving subjective freedom at its core (Weinstein and Weinstein 1993:101–129).

Similarly, he described the adventurer as a particularly modern social type. A person involved in an adventure seeks to step out of the mundane routines of daily life into a domain of activity with its own distinctive rules and rhythms. If the realm of work is the world of necessity, it is in the realm of leisure time that the adventure occurs. In a bureaucratized, rationalistic, and disenchanted world, the adventure provides the individual with the opportunity to be released—if only for a relatively short time—from the constraints of such a social order. The adventure promises excitement, innovation, and self-realization. The example Simmel cited to illustrate this is the clandestine love affair, with its alluring combination of eroticism and risk (Simmel 1971:187–198; Lyman and Scott 1975:147–158).

What he was addressing was a far more significant and pervasive aspect of modern life, an aspect heretofore generally neglected by sociological inquiry. Encompassed in the idea of adventure was a range of activities, including travel, sports competition, gambling, and outdoor activities such as sailing and mountain climbing. In short, Simmel's sociology argued that modernity could be understood only if we sought to comprehend the dialectical relationship between work and play—between the realm of necessity and the realm of leisure (Simmel 1971; Sellerberg 1994:75–82).

Should Simmel be viewed as someone who articulated the contours of a new social formation without actually calling it postmodern, or should he be seen as someone who captured the impact of the transition from a premodern to a modern social formation in an era of rapid social change (Pescosolido and Rubin 2000)? With regard to whether we should consider Simmel to be a modernist or a postmodernist, I hope it is apparent, referring to the provisional definitions, that he does not appear to neatly fit the mold of either cultural orientation. This, as the long-time Simmel scholar Donald Levine (1985) has contended, is because the world we live in is one that is inherently ambiguous, and thus neither excessive optimism nor pessimism is warranted. Moreover, perhaps what we referred to as postmodern is, in fact, an aspect of the modern age: its dark side. Simmel, perhaps more than any other of the classic theorists we have considered, seemed to have appreciated the ambiguity of his age, and his sociology is, in effect, a profound reflection of this recognition.

Robert E. Park and the Chicago School

Simmel realized that because he did not bequeath a systematic sociological theory or method, his intellectual heritage would be, like coins, distributed to subsequent sociologists who would use them in many different ways and for many different purposes. Among the scholars most influenced by Simmel's thought was one of the most consequential figures during the formative stage in the development of American sociology, Robert E. Park. Although the way in which he was to become a pivotal figure in shaping what became known as the Chicago School of Sociology was a long and circuitous process, Park's singularly important role is beyond dispute.

Born in 1864, the same year as Max Weber, Park spent his formative years in the rather bucolic surroundings of Red Wing, Minnesota. The one significant event from his youth that Park enjoyed recalling in his later years was his encounter with Jesse James, when he provided the bandit with directions to the local blacksmith's shop (Raushenbush 1979:6). Park left Minnesota to pursue his undergraduate studies at the University of Michigan, where he took courses from the philosopher John Dewey. After graduation, he worked as a journalist for a number of metropolitan newspapers. This phase of his life ended when he returned to school, entering Harvard to continue his studies in philosophy. His mentors included such illustrious scholars as William James, George Santayana, and Josiah Royce.

Park's first encounter with sociology occurred when he, like so many of his compatriots of the era, traveled to Germany to study. It was at the University of Berlin in 1899 that he first encountered sociology, doing so by attending Simmel's lectures. In fact, these lectures would comprise the sum total of Park's formal instruction in sociology. Not surprisingly, Simmel was, as intellectual historian Fred Matthews (1977) wrote, "the most important single influence on Park's substantive sociological theories" (p. 34).

Park came to share Simmel's conviction that modernity would express itself most tangibly in the city. Apropos of this, Park (1950) once contended that the world could "be divided between two classes: those who reached the city and those who have not yet arrived" (p. 167). Park (1952) also wrote, in words that read as if they might have been penned by Simmel, that "in the city all the secret ambitions and all the expressed desires find somewhere an expression. The city magnifies, spreads out, and advertises human nature in all its manifestations" (p. 87).

Park's sociology of modernity would focus on the extraordinarily heterogeneous subgroups of urban dwellers. What set Park apart from his mentor was his keen interest in the racial and ethnic groups that migrated to cities during the late 19th and early 20th centuries. This was a reflection of his

American roots because the significance of racial and ethnic differences was far more pronounced in American cities than in those in Simmel's Germany (Park, Burgess, and McKenzie 1925; Park 1950; Lal 1990; Kivisto 1990).

Before embarking on developing his own sociological vision, however, Park made another extended departure from academe. After returning from Europe to Harvard, he completed his dissertation based on a project he had begun in Germany. With a freshly minted PhD in hand, Park might have been expected to seek academic employment. Instead, he returned to his former profession as a journalist, this time as a freelance writer concerned with social reform.

During this time, Park became involved in the activities of the Congo Reform Association, an organization committed to educating the public about the cruel colonialist exploitation of the inhabitants of the Congo by Belgium, then under the leadership of King Leopold. He served as secretary of the organization and penned a series of muckraking journalistic exposés with provocative titles, such as "Blood-Money of the Congo" and "The Terrible Story of the Congo," which appeared in such popular publications as *Munsey's Magazine, Everybody's Magazine,* and *The World Today* (Lyman 1992; Kivisto 1993).

What was particularly revealing about these essays was the author's endorsement of his former professor William James's assertion that "progress was a terrible thing." Stanford Lyman (1992) referred to Park's critique as a "Gothic perspective," by which he meant that it "teaches its readers about the actual horrors that produce and prevail in the social construction of modernity" (p. 44).

Through his involvement in the association, Park met Booker T. Washington, the most important black leader of his era. Washington invited Park to work for him as a press agent at his educational institution in Alabama, the Tuskegee Institute. Park accepted and thus began a seven-year stint in the Deep South, where he functioned as a public relations officer and ghostwriter for Washington. During this extended period, the white northerner would learn much about the racial conditions of the American South and about a rural-based, African American culture (Matthews 1977:57–84; Raushenbush 1979:36–63). As a consequence of his involvement with Washington, he kept his distance from the most important African American intellectual of his era, W. E. B. Du Bois, whose political radicalism was antithetical to the reformism of Washington. Nonetheless, Park agreed with Du Bois about the importance of developing a leadership cadre for the black community, what Du Bois referred to as the "talented tenth."

Park's academic career began only after this extended apprenticeship. At age 49, he was hired by W. I. Thomas, then head of the sociology department at the University of Chicago. Thomas's forced departure from the university a few years later due to his arrest on a morals charge (he was seen leaving a hotel with a woman who was not his wife) paved the way for Park to be elevated to the chair's position. For the next quarter of a century, he was perhaps the central figure in shaping American sociology. The Chicago School would be, in effect, the center of the sociological universe, with the city of Chicago serving as a laboratory for faculty and students alike. Near the end of his life, Park (1950:viii–ix) wrote that early in his career he came to view the sociologist as "a kind of super-reporter," one committed to studying the "Big News," by which he meant large-scale patterns and social processes. In a recent reconsideration of the approach to sociological research as urban reportage that Park instilled in his students, Rolf Linder (2006) has appropriately suggested that in this regard he viewed himself as "the city-editor."

Race Relations in the Modern World

Central to Park's sociology was an awareness that the modern world brought together, via mass migration, a wide array of racial and ethnic groups from throughout the world who migrated to those nations at the center of the newly emerging economic world system, particularly the United States (for a recent account, see Kivisto and Faist 2010:13–33). Although some headed for rural frontiers in search of land, a majority of the immigrants arriving in the 20th century located in the burgeoning industrial cities, because it was there that genuine employment possibilities existed. Immigrants were compelled to adjust to their new social and cultural milieus and to the diverse groups they encountered (Park 1950, 1972).

Park was particularly concerned with delineating the processes of immigrant adjustment. Like political progressives of the era, he understood that in making the transition from their old world to the new, immigrants frequently experienced painful dislocations. The newcomers lived between two cultural spheres: No longer a part of their old culture, they were also not genuinely part of the new. This could result in what Park at various times called either "demoralization" or "personal disorganization," which meant that neither social controls nor cultural values were effective in integrating the individual into society. This contributed to a variety of potential problems, such as mental illness, suicide, and criminal activity (Park and Miller 1921). Somewhat resembling Simmel's characterization of the stranger, Park saw the immigrant as a "marginal man" [sic].

Writing at a time when anti-immigration sentiment was at a peak in the United States, Park was a sympathetic defender of immigrants. He opposed conservatives who demanded the rapid Americanization of the newcomers.

From the view of these nativists, the new strangers at the door should be expected to abandon, quickly and entirely, their cultural roots. Like progressives such as Jane Addams at Hull House, Park urged tolerance and acceptance as an antidote to ethnocentrism (Deegan 1988).

Thus, in key respects, Park's thought also resembled that of contemporaries such as Horace Kallen and Randolph Bourne, both advocates of what the former termed "cultural pluralism." The cultural pluralists sought to preserve distinctive ethnic and racial groups; Kallen (1924) went so far as to suggest that democracy required such diversity. Bourne saw a particular vibrancy in immigrant culture that he hoped would revitalize what he perceived to be a rather static and unimaginative culture. Park thought of himself as a hardboiled realist, and he probably thought that Kallen and Bourne were in some ways hopeless romantics. Like this duo, Park appreciated cultural diversity and was an opponent of Anglo conformity. Unlike these two intellectuals, however, Park largely confined himself to depicting current realities and future trends, avoiding discussions that elaborated on his pluralist preferences.

Park also differed from cultural pluralists because he thought that, over time, it was unlikely that in many instances—particularly among European-origin groups—distinctive ethnic cultures could be preserved. When they did, they would likely become watered-down versions of the original. They were subject to change and to erosion because of interaction with other groups and because of the influence of the dominant national culture of America. Though he did not think it was inevitable, it was Park's conviction that assimilation was a very powerful force in America, casting into question the ability of distinct groups and cultures to persist into the indefinite future (Kivisto 2005:5–15).

In this regard, as Barbara Ballis Lal (1990) observed, Park was inclined to emphasize processes of social change at the expense of examining the durability of social structures. Ultimately, the process of assimilation is one that entails the gradual erosion of social and cultural heterogeneity. Lal refers to this as the "ethnicity paradox," by which she refers to Park's claim that active participation in ethnic communal life has the unintended consequence of assisting in the incorporation of groups and individuals into the larger host society. On this basis, Park challenged the forced assimilators noted previously, arguing instead that policies of cooperation, tolerance, and voluntary action would over time ensure the incorporation of ethnics into the mainstream of American society and culture (Park and Miller 1921; Park 1922, 1950; Lal 1990).

At the same time, Park thought that ethnic identities could persist into the future, contending that many of his contemporaries had "greatly exaggerated" the extent to which assimilation was based on homogeneity and like-mindedness. Indeed, under the clear influence of both Simmel and Durkheim, he understood modern civilization as entailing the freeing of individuals from many of the constraints imposed by both ethnic groups and the national society as a whole. What this meant for group life was the emergence of what Park (1914) called "cosmopolitan groups" (p. 606; see also Winant 2000; Kivisto 2003a). Park's thought has more in common with contemporary discussions about multiculturalism than has been heretofore appreciated.

Race as a Social Construct

It is a truism among contemporary scholars that race is a social construct. This can be seen, for instance, in the approaches of scholars such as Stuart Hall, Patricia Hill Collins, Homi Bhabha, Paul Gilroy and many others who emphasize the fluid, hybrid, and contested character of racial identities. In this regard, Park was a path breaker insofar as he was one of the first sociologists to abandon biological explanations of race relations. He insisted that people of color must be understood in cultural, rather than biological, terms (Kivisto 2003b). For example, he observed that at the same time that mass immigration of Europeans across the Atlantic was taking place, a parallel migration was occurring as African Americans were migrating from the rural South to the urban North. It was his view that these two migrations could be understood in fundamentally the same way. In both cases, an essentially peasant folk from premodern, preindustrial communities was entering, and being forced to adapt to, a modern, urban, industrial milieu.

Earlier in his career, Park thought that assimilation was so powerful a social force that as diverse peoples came into contact with each other in the modern world, they would inevitably be caught up in what Park once called the "race relations cycle." This was a four-stage process leading from initial contact to intermediary stages of conflict and cooperation and resulting in assimilation (Park 1950; Lyman 1968). Thus, modernity was viewed as a great force promoting societal integration. Park also saw, however, that conflict and resistance to inclusion seemed to be capable of persisting indefinitely. He was acutely aware of the fact that race and racial differences—as social constructs and not as biological realities—played a profound role in perpetuating group differences and in putting a break on assimilation.

At the interpersonal level, Park understood what race differences could mean for intergroup relations. In an insightful essay titled "Behind Our Masks" (1950), he explored the implications of race relations in situations in which people are compelled to wear their race like a mask. The essay is in part indebted to his former teacher, Simmel, particularly his essay "The Aesthetic Significance of the Face" (Simmel 1959:276–281), and in part to the pre–Harlem Renaissance poet Paul Laurence Dunbar's poem, "We Wear the Mask" (1974). Park contended that in societies in which racial differences are considered especially significant, people wear their race like a mask. As a result, people from other races see the person merely as an essentially interchangeable representative of the race. In effect, people look across racial divides and proclaim, "they all look alike to me." Thus, racial masks prevent people from being seen as individuals. Park concluded by suggesting that in such societies, race relations will be characterized by considerable tension and conflict.

Because Park agreed that individualism was a characteristic feature of modernity, racialized barriers to its expression could appropriately be seen as vestiges of premodern, or traditional, culture. Earlier in his career, Park thought that as modernity uprooted tradition, race would decline in importance and class would become more important. Park emphasized the inevitability of conflict in social life and thought that race conflict would increasingly give way to class conflict as a divisive factor in contemporary life. In his later years, however, he seemed to realize that race could potentially continue as a potent social force long into the future. He did not share Parsons's idealism about the prospects for resolving America's racial dilemma.

Park was not so pessimistic, however, as to conclude that race was an intractable social problem. He saw in the crucible of the modern life, the city—with its social differentiation, mobility, and fragmentary characteristics—new kinds of social relations emerging that had the potential of rendering race a less salient force in social life. Likewise, advances in mass communication were seen as having the potential to reduce levels of group isolation and encourage greater tolerance (Matthews 1977:157–174; Smith 1988:123–131). Thus, like Simmel, Park's understanding of modern culture does not contain an unbridled optimism. Rather, its tempered endorsement of modernity was the result of his awareness of the paradoxical character of the age.

Park trained a generation of sociologists, many of whom would in turn become major forces in the discipline, including Herbert Blumer, the founding figure of the theoretical perspective known as symbolic interactionism, and Everett C. Hughes. Both in turn trained another generation of graduate students. A hallmark of Chicago School sociology was its devotion to ethnographic research, which entailed careful and rich descriptions of discrete slices of social life. Thus, a partial list of research by Chicago School graduates includes accounts of hoboes, race relations in small towns, the taxi dance hall (usually a front for prostitution), the real estate industry in Chicago, the medical profession, gangs, jackrollers (i.e., muggers), the public school, and the medical profession. One of the characteristics of the research tradition that was in no small part initiated by Park was its recognition of the Janus face of modernity. Chicago School sociologists saw the positive features of modernity, and they embraced its cosmopolitan and universalistic features. At the same time, they were sensitive to the negative aspects of the modern condition and the discontents that it generated.

Postmodernism and Sociological Theory

The word postmodernism has been around for some time. For example, C. Wright Mills (1959) proclaimed, without much elaboration about what he meant, that "the Modern Age is being succeeded by a postmodern period" (p. 166). Although the word has surfaced in various other places since Mills's proclamation, postmodernism did not burst onto the academic stage in the United States until approximately a quarter of a century ago—imported from its French literary and philosophic progenitors. Nevertheless, in its brief and highly contested history, it has had a pronounced impact on certain fields, particularly in literature, in which many of its most influential advocates occupied at various points in the recent past prestigious chairs at elite universities, such as Stanley Fish at Duke University and Huston Baker, Jr., at the University of Pennsylvania and later at Vanderbilt University. Postmodernism, however, filtered into sociology slowly and with less impact than on some other fields (Rosenau 1992; Gottdiener 1993; Kivisto 1994; Seidman 1994).

Insofar as postmodern theorists focus particular attention on culture, they are located in a lineage of sociological thought dating back to the cultural sociology of the formative period, particularly in the work of Simmel but also in that of Durkheim. This lineage also includes various subsequent theoretical approaches, such as those contained in the German Frankfurt School (especially the work of Theodor Adorno and Walter Benjamin) and the French College of Sociology (particularly Georges Bataille and Roger Callois) and those of mass society cultural critics (Eagleton 2000; Cormack and Cormack 2002; Richman 2002). It is important to note that we are interested in what it means to speak about the postmodern as a theory of culture (Lash 1990; Touraine 1995). Thus, we are not interested in the epistemological claims of postmodernism. Likewise, the postmodernist mode of literary criticism, known as deconstruction, is not of concern here (Derrida 1981; Agger 1990; Jameson 1991; Rosenau 1992).

There are a number of interpretive difficulties entailed in coming to terms with the idea of postmodern culture. First, postmodernist theorists often disagree with one another about the parameters of postmodernism. For example, Norman Denzin (1991), a sociologist whose thinking took the postmodern turn, provided a number of definitions of the term postmodern, one of which was that it is "undefinable" (p. vii). Second, postmodernists all too frequently write and speak in an impenetrable jargon, and thus their ideas sometimes appear to be comprehensible only to those who are initiates into the mysteries attached to such concepts as antifoundationalism. Logocentrism, hyperreality, and simulacra. A third reason, clearly related to the second, has to do with the French intellectual origins of postmodernism. In these there is a tendency to accentuate the novelty of the claims being made and the positions being staked out—phenomena resulting from the peculiar intellectual fashion consciousness in France.

We examine two interrelated themes that have, in varied ways, preoccupied some of the central figures associated with postmodernist thought: the critique of "grand narratives" and the blurring of the distinction between the real and the "hyperreal."

The Exhaustion of Grand Narratives

Grand narratives, in postmodernist discourse, refer to large, panoramic accounts or explanations of current social circumstances and future trends: Marx on the logic of capitalist development, Weber on rationalization, Durkheim on the development of organic solidarity, and Parsons on the progressive inclusion of marginalized groups in the social and cultural mainstream are examples of grand narratives that we explored in previous chapters. However different these theories might be, they share the Enlightenment conviction that we have the ability to make sweeping generalizations about the social world we inhabit, and with the understanding obtained by these grand narratives, we have the power to change society for the better (Best and Kellner 1991:8).

Postmodernists cast suspicion on these convictions. The French theorist Jacques Derrida, for example, sees the construction of grand narratives as the product of what he refers to as "logocentrism," by which he means modes of thinking that refer truth claims to universally truthful propositions. In other words, our knowledge of the social world is grounded in a belief that we can make sense of our ever-changing and highly complex societies by referring to certain unchanging principles or foundations. The postmodernist stance articulated by Derrida (1976, 1978) calls for a repudiation of logocentrism, which entails taking what postmodernists refer to as an antifoundational stance. In its most extreme versions, postmodernism constitutes a profound repudiation of the entire Western philosophical tradition and represents a form of extreme skepticism about our ability to carry on the sociological tradition as it has been conceived since the 19th century.

One might reasonably conclude that postmodernism is a contemporary form of nihilism—an anomic state characterized by a loss of meaning and a loss of faith in our ability to translate theory into practice. The Enlightenment belief that a more rational world would lead to a more humane world is abandoned. Given this, postmodernism could be seen as encouraging escapism and political passivism or an irrationality that promotes reactionary political positions (Callinicos 1989; O'Neill 1995).

Political Orientation of Postmodernists

What is somewhat surprising is that many postmodernists see themselves as situated on the political Left and, as such, as sympathetic to various progressive political movements: anti-imperialism, feminism, gay liberation, and so on. An example of how such a deconstructionist postmodernism proceeds, however, can provide a sense of its limited utility for leftist politics. In an essay titled "Can the Subaltern Speak?" (1988), Gayatri Spivak contends that it is important to hear the voices of powerless, marginalized people rather than allowing more privileged and powerful voices to attempt to speak on their behalf. Spivak is an Indian feminist teaching in the United States, and she has served as a translator of Derrida's work. In this particular essay, she addresses the traditional Hindu practice of *sati* (or *suttee*), in which the widow climbs onto her dead husband's funeral pyre and immolates herself.

During British colonial rule, the practice of sati was outlawed by colonial authorities. Spivak criticizes this act, claiming that it is a reflection of a desire to impose Western values on Indian society and as such is a form of cultural imperialism. The result was that the voices of the subaltern women were not heard. The colonial authorities failed to comprehend the women's belief that they were acting virtuously in performing this moral obligation. Spivak does not purport to defend sati. Rather, her intention is to criticize the British for presuming that their values should be seen as universal values, applicable to people everywhere. Such universalistic claims, she suggests, can only be the product of a worldview that is thoroughly logocentric.

In Spivak's thesis, one sees the linkage between postmodernism and those multiculturalists who contend that differing cultures can only be understood and evaluated on their own terms. Antifoundationalism thus merges with extreme cultural relativism. In the process, critics contend, it becomes impossible to make a case for universal human rights or to respond to charges of Eurocentrism. Antifoundational postmodernism undercuts the moral grounds to challenge such phenomena as the torture of political dissidents by African military strongmen, infanticide in China, and female genital mutilation practiced in many Islamic countries (Callinicos 1989:78–79; Kivisto 1994:726–727).

Ultimately, cultures are viewed as being discrete and incommensurate. There is no shared language that permits people to transcend local cultures and the parochialisms they embrace. In other words, if postmodern theorists are correct, we have entered an era characterized by what Todd Gitlin (1995), a critic of postmodernism, plaintively describes as "the twilight of common dreams."

Thus, the end of grand narratives signals the exhaustion of the modernist project, with its conviction that human knowledge could be used to remedy problems in both nature and the social world and, in the process, to facilitate more humane and sustainable societies. We arrive at a state of, as Durkheim called it, pervasive anomie.

The Real and the Hyperreal in Postmodern Culture

Whereas Marx and a tradition of sociological inquiry stemming from his thought have been preoccupied with the realm of production (e.g., with the factory system and with the conditions confronting the working class), postmodern theorists have turned their attention toward the realm of consumption. Indeed, one of the main claims of postmodernists about the transition from modern culture to postmodern culture is that people should be perceived as consumers rather than producers. Moreover, in advanced industrial (or postindustrial) societies, the sheer plenitude of goods and services available is seen as creating heretofore unimaginable consumer choices and with these choices a proliferation of new means of consumption (Ritzer 1999). Jean-François Lyotard (1979) wrote,

> Eclecticism is the degree zero of contemporary general culture: One listens to reggae, watches a Western, eats McDonald's food for lunch and local cuisine for dinner, wears Paris perfume in Tokyo and "retro" clothes in Hong Kong; knowledge is a matter for TV games. (p. 76)

Baudrillard on Disneyland as Paradigm

Contemporary culture in the advanced industrial societies is often characterized as being saturated by the media, entertainment, and new information systems. What are the implications of this saturation? Jean Baudrillard (1981), a former professor of sociology at the University of Nanterre who broke from his Marxist past to stake out his place among postmodern theorists, has argued that this saturation has resulted in a world in which the difference between the real and the images, signs, and simulations of the real has dissolved. This leads to the creation of what Baudrillard refers to as *simulacra*—reproductions or simulations of the real that are difficult or impossible to distinguish from the real. His argument parallels that of his contemporary Guy Debord, author of *Society of the Spectacle* (1983), which begins with the claim that today "all of life presents itself as an immense accumulation of spectacles" (para. 1).

The result is the emergence of what Baudrillard refers to as *hyperreality*. The term is meant to imply something that is at once not real and more real than real (Baudrillard 1983). Steven Best and Douglas Kellner (1991) provide the following illustration of what Baudrillard means with regard to hyperreality:

> In "TV World," for instance, the image or model of the Doctor (the simulated Doctor) is sometimes taken for the real doctor; thus Robert Young, who played Dr. Welby, received thousands of letters asking for medical advice and later appeared in ads where he advised readers on the wonders of decaffeinated coffee. (p. 119)

Although this example illustrates how the image comes to be seen as real—to merge with the real—Baudrillard also asserts that the postmodern era is characterized by the creation of simulacra, hyperreal social worlds that do not rely or depend on a "real" referent. Although one can point to the food in fast-food restaurants, theme parks, and shopping malls as instances of simulacra, the purest example, according to Baudrillard (1988), is Disneyland because the Magic Kingdom is not a copy and does not purport to refer to a reality outside of Disneyland.

Although nonpostmodern analysts of culture can concur with much of what Baudrillard has stated to this point, he proceeds to make sweeping generalizations that leave him open to criticism. This penchant for gross generalization is evident when Baudrillard (1983) remarks,

> Disneyland is presented as imaginary in order to make us believe that the rest is real, when in fact all of Los Angeles and the America surrounding it are no longer real, but of the order of the hyperreal and of simulation. (p. 25)

Recall that although Simmel saw leisure as an increasingly important arena of social life, he nonetheless maintained that leisure activities were set apart and distinct from the mundane world of work. In stark contrast,

Baudrillard suggests that this distinction today is meaningless because he views the world almost entirely in terms of consumption. Thus, in making a complete break with his own Marxist past, Baudrillard (1983) writes,

> You are no longer brutally removed from daily life to be delivered up to machines. But rather you are integrated: your childhood, your habits, your human relations, your unconscious instincts, even your rejection of work. . . . In any case, you will never be left on your own . . . the die is cast . . . the system of socialization is complete. Labor power is no longer violently bought and sold; it is designed, it is marketed, it is merchandised. Production thus joins the consumerist system of signs. (p. 134)

It is not easy to determine what Baudrillard's attitude is about postmodern culture. Jeffrey Alexander (1995) considers him to be "the master of satire and ridicule, as the entire Western world becomes Disneyland at large" (p. 27). Stuart Hall thinks that Baudrillard celebrates postmodernity, whereas Douglas Kellner sees in his work a fatalistic bemoaning and acceptance of the existing new social order, although it is a nightmare (Gane 1991; Smart 1992:131) (Figure 5.2). What is clear is that Baudrillard is less inclined to develop the conceptual tools that others might find useful in cultural analysis and more inclined, as Kellner (2000:751) suggests, to serve as a "provocateur," challenging much of classical and contemporary social theory.

Figure 5.2 Competing Assessments of the Fate of Modernity

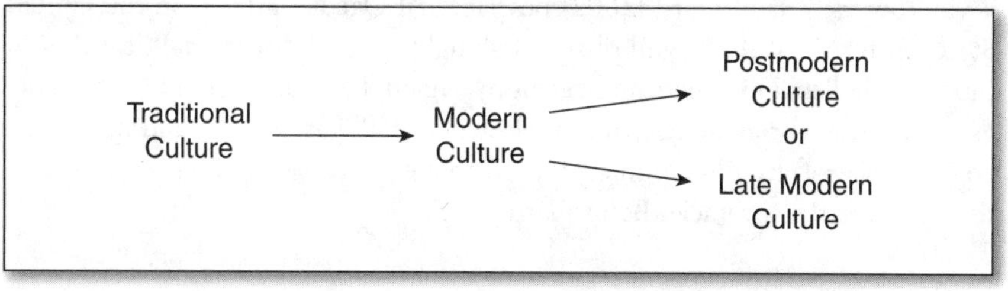

Easier to discern is Baudrillard's rather unflattering portrait of the role of individuals in postmodern culture. We appear to have been reduced to the roles of mall rats in quest of objects of desire and excitement, couch potatoes playing with the TV remote control, and voyeurs peering into the private lives of the rich and famous. We are, as the previous quotation indicates, thoroughly enmeshed in our social worlds but incapable of controlling them or of operating in a genuinely autonomous way.

This view of social actors is far removed from Marx's vision of the potential for beneficial change arising from collective action. It signifies the demise of the autonomous individual at the center of attention in a tradition of thought from Durkheim to Bellah. It goes beyond Weber's pessimistic assessment because Weber still held out hope that people could act in constructive ways to resist the iron cage. Finally, Baudrillard's views are distinctly at odds with Simmel's appreciation of the individual choices people can make in the ongoing dialectical tension between life and form. The implicit message of Baudrillard's work seems to be that we should passively accept—and even enjoy to the extent that we can—the spectacle and the carnival that is postmodern culture.

Because signs no longer refer to real referents, because the real has collapsed into the hyperreal, meaning has evaporated. In a rather notorious instance of applying this thinking to a concrete event, Baudrillard (1991) claimed that the Gulf War was nothing more than a television and computer graphics spectacle—the difference between this war and the war games in a video arcade presumably having essentially disappeared. Of course, there is an element of truth to this claim. Indeed, a similar claim was made by Slovenian theorist and fellow provocateur Slavoj Žižek (2002) about the war in Afghanistan that took place in the aftermath of September 11, 2001, which he depicted as "a virtual war fought behind computer screens" (p. 37). Lost in Baudrillard's vision, however, as David Lyon (1994) pointedly noted, is the fact that there really (i.e., not hyperreally) were "blood-stained sand and bereaved families" (p. 52). Lost, too, are beliefs about patriotic duty, geopolitical realities, the economics of oil, and similar very real considerations that lead nations into war. In his book on terrorism, which is described in the subtitle as a "Requiem for the Twin Towers," Baudrillard (2002) describes Al Qaeda's attack on the United States in terms of the "symbolism of slaughter" and "sacrificial death" as a mode of challenging American hegemony. Again, he treats a bloody event only as a spectacle—or as he describes it elsewhere as "war porn"—and not as the consequence of a complex interplay of political, economic, and social forces that underlie the spectacle (Baudrillard 2005).

Forget Baudrillard?

Baudrillard, who once urged readers to "forget Foucault," was himself the subject of an edited collection titled *Forget Baudrillard?* (Rojek and Turner 1993). The difference was the question mark, for the contributors in a sympathetic but critical way attempted to determine whether or not his work would manage to exert an influence over social theory in the foreseeable future.

My criticism of Baudrillard revolves around the obvious point that there is a reality that people experience, emotionally respond to, and attempt in some fashion to shape. There is a life outside the television set and outside cyberspace. The emotionless and meaningless worlds depicted in films such as David Lynch's *Blue Velvet* and Quentin Tarantino's films, from *Pulp Fiction* to *Inglourious Basterds,* are not synonymous with our lived experiences, nor do most people confuse the two (Best and Kellner 1991:137–144; Bauman 1992:149–155; Denby 2009).

Although it is certainly true that the world of consumerism has changed considerably in recent years, and that this world deserves more sociological attention than it has previously received, little evidence can be mustered to claim that we have left modern culture for postmodern culture. The continued potency of religious belief, for example, calls into question the pervasiveness of meaninglessness Baudrillard envisions. The existence of the new social movements concerned with such issues as the environment, peace, feminism, civil rights, and poverty also calls into question the extent to which people in advanced industrial societies have opted for political passivity and escapism.

By claiming that we have moved from production to consumption, this version of postmodernism shows evidence of a serious blind spot. It is obvious that goods continue to be produced, although in a global economy this might mean that they are being produced in poor countries, where workers (frequently including children) are paid abysmal wages and are forced to work exploitatively long hours in unsafe and unsanitary factories. The clothes purchased at the mall and the athletic shoes pitched in television and magazine ads by celebrities such as Spike Lee and a cast of NBA stars are the products of this darker side of our contemporary culture. Moreover, as Alex Callinicos (1989) has pointedly noted, most of the world's inhabitants are excluded from the consumerism Lyotard and Baudrillard describe, including poor people in the advanced industrial societies, who have only a limited involvement in this kind of consumption.

In a generous assessment of Baudrillard that appeared shortly after his death in 2007, Robert Antonio (2007) pointed out that Baudrillard's abandonment of leftist politics was a reflection of his assessment of the failure of the 1968 student/worker protests. This event led to his the abandonment of the Marxist dream of a radiant future. Unlike Žižek (2008), whom some continue to describe as a Marxist, Baudrillard was not inclined to argue "in defense of lost causes." Nor was he prepared to endorse the anti-utopian pragmatism of liberal democracy. Rather, in relentlessly promoting his often contradictory but deeply pessimistic diagnoses of our times, he became a media star, which included homage to him in the first movie of the *Matrix* trilogy and a U.S. lecture tour that was part of the Institute of Contemporary Arts' "Big Thinkers" series. He played a major role in creating and sustaining the postmodern moment, but near the end of his life he claimed that the term that best defined him was nihilist.

Liquid Modernity

Baudrillard was the most explicit and insistent advocate of radical postmodernism (Lemert 2005). It's important to note that other postmodernists have offered more tempered assessments of the postmodern condition, viewing it in many respects as a new phase of modernity rather than constituting a radical rupture between past and present. No one better exemplifies this position than the Polish-born sociologist Zygmunt Bauman. Born in 1925, he lived through the dark times of the Nazi era and supported the communist takeover of Poland after World War II. His intellectual trajectory led him from orthodox Marxism to critical neo-Marxism, which also entailed a shift from being complicit in the regime to becoming a dissident intellectual whom the authorities viewed with deepening suspicion (Edemariam 2007). When he lost his job as a result of anti-Semitic purges of universities in 1968, he and his family settled in England, where he took up an academic post at Leeds University, remaining there until his retirement.

A prolific author, Bauman commenced on what appeared to be virtually a new career once he had retired, rapidly churning out book after book. During the 1990s, he published a series of books explicitly devoted to postmodern concerns, writing, for example, about postmodern ethics and morality, as well as the discontent generated by the postmodern condition (Bauman 1993, 1995, 1997). Of particular emphasis in these theoretical reflections is an appreciation of the significance of ambivalence in postmodernity. Peter Bielharz (2009) sees a parallel between Bauman's thought and that of Simmel, contending that in both one finds a commitment "to the idea of *ambivalence* as a central orienting device and motif of modernity" (p. 97).

By the turn of the century, Bauman (2000) opted to replace the term postmodern with the idea of "liquid modernity." Perhaps to avoid the confusions and incessant debates about postmodernism and perhaps also to distance himself from postmodernism's more radical proponents, this original term can be seen as useful in carving out an intellectual space in which to articulate his own position. Agreeing with the claim that grand narratives have ceased to be compelling, Bauman (2007) sees the present as an "age of uncertainty." The preceding stage of modernity can be characterized as "solid." In contrast, the current stage is "liquid" insofar as patterned social conduct and the social structures essential to making such forms of everyday social relations durable no longer exist. Instead, we live during times in which these structures no longer keep their shape for very long, "because they decompose and melt faster than the time it takes to cast them." The consequence is that structured forms today "cannot serve as frames of reference for human actions and long-term life strategies because of their short life expectations" (Bauman 2007:1).

In short, people in the contemporary world are consigned to living out their lives with a far greater focus on the present and immediate future rather than with the "open horizon of the future" that Wagner (2008:1) associated with the early phase of modernity in a passage cited at the beginning of this chapter. Today it is essential to be flexible in order to address the more immediate contingencies of situation. Our lives cannot be seen as epic novels, but rather as a series of discrete short stories.

What makes Bauman so dramatically different from someone like Baudrillard is that his assessment of our current condition does not lead him to nihilism. On the contrary, he thinks that, today more than ever before, ethical conduct must be grounded in a sense of personal responsibility. We may live in uncertain times, but we don't live in amoral times. It's for this reason that Bauman continues to define himself as a socialist. In an interview in *The Guardian*, he explained to Stuart Jeffries why his commitment persists by contending that he has always believed that "you do not measure the health of a society by GNP but by the condition of the worst off" (quoted in Jeffries 2005:31). He would thus likely agree with Bielharz (2009:140) that socialism today should be viewed, not so much as an alternative economic system to capitalism, but as its "alter ego."

Anthony Giddens and the Late Modern Age

Given the severe criticisms discussed previously, one might reasonably ask why postmodern cultural theory has had such an impact in some quarters of sociology. One answer is that postmodernists have addressed new cultural conditions that had not, until recently, received adequate attention from modernist theorists. Second, many postmodernists similar to Bauman have backed away from the extreme positions articulated from a sociological vantage point by Baudrillard and from a more philosophical orientation by figures such as Lyotard and Derrida. Some creative thinkers, such as Frederic Jameson, Ernesto Laclau, Chantal Mouffe, and Nancy Fraser, have sought to selectively fuse elements of postmodernist theory with various modernist theories, particularly those emanating from Marxism and feminism. By continuing to employ the term postmodernism, however, they persist in conveying the sense that a radical cultural break has recently occurred or is in the process of occurring. Put another way, they resist the idea that the world we live in "is not *all* about flux," and that "[w]e remain firmly stuck within modernity" (Bielharz 2009:27).

This idea of a radical break has been criticized by a number of theorists (including Jürgen Habermas), nowhere more cogently than in the work of Anthony Giddens. It is fitting that we end our discussion of major themes in sociology with Giddens for two reasons. First, he is recognized as one of the best—perhaps the best—textual exegete of sociological theory in the world today. Giddens's (1971, 1979, 1987, 1995b) treatments of the sociological classics and of major contemporary theorists are known for their incisiveness and judiciousness, and they clearly reveal his conviction that sociological theorizing is both polemical (i.e., critical of the perceived shortcomings of the work of others) and forensic insofar as it builds on the work of others (for a general discussion of exegetical dilemmas, see Lybrand 1996). Second, Giddens brings us full circle because, as you may recall, he was one of the theorists mentioned in Chapter 1 who, in the face of considerable criticism, provided a vigorous defense of sociology.

Born in North London in 1938, Giddens did not distinguish himself as a student during his early years in school. Thus, rather than entering the elite Oxbridge world, he pursued undergraduate studies at Hull University. Denied entrance into the English department, he chose philosophy as an alternative major. When too few course offerings in philosophy were available, he took up sociology and psychology. Thus, this preeminent social theorist seems to have stumbled into the discipline. Giddens quickly became fascinated with these social sciences, and this interest had a positive impact on his academic success because he graduated with first honors.

Giddens then attended the prestigious London School of Economics, where he obtained a master's degree, and subsequently obtained a lectureship at Leicester University. He left Leicester in the late 1960s to teach in Canada at Simon Fraser University, after which he moved to the United States, where he taught at UCLA. His encounter with Southern California during the height of the 1960s' student revolts and the counterculture was an eye-opening experience. Bryant and Jary (1991) describe the impact of this encounter on how Giddens envisioned sociology as follows:

> Old European sociologies of class and authority shed little light on the revolution of everyday life associated with the hippies and with the new social movements including the student and anti-Vietnam movements. He recounts how a

> trip to a beach populated with large numbers of people in strange garb brought home to him that European sociology, and the agenda of the European Left, had their limitations. (p. 5)

Giddens returned to England at the end of the tumultuous decade of the 1960s, where he both completed his doctorate and was appointed to a lectureship in sociology at Cambridge University. Despite numerous visiting appointments abroad, including a stint at the University of California at Santa Barbara and, perhaps, a return to the beaches of southern California (he took a sociological interest in the body at approximately this time), he stayed in England, where he served as the director of the London School of Economics until his retirement in 2003.

During this time, he translated theory into praxis by serving as the intellectual guru of Prime Minister Tony Blair, who steered Britain's Labour Party toward the political center, transforming it into what he has dubbed "New Labour." Giddens was rewarded for his contributions to this political project by being named a life peer in the House of Lords.

The principal architect of a theoretical framework for a politics of what he calls "the Third Way" (Giddens 1998), Giddens envisions the Third Way as an alternative both to the neoliberal policies of Margaret Thatcher and to the welfare state created and defended by "Old Labour." He sees the Third Way as a new version of social democracy that, although connected to the Left, is actually located in what he refers to as the "radical center." Although many features of Third Way politics are ambiguous, Giddens is quite clear in two fundamental respects: (1) He is certain that after the collapse of communism, market capitalism is the only viable economic system. (2) Although the state is portrayed as continuing to play a role in combating the inequalities generated by the market, protecting individual rights, and confronting ecological problems, he is especially concerned about the strengthening of civil society. The success of Third Way policies rests mainly with the capacity of a vibrant civil society to emerge and to contain the excesses both of the unbridled market and of the bureaucratic state (Giddens 1998, 2000, 2002).

Structuration Theory

Giddens has written prolifically on all the topics discussed in this book. Of relevance to his understanding of modernity, in *The Class Structure of the Advanced Industrial Societies* (1973), he sought to depict the ways the class configurations of contemporary industrial societies were similar to and differed from the earlier industrial society analyzed by Marx. In this work, he was critical of postindustrial theorists, such as Bell and Touraine, for postulating a radical discontinuity between industrial and postindustrial societies. Instead, Giddens argued for historical continuity; change had certainly occurred, but he thought it more accurate to speak about an advanced industrial society rather than a postindustrial one. As we shall see, he makes a similar claim in confronting the claims of postmodernists.

Before discussing the specific contours of what Giddens refers to as "high modernity" or the "late modern age," one needs to link this work to his general attempt to reorient sociological theory. Although Giddens contends that he has been engaged in the development of what he calls "structuration theory" throughout his entire career, his efforts at theory construction are most clearly revealed in two works, *The New Rules of Sociological Method* (1976; the title is an explicit response to Durkheim's [1938] much earlier *Rules of Sociological Method*) and, especially, *The Constitution of Society* (1984).

The second book is the crowning achievement in Giddens's efforts at theory construction. Citing an often-quoted passage from Marx's "The Eighteenth Brumaire" ([1852] 1996), Giddens agrees that people create their own social worlds, although they do so in circumstances not of their own choosing. In his view, the major problem confronting social theory revolves around offering an adequate linkage between actors and social structures. The theory of structuration is an attempt to overcome the dualism that he sees as plaguing other theories—a dualism that gives priority either to actors or to social structures. Although various interpretive sociologies, including symbolic interaction, have tended to accord too much to agency at the expense of structure, the reverse is true in various structuralist theories, including Parsonian and neo-Marxist versions (Giddens 1984; Cohen 1989).

Given the scope of Giddens's concerns and the range of theoretical resources he brings to bear on the project, it is impossible to provide a brief summary of structuration theory. For our purposes, it is important to note that Giddens's proposed solution to the actor-structure problem is arrived at by focusing on social practices. He argues for what he calls the "duality of structure," which means that structures both are produced by human actors and are the means by which such action takes place. Structures are created by humans, but they in turn constrain and enable human action (Giddens 1976, 1984; Craib 1992:33–72; Lemert 1995:146–156).

The significance of this perspective for his substantive contributions to our understanding of modernity is that embedded in his theory is a perspective that encourages what might be seen as a tempered optimism—a view that does not succumb to the pessimistic conclusions about the inability to change for the better the course of modern life. Actors are not rendered powerless and thus have a role to play—individually and collectively—in directing, shaping, and managing the forces of modernity. Modernity, however, is a "juggernaut" that we are forced to ride: We are not in a position to abandon or transcend it at will (Giddens 1990:151).

Consequences of Modernity

In a trilogy that appeared in the early 1990s, Giddens employed his theory of structuration to explore various facets of modernity, searching for continuities with the recent past as well as those aspects of contemporary social life that suggest we have entered a new phase or stage of modernity, which he refers to as late modernity or high modernity. Taken as a whole, these works constitute an implicit response to Latour's question posed at the beginning of the chapter. Giddens's answer is that we are indeed modern and have been so for quite some time. Apparently, we will continue to be modern well into the foreseeable future. Giddens stated, "What other people call postmodern I think of as the radicalizing of modernity" (Giddens and Pierson 1998:116).

In the first and most systematic of these books, *The Consequences of Modernity* (1990), Giddens contends that modernity arose in the West under the twin impact of the modern expansionist nation-state and the system of capitalist industrialism. In its relatively brief history, modernity became a global phenomenon infiltrating non-Western cultures throughout the world.

The modern world is composed of nation-states that are crucial in directing a society's allocation of resources. The centralization of power in the state gives it military might as well as far-ranging administrative control over its citizenry. Nation-states make a major contribution in creating the modern information society because this institution paves the way for new and more pervasive modes of surveillance and control. Moreover, the nation-state is intimately linked to a capitalist industrial economy. Capitalism refers to a highly competitive system of production with labor markets operating on a global scale, whereas for Giddens, industrialism basically refers to the use of machine technology to control and transform nature and to develop a "created environment." In combination, they profoundly transformed social relations and humanity's relationship to the natural world.

Modernity results in a process of what Giddens (1990:19) calls "distanciation," which means that social relations are no longer tied to particular locales. Relationships with those who are not physically present become increasingly more characteristic of the modern world. An appreciation of this phenomenon is evident in AT&T's old advertising jingle, "Reach out and touch someone." It is also the topic of considerable speculation in discussions about virtual relationships established in cyberspace.

Modernity also entails a related process known as "disembedding" (Giddens 1990:21–27). This involves "the 'lifting out' of social relations from local contexts of interaction and their restructuring across indefinite spans of time-space" (p. 21). Like Simmel, Giddens sees one major type of disembedding in the expansion of a money economy. In some respects, like Durkheim, he sees a second type of disembedding in the increasing reliance on professional and technical experts. In both types, it is essential for people to operate with sufficient levels of trust, which Giddens (1991b) defines as "the vesting of confidence in persons or in abstract systems, made on the basis of a 'leap into faith' which brackets ignorance or lack of information" (p. 244). How is trust established and maintained? What are the threats to trust? Giddens treats these as crucial and unresolved questions in his discussions of late modern society as a risk society.

Risk in Late Modernity

Giddens (1990:55–63) identifies four risks of modernity embedded in this politicoeconomic institutional framework (Table 5.1). The first is the expanded ability of those with power to engage in surveillance in the interest of controlling information and monitoring and controlling people. Because the surveillance capabilities of the state and of capitalist enterprises have expanded dramatically in recent years, this ability creates the increased risk of the growth of totalitarian power.

The second risk is associated with the rapid escalation in military power brought about by the "industrialization of war," a phenomenon that, beginning with World War I, signaled the end of "limited wars" and the dawn of

Table 5.1 Giddens on the Risks and Promise of Late Modernity

Risks	Promise
Growth of totalitarian power	Multilayered democratic participation
Nuclear war or large-scale warfare	Transcendence of warfare
Collapse of economic growth	Postscarcity economy mechanisms
Ecological disaster	System of planetary care

the era of "total" wars. The development of weapons of mass destruction, including nuclear weapons, has created heretofore unimaginable threats to human survival and has led to far more war-related deaths in the 20th century than in any other century (e.g., the number of war-related deaths in the 20th century was at least 15 times more than that in the 19th century) (Giddens 1991a:429–431).

The third risk relates to the potential collapse of economic growth systems. This risk is connected to the fourth, which involves the potential for ecological decay or disaster. Giddens's politics are on the political Left, and thus it is not surprising that he contends that capitalism must be regulated to remedy its "erratic qualities" or, as Marxists would say, its crisis tendencies. He also sees modern capitalism as yielding gross inequalities at the national and global levels. Added to these problems, and going beyond Marxism, Giddens argues that capitalism's need to constantly expand productive capacity comes up against ecological limits, and thus the pursuit of capitalist accumulation is a major cause of environmental degradation (Giddens 1990:163–170; Beck 1992, 2009).

In summary, separately and in combination, these risk factors define the dark side of the late modern condition, and the seriousness of these threats might seem to justify a pessimism not unlike that expressed by many postmodernists. Indeed, Giddens (1990) concludes *The Consequences of Modernity* with the following bleak prognosis:

> On the other side of modernity, as virtually no one on earth can any longer fail to be conscious, there could be nothing but a "republic of insects and grass," or a cluster of damaged and traumatized human social communities. . . . Apocalypse has become trite, so familiar is it as a counterfactual of day-to-day life; yet like all parameters of risk, it can become real. (p. 173)

Giddens (1990:154–163), however, does not succumb to pessimism because he sees these risks as potential and not as inevitable. Preventing this dreadful scenario from unfolding and ensuring that solutions to the four types of risk can be found are distinctly possible. In particular, Giddens sees considerable promise in various social movements that operate with an orientation that he refers to as "utopian realism." The labor movement (the movement with its origins in the earliest stages of industrial society) seeks to address the risk tendencies of capitalism, whereas democratic movements challenge authoritarianism, peace movements challenge militarization, and ecological movements seek to remedy threats to the global environment. Although the success of these movements is not guaranteed, neither is their failure. What is essential for the viability of these movements is a worldview that considers plausible utopian realism. To that end, Giddens has become increasingly focused on explicating pragmatic political and policy choices, whether in examining the ways to enact what he sees as necessary reforms to Europe's social welfare model (Giddens 2007) or finding solutions from a center-left position to the ecological threat posed by climate change (Giddens 2009).

Modernity as Lived Experience

In the two books that followed *Consequences* (1990)—*Modernity and Self-Identity* (1991b) and *The Transformation of Intimacy* (1992)—Giddens turned to more Simmelian concerns, that is, to how people experience the modern condition. He attempts to indicate the growing connection between global developments and changes that are occurring in the shaping of self-identities and in establishing interpersonal relationships. Although attuned to the fact that these changes will likely be experienced differently based on such factors as gender identity and sexual orientation, Giddens does not explore in-depth the potential differences or their implications the way that feminists such as Luce Irigaray, Julia Kristeva, and Judith Butler have done.

For Giddens, the self becomes a project to be created rather than something decisively determined by tradition or habit. This project brings with it the possibility of considerable doubt and the threat of a sense of meaninglessness. It also, however, grants to individuals the possibility of engaging in life planning—in adopting a variety of lifestyle options. Whereas some critics of self-help manuals, 12-step programs, and so on see in this lifestyle exploration a form of contemporary narcissism, Giddens has a more positive assessment. Indeed, he depicts this trend in terms of the emergence of "life politics," which is concerned with the freedom of individuals to make choices and to create answers to the existential question of how a person should live his or her life. In other words, life politics involves the promotion of individual self-actualization (Giddens 1991b:209–231).

Life politics has far-ranging implications for interpersonal relationships, especially intimate ones. The democratization of intimate relations and the quest for emotional self-fulfillment have transformed intimacy, creating the possibility in late modernity of "pure relationships," which are relations determined and defined solely on their own internal terms and not in terms of any external factors. Giddens (1992) claims that "the transformation of intimacy might be a subversive influence upon modern institutions as a whole" (p. 3). Given the fact that his thought remains a work in progress, much remains unclear about what this transformation might entail outside the realm of intimate relations. It is certain, however, that the modern age is one characterized by reflexivity, which means that it is an age in which our acts and beliefs are constantly subjected to examination and reflection.

Summary

Anthony Giddens is part of a community of sociological discourse—involving sociologists past and present—that has played and will continue to play a singularly important role in the ongoing act of examining and reflecting on the human condition in the contemporary world. Although all the classical theorists discussed in this book have much to say about modernity, this chapter reveals the unique insights of Georg Simmel—insights that have shaped our understanding of what it means to be modern and what it means to be postmodern. Indeed, the uneven reception of Simmel's work meant that both theorists of modernity and those of postmodernity have benefited from his thinking. His former student, Robert Park, extrapolated his ideas and incorporated them in his own work on both the city and race relations in the modern age. Postmodernists such as Baudrillard build on his legacy in their focus on leisure and consumption. Bauman and Simmel share a conviction concerning the centrality of ambivalence to the contemporary human condition. Finally, theorists of modernity such as Giddens have learned much from Simmel's attention to the lived experience of modernity.

6

Globalization

Key Ideas in a Global Framework

The British Broadcasting Corporation (BBC) invited Anthony Giddens to be the last person in the 20th century to deliver its annual Reith Lectures over BBC Radio 4 and the World Service. Rather than presenting the series of lectures in the BBC's London studios, as was the custom, Giddens decided to deliver them as open lectures at four different venues throughout the world: London, Washington, D.C., Delhi, and Hong Kong. Moreover, making use of the Internet, he made downloading the lectures possible and arranged to have a global question-and-answer session after each presentation. In other words, he made good use of current technological developments in communications and transport to illustrate the fact that globalization is having profound impacts on all facets of social, political, and cultural life throughout the world. Appropriately, his lectures were concerned with this very topic, as their published version indicates by the title, *Runaway World: How Globalization Is Reshaping Our Lives* (Giddens 1999). Giddens quickly made clear that he thinks we are only at the beginning of what has already proven to be a major turning point in human history. Explaining the choice of the title for the book, he describes his take on the present in the following way:

> We are the first generation to live in this society, whose contours we can as yet only dimly see. It is shaking up our existing ways of life, no matter where we happen to be. This is not—at least at the moment—a global order driven by collective human will. Instead, it is emerging in an anarchic, haphazard fashion, carried along by a mixture of influences. (p. 10)

If this is true, what exactly has been the impact of globalization on your life thus far? What does the future hold in store for you at the dawn of the 21st century? A brief look backward indicates how different the world is today from what it looked like at the beginning of the 20th century. The sheer rate and scope of change render the 20th century distinct from its predecessors. Will social change continue to transform social life with the same intensity in the next century? Although it is impossible to predict with any certainty exactly what the world will look like in 25 years, 50 years, or at the end of the 21st century, if you carefully examine some of the most consequential current events that are captured in the daily news—those close to home and those in places far removed from where you live—you will see that they point to a number of possible future outcomes. In the process, they suggest that we are in the midst of dramatic changes that create new possibilities and new potential problems. These events raise all kinds of questions that stimulate the sociological imagination.

For instance, given the changes that continue to transform industrial societies (inherent in the idea of postindustrial society and in the concept of deindustrialization), what is your economic future? What about the economic futures of those in the United States who will not graduate from college and thus cannot expect to enter the ranks of the professional middle class? What about the economic futures of elites living in the developing nations? What about the futures of poor people living in those same countries?

Turning to the political realm, a number of similar questions quickly come to mind. Will democracy in America continue to alienate large segments of the population (i.e., those Americans who do not even bother to vote), or will new modes of citizen participation emerge to revitalize democracy—possibly via the Internet? Will democratic institutions in existing liberal democracies flourish or erode? What are the chances of democratic change in nondemocratic regimes? Will new waves of democracy sweep across the globe, or will new and powerful forms of totalitarianism arise to crush aspirations for self-determination? How robust is the international human rights regime? Can we speak about the emergence of a global civil society (Keene 2003)? To what extent have people been able to shift from outlooks defined in national terms to what Ulrich Beck (2006) calls a "cosmopolitan vision"? Is it possible to conceive of a citizenship that, rather than being rooted in the nation-state, is instead a world or global citizenship (Heater 2002)?

With regard to culture and the psychological aspects of the modern condition, equally important questions arise. Will individualism in the advanced industrial nations be shaped in ways that mesh with a sense of attachment to and obligation toward community, or will individualism take the negative course that Tocqueville predicted it would more than 150 years ago? Will religious fundamentalists in non-Western nations and others hostile to modernity succeed or fail in their efforts to prevent modern individualism from taking root in their respective cultures? What type of individualism will take root in former communist lands?

The following crucial information is linked to the above concerns. Will modern culture increasingly become the dominant global culture, eroding the influence of local traditional cultures, or will these traditional cultures manage to stave off the impact of Western cultural influences and persist into the indefinite future? Can we expect a growing homogenization of culture globally—what George Ritzer (1996) refers to as "McDonaldization" and Benjamin Barber (1992) calls "McWorld"? If not, will we witness a growing syncretization of popular cultures and thus greater diversity, as can be seen in the case of rock and roll? Conversely, can we expect a growing fragmentation, or a tribalization of cultures, along ethnic or religious lines as is evident in the violent civil wars in Bosnia and Rwanda or the more peaceful struggle in Canada regarding whether the Francophone community of Quebec will remain a part of the nation or go its separate way?

These are but a few of the crucial topics of inquiry that arise in pondering the kind of society we will soon inhabit. When looking around us today, we find plenty of evidence that can encourage us to be hopeful about the future. At the same time, we also see troubles that provide ample cause for genuine alarm. In attempting to sort out the positive from the negative, people—perhaps especially students like you who are about to launch out into their chosen careers and are beginning to think about what kind of obligations they will have as responsible citizens—are often highly perplexed. The tumultuous social changes that we explored in Chapters 2 through 5 have accelerated their pace in recent years, and it is not surprising that many people view the world around them anxiously and ambivalently. It is, quite simply, a confusing and complicated time; the eminent historian Eric Hobsbawm (1994) characterizes the current era as an "age of extremes."

This book has attempted to show how social theory can make sense of those extremes. It has revealed how four key ideas and a number of related concepts have been used profitably by social theorists since the 19th century to help people better understand the societies they inhabit and to provide reasonable clues as to what they can expect to experience over time. As you have seen, as those societies have changed, the ideas used to comprehend them have been modified accordingly. They will continue to be reshaped in the future (Halliday and Janowitz 1992; Wolfe 1996).

The Need to Think Globally

To illustrate some of the ways that this rethinking is evolving, I point to some major theorists who have attempted to provide theoretical tools for understanding globalization in its varied guises (Robertson 1992; Sklair 1995; Waters 2001; Ritzer 2007). It is something of a truism to suggest that the world is getting smaller and that we have come to appreciate how interconnected it actually has become. Building on this view, the iconoclastic social thinker Marshall McLuhan (1964) argued more than one third of a century ago that what was emerging was what he called the "global village," made possible by a revolution in communication and transportation systems that has transformed our experience of time and space. However suggestive this notion of the global village is, it needs to be examined in light of the ideas we have been discussing.

Perhaps the major impediment in coming to terms with globalization theoretically is that our key ideas have been, either explicitly or often implicitly, defined in terms of the nation-state. Indeed, when sociologists write about society, they tend to be writing about the nation-state, with the two terms treated as virtual synonyms (see the discussion of Parsons in Chapter 3). Alberto Martinelli (2002) sees this as a problem insofar as a "focus on the country level today risks obscuring the basic interconnectedness of the world system" (p. 1). Thus, for globalization theorists the task is to create an unbounded social theory that recognizes the expanding reality of global fields of action, networks of interaction, and organized institutional practices. Although a number of social theorists have suggested that these changes make necessary a reconsideration of our received understanding of what society is, none have been more persistent than British sociologist John Urry (2000) in his call for a "sociology beyond societies" and for the development of a "mobile sociology." Although his call for replacing the study of society with the study of mobilities strikes me as misplaced, it does call attention to the need to reckon with the networked, fluid, and globalizing character of much of contemporary life. Rather than replacing society, globalization calls for a conceptualization of, in the words of Roland Robertson (1992), "the world as a whole" or, in other words, as a single society (p. 8).

Globalization has brought about a redefinition of traditional understandings of space and time. Giddens (1990, 1991) has referred to this, somewhat misleadingly, as "time-space distanciation," whereas geographer David Harvey (1996) calls it "time-space compression." What both are getting at is the fact that, due to the impact of improved transportation networks and enhanced communications systems, we are witness to the dramatic undermining of what Harvey (1996) calls the "monopoly power inherent in place"

(p. 297). In a similar vein, Giddens (1990) refers to the rapid growth of social relations that are no longer tied to "local contexts of interaction" but instead are constructed "across infinite spans of time-space" (p. 21). Although Giddens, the theorist of late modernity, sees this in terms of a continuation of trends evident in the earlier phases of modernity, Harvey, the postmodernist, depicts it in terms of a radical rupture with the immediate past (Waters 2001:64–65). Whereas Giddens views the economic, political, and cultural aspects of globalization as operating with relative autonomy, the neo-Marxist Harvey sees the process in terms of the changing dictates of the capitalist system, which means that economic factors drive globalization in all its aspects. Despite their differences, both theorists agree that we are on the cusp of a new epoch. Both would concur with Malcolm Waters's (2001) succinct definition of globalization as a "social process in which the constraints of geography on economic, political, social, and cultural arrangements recede, in which people become increasingly aware that they are receding and in which people act accordingly" (p. 5). It is precisely this social process, in its various manifestations, that has begun to receive increasing attention from social theorists.

The Emerging Global Economy

More than 150 years ago, in *The Communist Manifesto*, Marx and Engels ([1848] 1967) argued that "modern industry has established the world market, for which the discovery of America paved the way" (p. 81). Later in the 20th century, this focus on the expansionist character of industrial capitalism would become the hallmark of the world system approach pioneered by Immanuel Wallerstein (1974, 1980, 1989) in his magisterial trilogy. Wallerstein (1998) locates the origin of the system in the 16th century but sees it as becoming "global only in the latter half of the nineteenth century, and it has only been in the second half of the twentieth century that the inner corners and remote regions of the globe have been effectively integrated" (p. 9). Rooted in the Marxist tradition, Wallerstein depicts the world system as a single powerful economic entity supported and sustained by a shifting group of strong nation-states that constitute the wealthy core. The remainder of the world is divided into the periphery and the semiperiphery, both of which are exploited as sources of cheap labor and raw materials by the core.

Although some commentators seek to distinguish world system theory from globalization theory proper, viewing the former as a precursor to the latter, for our purposes the two approaches reveal more than a family resemblance insofar as they take the globe as the proper unit of analysis (Giddens

1990:68–70). Many recent theorists of globalization dispute what they consider to be Wallerstein's economic determinism and disagree with his Marxist-inspired predication that the crisis tendencies of the world system signal the limits of a capitalist-dominated system and the embryonic development of a new postcapitalist world system. They concur with him, however, about the global reach of capitalism.

The initial questions in any attempt to understand the implications of this reach are as follows: What exactly do we mean by a global economy, and what are some of the implications of globalization? A global economy is one in which corporations compete internationally while severing the attachments to the nations in which they originally operated. Saskia Sassen (1996) described this trend as a reflection of the "global footlooseness of corporate capital" (p. 6). Thus, in the quest for sources of cheap labor (and weak or nonexistent labor unions), manufacturers have closed plants in the industrial heartlands of America and have relocated in developing nations. As a consequence, deindustrialization has produced a "rust belt" and severe social and economic distress in many communities heretofore reliant on manufacturing as hundreds of thousands of blue-collar jobs have been eliminated. At the same time—as in Europe at the advent of the Industrial Revolution—peasants in the nations of the South (the new term for the Third World after the collapse of the communist Second World) have flocked to burgeoning cities in search of work in factories founded by multinational corporations. These are the new proletarians.

Corporate giants in America and the other nations that constitute the North (i.e., the old First World) have invested heavily in new facilities outside of their national borders. In the case of American corporations, this has taken place both close to the United States (e.g., *maquiladora* industries in Mexico's territories along the U.S. border) and in a vast number of overseas nations. This has led to a situation in which currently more than 50% of the workforces of firms such as Ford, General Motors, IBM, and Exxon reside outside the United States (Sassen 1994).

At the same time, a restructuring of the U.S. economy is under way. Foreign firms, such as Japanese automobile manufacturers, have built plants in the United States and have begun to introduce new management styles and corporate cultures. They are also entering into innovative cooperative agreements with American companies. These trends have made for a very complicated and novel situation: Which is the American car—the Toyota built in Alabama or the Ford largely assembled in overseas facilities? Moreover, despite the loss of hundreds of thousands of manufacturing jobs, immigrants from developing nations continue to seek entry into the United States, believing that their economic futures are brighter here than in their homeland (Kivisto and Faist 2010:80–83). Some of these immigrants, too, are the new proletarians. Not all are members of the blue-collar workforce, however. New immigrants also include educated professionals with skills needed in the technology, information, and health sectors of the economy. This latter category is sometimes referred to as "brain-drain" immigrants (Kivisto 2002).

Looking elsewhere, with the collapse of communism in the former Soviet Union and Eastern Europe, capitalist firms have rushed into several of these nations to establish bases of operation. Poland, for example, is often portrayed as a country that has succeeded in making the transition from communism to capitalism. Due to this perception, it has experienced a dramatic influx of foreign investment. Businesspersons converge on Warsaw's Marriott Hotel and "do deals" in the hotel's lobby. Dubbed the "Marriott brigades" by some acerbic Polish commentators, these capitalist entrepreneurs believe that there is sufficient political stability in Poland's fledgling democracy to ensure that the country is a good place to invest. Thus, in less than a decade, dramatic changes occurred in the Polish economy. Industrial modernization has progressed relatively quickly, and a consumer culture is taking root. Warsaw, for example, is now home to McDonald's and numerous other fast-food enterprises as well as to major clothing outlets whose home bases are located in either North America or Western Europe. Its main shopping streets are quickly beginning to resemble their counterparts in major Western European cities.

At the same time, due to the relative political instability of some other Eastern European nations, including Russia, Western capitalists have been somewhat more restrained in their willingness to invest. Many investors, quite reasonably, are uncomfortable with the levels of corruption endemic in such nations. The Swedish chain IKEA, for example, has been forced to provide its stores in Russia with electrical generators in order to avoid having to pay bribes to obtain electrical service. Similarly, investors are waiting to see if these countries actually manage to establish relatively free and open political systems while at the same time addressing major social problems (particularly crime) before they establish bases of operation.

Given these recent developments, it is not surprising that we can see a growing consensus that economic globalization is occurring rapidly. There is less agreement about how best to explain these trends. Some sociologists consider the examples cited previously and similar manifestations of economic globalization to be the result of processes that are beyond the control of any social actors, even the leaders of giant corporations and powerful nations. Giddens's image of a "runaway world" captures this perspective very well. Others dispute this claim by arguing that the trends should be viewed in terms of the emergence of global capitalism, which in turn should be seen as guided by an increasingly powerful corporate elite no longer tied to the traditional boundaries of nation-states. British sociologist Leslie Sklair, a former colleague of Giddens at the London School of Economics, is perhaps the key spokesperson for this position.

Sklair's (2001) analysis begins by introducing the term *transnational*, which in his work refers to "forces, processes, and institutions that cross borders but do not derive their power and authority from the state" (p. 2). Driven by the quest for profit, the goals of what Sklair refers to as the "transnational capitalist class" include "the establishment of a borderless global economy, the complete denationalization of all corporate procedures and activities, and the eradication of economic nationalism" (pp. 2–3). From this perspective, what we are currently witnessing is an unfolding process that is far from complete but constitutes a qualitative shift in capitalism from "an inter-national to a global system" (p. 59). To provide a structure to channel and shape the changes underway, the global economic elite has created organizations such as the World Bank, the World Trade Organization (WTO), and the International Monetary Fund and institutional frameworks such as the General Agreement on Tariffs and Trade. In a theoretical argument located within the Marxist tradition, Sklair seeks to counter the view of globalization that emphasizes its anarchical character by indicating the capacity of the most powerful social actors in what Giddens (1999:19) calls the "mixture of influences" to seek to impose the sort of order they prefer onto the global system.

Globalization and Democracy

All this suggests the following: Economic globalization is connected to political developments, and the footlooseness of corporate capitalism illustrates the fact that nations cannot adequately regulate or establish viable rules of the game for the emerging economic order. As a result, transnational institutions, such as the European Union, and governmental agreements, such as the highly controversial North American Free Trade Agreement, take on added salience.

As noted previously, whether democracy will genuinely take root in former communist lands in Europe is a major unanswered question. Of course, this question is relevant to other nations as well. For example, this is an open question in non-European communist countries. In the case of China, Western capitalists have played a major role in transforming it into an industrial powerhouse. For their part, the Chinese authorities appear to have decided that, given the glaring failures of their rigid command economy, market capitalism must be introduced if popular discontent with the regime's chronic inability to meet basic material needs is to be contained. At the same time, they apparently seek to promote private enterprise without transforming the authoritarian character of the Chinese state. In other words, they want to introduce capitalism without introducing democracy, thus raising anew the issues that Lipset in particular addressed concerning the relationship between political regimes and economic systems.

Democratization is also an issue in noncommunist nations that have either weakly institutionalized democratic institutions or no historical tradition of democratic rule. A cursory examination of current affairs reveals how difficult it is to unequivocally assess the democratic prospects in such nations. On the one hand, one can point to the replacement of military juntas by democratic regimes in a number of places—notably in such Latin American nations as Argentina, Uruguay, and Chile—and the apparent blossoming of democracy in the Czech Republic, Hungary, Poland, the Philippines, and South Africa. On the other hand, there is abundant evidence to suggest that democratic prospects are exceedingly bleak in many nations, including the autocratic regimes of several new states that were once part of the Soviet Union and many Middle Eastern nations, such as Syria, Iraq, Iran, and Saudi Arabia; military regimes in nations such as Burma; and in nations divided by civil strife, including Sri Lanka, Burundi, Rwanda, and (once again) Bosnia.

In the last three cited cases, the involvement of the world community points to a growing sense that the rights generally associated with citizenship in nation-states need to be rethought. In other words, civil rights that are guaranteed by nations are increasingly being seen as a manifestation of more universal rights—or human rights. In 1948, soon after the founding of the United Nations, the representatives of the member states passed a Universal Declaration of Human Rights, which asserted for the first time in history that every person has inalienable rights. Among other things, the declaration contended that everyone should be protected from being punished for expressing in nonviolent form their political and religious beliefs and in all cases should not be subjected to torture or execution. When Amnesty International was founded in 1961, it took seriously the idea of universal human rights, and insofar as the thousands of people who volunteer their services for the organization are concerned, this means that they are dedicated to challenging political regimes that violate those rights.

Amnesty International is but one example of a new type of organization that is having an increasingly significant impact globally. Usually referred to as INGOs (i.e., international nongovernmental organizations), they have exhibited a willingness to challenge the policies of various nations directly and not through state-to-state diplomatic channels. They have also challenged the activities of transnational capitalists. In this regard, Michael Hardt and

Antonio Negri (2000) are correct in concluding that they represent "the newest and perhaps most important forces in the global civil society" (p. 312). Thus, Greenpeace activists have intervened to attempt to prevent France from testing nuclear weapons in the Pacific, feminist organizations have urged various governments to take steps to end the practice of female circumcision, and others have engaged in campaigns to press multinational corporations to improve conditions in their global sweatshops. In their relatively short histories, INGOs such as these have proven, even when they have failed, that governments need to reckon with them, and in so doing the boundaries between the state and the rest of society are being reshaped.

At the same time, more grassroots social movements have arisen that, although addressing local political matters, have had transnational influences and ramifications. Such was the case, for instance, with the Chinese pro-democracy movement in 1989. The Chinese government's violent repression of the movement led to international condemnations of the regime (Calhoun 1994). Likewise, the reformist movement in Iran that continues to challenge the legitimacy of the reactionary regime in power has far-reaching geopolitical implications. Other popular movements, such as the peasant revolt in Chiapas, Mexico, against political oppression and economic exploitation and the protests against the environmental degradation caused by international oil companies (including Royal Dutch/Shell, Mobil, and Chevron) in Nigeria's Niger Delta, also became issues of global concern. Counterparts to these "glocalized" mobilizations have occurred when coalitions of labor, environmentalists, and other groups have mobilized, beginning in Seattle in 1999 when they demonstrated against the WTO at the organization's annual meeting and two years later in Genoa at the Group of Eight meeting. The World Social Forum, which was launched in Porte Allegre, Brazil in 2001, serves as a meeting place for people from around the world committed to the global social justice movement.

In grappling with the implications of these and similar indications of the political consequences of globalization, scholars have begun to offer ways of thinking about the prospects for democracy in the international sphere and not simply at the nation-state level. One such effort derives from the work of Stanford University sociologist John Meyer and colleagues, which employs a neo-Weberian perspective on rationalization to account for what they refer to as a "world society." From their perspective, the combined impact of global structural frameworks created by international organizations such as the United Nations, the diffusion of cultural values supportive of legal-rational political institutions from the world's Western liberal democracies to the rest of the world, the impact of the promotion of rationality by international scientific and professional associations, and the role

Figure 6.1 Protesters Demonstrate Against the World Trade Organization in Seattle, 1999

SOURCE: Photo © Christopher J. Morris/CORBIS.

of social movements in seeking to correct social problems have led to the emergence of a world society (Meyer et al. 1997).

According to Frank Lechner (2005), in a passage reminiscent of Goffman, in a world society "the individual universally acquires a sacred state" (p. 332). The component members of the world society are thus increasingly judged by their adherence to universally held values, which in particular include a respect for human rights. In this regard, this thesis bears more than a family resemblance to the thought of Talcott Parsons. In such a scenario, nation-states do not lose their efficacy but instead become increasingly similar and a part of a decentralized global polity. Meyer and associates (1997) explain deviant cases that systematically violate human rights and/or are engaged in corrupt practices, such as the former regime of Saddam Hussain in Iraq and the military junta in Burma, as instances in which "decoupling" has occurred, by which they mean that the nation has separated from the world society. Given the growing capacity of the world society to absorb nations into its orbit, from this perspective such deviant examples are generally regarded as temporary.

Another line of thought that has explored the globalization of democracy focuses on social movements. Although not absent in the preceding account, social movements appear from that perspective to represent something of a mopping-up operation, pointing out where the general trend promoting rationalization and democratic principles encounters obstacles or problems. In contrast, an approach advanced by John Guidry, Michael Kennedy, and Meyer Zald (2000) is rooted in social movement theory and a Habermas-inspired version of the public sphere. Rather than viewing global democratization as a relatively smooth and seamless process, they see it as the product of contestation between dominant and subordinate collective social actors, with the new social movements reflecting the demands made by segments of the latter for increased democratization, emancipation, and self-determination. These demands are increasingly being made in what they term the "transnational public sphere," which they define as "a space in which both residents of distinct places (states and localities) and members of transnational entities (organizations or firms) elaborate discourses and practices whose consumption moves beyond national boundaries" (pp. 6–7).

Ulrich Beck (2000:64–86) has advanced a parallel line of argument in his depiction of the rise of "transnational civil society," as has Manuel Castells (1996–98) in his discussion of the impact of the "information age" on the development of a global "network society." In all three cases, the argument being advanced is that new global social spaces have appeared that constitute forums wherein democratic demands are articulated and practices enacted, and that as a consequence our conceptual tools need to be redefined to reflect this novel situation.

Globalization's impact on democracy can also be seen in recent developments regarding conceptions of citizenship that have arisen as a consequence of the immigration of millions of people from the poorer nations of the South (and East) to the advanced industrial nations of the North (and West) during the second half of the 20th century. Many of these immigrants are attempting to define their identities in terms of both their homeland and their settlement destination, living in effect with one foot in both places. The term *transnational immigration* is increasingly used to describe this type of migration. It is assumed that such immigrants constitute a more significant phenomenon today than was the case with earlier migratory waves, due mainly to new communication technologies and modes of transportation (Kivisto 2001, 2003a). Moreover, they live in an era in which the idea of the rights of individuals is increasingly no longer solely tied to particular nation-states. Rather, rights are increasingly being shaped by international organizations, such as the United Nations and the International Labour Organization; by regional transnational organizations, such as the European

Union; by intergovernmental organizations, such as the Organisation for Economic Co-operation and Development and the WHO; and by such INGOs as the International Committee of the Red Cross and the World Council of Churches (Soysal 1994; Delanty 2000).

Out of this confluence of factors, new types of citizenship have appeared that no longer limit the idea of being a citizen to a particular nation. Perhaps the most common type is dual citizenship, a situation in which individuals maintain citizenship in their nation of origin but also become citizens of their new homeland. Approximately half of the nations of the world permit dual citizenship, and those that in many respects do not (including the United States) are not inclined to prosecute individuals holding dual citizenship. Nested citizenship is another transnational form of citizenship. Here, the European Union is the significant test case because increasingly European residents are beginning to see their national citizenship identities as located—and thus "nested"—within the larger framework of being a citizen of Europe. Some theorists concur with Derek Heater (2002) that what the future holds in store is the birth of the world citizen, although this remains more an aspiration than a reality. Taken together, these globalized notions of citizenship reflect what Aihwa Ong (1999) describes as a growing demand for "flexible citizenship." Conceptions of citizenship are, quite simply, in a state of flux. Although it would be a mistake to conclude that the expanded role of transnational citizenship practices and political entities signals the demise of the nation-state, it would also be a mistake to ignore these novel phenomena because they are changing the rules of the game (Spinner-Halev 1999).

Toward a Global Culture

The process of redefining political boundaries and definitions of membership is linked to a rethinking of cultural boundaries. What the idea of human rights points to are claims about universalistic values that can come into conflict with the values of local cultures. For example, some cultures resist such notions as modern individualism. Intimately related to the topic of individualism is the question of the appropriate role of women in society.

A revealing example that highlights this tension is the Taliban's capture of power in Afghanistan in 1996: They immediately implemented laws based on their distinctive fundamentalist interpretation of Islamic law. Unsympathetic to notions of modern individualism and, relatedly, to the idea of women's rights, the Taliban quickly mandated a law that forbade women from working outside the home. Although accepted in some quarters, this policy was not well received in other segments of Afghan society. For the residents of Kabul, the nation's capital, the elimination of women from the workforce would have profound implications. More than 40% of the city's teachers were women, and they also occupied key positions in many government offices. The policy would create serious labor power problems and would conflict with the desire of women to pursue careers. In short, the Afghan people were sharply divided over whether to embrace or resist cultural values associated with the forces of modernity centered in the advanced industrial nations.

Similarly, Islamic immigrants to Western nations have often found that their traditional values come into conflict with those of the receiving nation. This can be seen in the numerous instances of immigrant parents who find that the practice of arranged marriage, especially if the arrangement lacks the consent of the child, is looked on unfavorably by the host society. The ongoing conflict in France and some other European nations over the wearing of the Islamic head scarf represents yet another example of the tension between secular societies and conservative religious believers (Joppke 2009).

It was also evident in the support that many Islamic immigrants in Britain gave to the call of a fundamentalist Iranian cleric to kill the author Salman Rushdie for publishing the novel *The Satanic Verses* (1989), which was considered to be blasphemous. Again, Westerners were highly critical of this threat, which from their perspective reflected a stark repudiation of ideals associated with freedom of expression and tolerance of opinions different from one's own. The July 7, 2005, bombings in the London Underground raised alarm bells for a society that was no longer certain of its ability to incorporate Muslim immigrants into the larger society.

Certainly, the vast majority of Muslims are not fundamentalists, and the conflict between modernity and antimodernity can be seen in many other traditional cultures as well. The high visibility of Islamic fundamentalism today, however, provides a particularly instructive illustration of some of the implications of and impediments to the development of a genuinely global culture.

This idea that some have called the clash of civilizations, but more appropriately should be viewed as a clash between supporters and opponents of modernity, was graphically on display on September 11, 2001. Osama bin Laden's call for a *jihad*, or a holy war, is but one instance of what Mark Juergensmeyer (2001) describes as "the global rise of religious violence." It reveals the capacity of globalizing forces to produce intense conflict and fragmentation. As Juergensmeyer observes, fundamentalist challenges to modernity—including values associated with it, such as tolerance, individualism, democracy, and rationality—can be found in fundamentalist movements in all the world's major religions and in religious sects as well.

At the same time, the impact of Western, particularly American, culture can be found in the most far-flung areas of the world. Hollywood films, popular music, sports celebrities, and such icons of globalization as McDonald's golden arches and the Nike swoosh are indications of the cultural penetration of the West throughout the entire world. Walter LeFeber (2002:14) recounts a story about an American college student traveling in a remote region of China near Tibet. He encountered some local people who invited him to eat with them. As they ate, they queried him about the United States, including asking how Michael Jordan was doing.

These examples suggest that the cultural consequences of globalization are dichotomous: on the one hand, fragmentation, and on the other hand, cultural homogenization due to the cultural imperialism of the West. This is what Benjamin Barber (1992) had in mind with the title of his article, cited in Chapter 1, "Jihad vs. McWorld." Increasingly, however, scholars are coming to the conclusion that this stark alternative fails to appreciate the give-and-take going on between the center and the periphery.

This is clearly the case in Orlando Patterson's (2000:465–480) claim that the global culture shaped in large part by American popular culture is nonetheless far more than the simple reflection of Western cultural hegemony. He argues that this view fails to appreciate the syncretistic character of these trends. Focusing on North America, Patterson makes his case by identifying four different regional cosmoses that have established new cultural boundaries transcending political boundaries: the West Atlantic, the Tex-Mex, the Southern Californian, and the Pacific Rim of the Northwest. His most sustained description of what he has in mind is devoted to the mutual influences and cross-fertilization of popular music in the West Atlantic. In his account, American rhythm and blues was introduced into Jamaica in the 1950s via radio and recordings, influencing the rise of reggae in that postcolonial nation. Reggae, in turn, was not only embraced by consumers in the United States but also served as an important source of inspiration for rap music, whose influence once again was not limited to its place of origin.

Patterson is not alone in calling for recognition of the hybrid outcomes that occur as a result of cultural diffusion. For example, Swedish anthropologist Ulf Hannerz (1992:217–267) argued that what we are witnessing is the emergence of a "global ecumene" characterized by a creolization of culture. Similarly, Arjun Appadurai (1996) points to the proliferation of cultural hybridization brought about by what he refers to as "global cultural flows."

Appadurai (1996) goes beyond this by developing concepts that are intended to assist us in making sense of cultural globalization. He identifies five dimensions of cultural flows in an effort to provide a framework for analyzing the cultural dimensions of globalization: (a) ethnoscapes, the impact of the migration of peoples, be they immigrants or refugees; (b) mediascapes, the dissemination of information by new communications technologies; (c) technoscapes, the flow of technologies across existing political boundaries; (d) financescapes, the flow of global capital; and (e) ideoscapes, images that constitute elements of a worldview. Appadurai contends that although each of these scapes has its own dynamic, all are obviously interconnected. As such, the outcomes of the globalization of culture will inevitably be highly complex and variable (Appadurai 1996:33–35). Much remains uncertain about globalization's impact on local cultures and on the processes of reconfiguring cultural boundaries and contents. For this reason, tools of cultural analysis, such as those provided by Appadurai, are being fashioned to aid our effort to make sense of these changes. As with the emerging global economy and with democratic developments throughout the world, the topic of global culture will increasingly occupy the attention of tomorrow's social thinkers.

The Lasting Impact of the Sociological Tradition

Thinking about the future requires reflecting on the past, including how social thinkers in the past sought to describe and assess the major societal trends they were living through. Sociologists cannot simply rely on the insights of earlier generations; they must build on the tradition of thought they have inherited. Although much about the future remains uncertain, it is clear that the future heirs of the legacies of Marx, Weber, Durkheim, and Simmel will continue to adapt the key ideas that have proven so essential to social inquiry in the past to meet the unique, and increasingly global, challenges of their times.

Review Questions

1. Marx contends that capitalism both alienates and exploits workers. Summarize and assess the main arguments he advances in making his case.
2. Review Marx's analysis of the principal classes in capitalist society. Is his perspective relevant today? Explain with reference to the other theorists discussed in Chapter 2.
3. In what ways can the members of the Frankfurt School be seen as heirs to Marx's intellectual legacy, and in what ways do they appear to part company with him?
4. Compare and contrast the counterimages of capitalist industrial society proposed by Joseph Schumpeter and Thorstein Veblen.
5. Critically evaluate C. Wright Mills's power elite thesis. Is this a Marxist analysis?
6. Describe what Daniel Bell means by postindustrial society. Do you find his thesis convincing? What do you think of the reactions of his critics?
7. Is bureaucracy in modern industrial societies inevitable according to Weber? Summarize his account, and in so doing discuss why he thought that the world of the future would increasingly become an iron cage.
8. Compare and contrast Weber's perspective on the prospects of democracy with that of Robert Michels.
9. What are the three types of legitimate domination that Weber identified? Which is most characteristic of the contemporary world? Why?
10. Are Marx's and Weber's ideas congruent or at odds with each other? Explain.
11. Review Talcott Parsons's understanding of citizenship, particularly as it was influenced by T. H. Marshall. How can this view be seen as a response to Weber?
12. Describe and offer a critical analysis of Seymour Martin Lipset's understanding of the relationship between democracy and class structure.

13. What does Jürgen Habermas mean by the public sphere, and how is it related to the idea of civil society? Why does he think the public sphere is threatened today?

14. Summarize Jeffrey Alexander's understanding of the civil sphere. In what ways does his position parallel that of Habermas, and how do the two differ?

15. What did Alexis de Tocqueville mean by individualism, and in what ways did he think it might be destructive? Relate his ideas to the work of both David Riesman and Robert Bellah.

16. Compare and contrast Ferdinand Toennies's distinction between *gemeinschaft* and *gesellschaft*. From his perspective, can they coexist, or are they mutually exclusive?

17. What did Durkheim mean by mechanical solidarity and organic solidarity? Which one is characteristic of modern industrial societies? What is the relevance of the division of labor to this argument?

18. Compare and contrast Marx's and Durkheim's understanding of the division of labor in industrial societies. Are these positions complementary or fundamentally at odds with each other?

19. What is anomie? Evaluate Durkheim's use of this term in his study of suicide.

20. What did Robert Merton mean by social strain, and how is it related to his understanding of a society's value system?

21. Discuss David Riesman's distinction between inner-directed and other-directed personalities. Relate his analysis to that of both Tocqueville and Bellah and associates.

22. Review and provide a critical analysis of Erving Goffman's contribution to our understanding of individualism in contemporary societies.

23. Summarize and evaluate the provisional definitions of modernity and postmodernity presented in the text.

24. What did Simmel mean by the tragedy of culture? Compare and contrast this idea with Weber's iron cage metaphor.

25. Discuss and evaluate Robert Park's discussion of race as a social construct and the significance of race in modern culture. What are some of the implications of viewing race as a social construct?

26. What are grand narratives? Discuss why postmodernists think that they have become exhausted.

27. What does Jean Baudrillard mean by the hyperreal, and how does this relate to a culture saturated by the mass media and by consumerism?

28. What does Zygmunt Bauman mean by liquid modernity? Is this concept essentially a synonym for postmodernity, or does it refer to a new phase of modernity?

29. Compare and contrast postmodernity with what Anthony Giddens calls late modernity.

30. What is the significance of risk in later modernity? Discuss this in terms of one of the four major risks Giddens identifies as characteristic of our age.

31. Provide an analysis of what Giddens means by globalization. What does it mean to depict it in terms of a runaway world?

32. Discuss the political implications of globalization, particularly concentrating on the idea advanced by Ulrich Beck about the potential for a transnational civil society and new conceptions of citizenship.

33. Compare and contrast the analyses of global culture proposed by Benjamin Barber and Orlando Patterson.

References

Adorno, Theodor W., Else Frankel-Brunswik, Daniel J. Levinson, and R. Nevitt Sanford. 1950. *The Authoritarian Personality.* New York: Harper & Row.

Agger, Ben. 1990. *The Decline of Discourse: Reading, Writing, and Resistance in Postmodern Capitalism.* London: Falmer.

Alba, Richard. 2009. *Blurring the Color Line: The New Chance for a More Integrated America.* Cambridge, MA: Harvard University Press.

Alexander, Jeffrey C. 1982/1983. *Theoretical Logic in Sociology.* Vols. 1–4. Berkeley: University of California Press.

______. 1987. *Twenty Lectures: Sociological Theory Since World War II.* New York: Columbia University Press.

______. 1995. *Fin de Siècle Social Theory.* London: Verso.

______. 1998. *Neofunctionalism and After.* Oxford, UK: Blackwell.

______. 2006. *The Civil Sphere.* New York: Oxford University Press.

Alexander, Jeffrey C. and Philip Smith, eds. 2005. *The Cambridge Companion to Durkheim.* New York: Cambridge University Press.

Althusser, Louis. 1970. *For Marx.* New York: Vintage.

Alway, Joan. 1995. *Critical Theory and Political Possibilities: Conceptions of Emancipatory Politics in the Works of Horkheimer, Adorno, Marcuse, and Habermas.* Westport, CT: Greenwood.

Anderson, Perry. 1976. *Considerations of Western Marxism.* London: New Left Books.

Antonio, Robert J. 2007. "The Passing of Jean Baudrillard." *Fast Capitalism* 4(1). (http://www.fastcapitalism.com).

Antonio, Robert J. and Douglas Kellner. 1994. "The Future of Social Theory and the Limits of Postmodern Critique." Pp. 127–152 in *Postmodernism and Social Inquiry,* edited by D. R. Dickens and A. Fontana. New York: Guilford.

Appadurai, Arjun. 1996. *Modernity at Large: Cultural Dimensions of Globalization.* Minneapolis: University of Minnesota Press.

Apter, David. 1987. "Parsons's Politics." *American Journal of Sociology* 93(2):451–456.

Aron, Raymond. 1985. *History, Truth, Liberty: Selected Writings of Raymond Aron,* edited by F. Draus. Chicago: University of Chicago Press.

Ashton, Thomas S. 1948. *The Industrial Revolution, 1760–1830.* Oxford, UK: Oxford University Press.

Avineri, Shlomo. 1968. *The Social and Political Thought of Karl Marx*. Cambridge, UK: Cambridge University Press.
Axelrod, Charles D. 1977. "Toward an Appreciation of Simmel's Fragmentary Style." *The Sociological Quarterly* 18(2):185–196.
Bannister, Robert C. 1987. *Sociology and Scientism: The American Quest for Objectivity, 1880–1940*. Chapel Hill: University of North Carolina Press.
Barber, Benjamin R. 1984. *Strong Democracy*. Berkeley: University of California Press.
______. 1992. "Jihad vs. McWorld." *Atlantic Monthly*, March, pp. 53–63.
Barnett, Vincent. 2009. *Marx*. London: Routledge.
Baudrillard, Jean. 1981. *For a Critique of the Political Economy of the Sign*. St. Louis, MO: Telos.
______. 1983. *Simulations*. New York: Semiotexte.
______. 1988. *America*. London: Verso.
______. 1991. *La Guerre de Golfe n'a pas eu lieu*. Paris: Galilee.
______. 2002. *The Spirit of Terrorism: And Requiem for the Twin Towers*. London: Verso.
______. 2005. "War Porn." *International Journal of Baudrillard Studies* 2(1). (http://www.ubishops.ca/BaudrillardStudies/vol2_1/taylorpf.htm).
Bauman, Zygmunt. 1992. *Intimations of Postmodernity*. London: Routledge.
______. 1993. *Postmodern Ethics*. Cambridge, MA: Basil Blackwell.
______. 1995. *Life in Fragments: Essays in Postmodern Morality*. Cambridge, MA: Basil Blackwell.
______. 1997. *Postmodernity and Its Discontents*. New York: New York University Press.
______. 2000. *Liquid Modernity*. Cambridge, UK: Polity.
______. 2007. *Liquid Times*. Cambridge, UK: Polity.
Bauman, Zygmunt and Tim May. 2001. *Thinking Sociologically*, 2nd edition. Oxford, UK: Blackwell.
Beck, Ulrich. 1992. *Risk Society: Towards a New Modernity*. Newbury Park, CA: Sage.
______. 2000. *What Is Globalization?* Cambridge, UK: Polity.
______. 2006. *Cosmopolitan Vision*. Cambridge, UK: Polity.
______. 2009. *World at Risk*. Cambridge, UK: Polity.
Becker, Ernest. 1971. *The Lost Science of Man*. New York: George Braziller.
Bell, Daniel. 1965. *The End of Ideology*. New York: Free Press.
______. 1973. *The Coming of Post-Industrial Society: A Venture in Social Forecasting*. New York: Basic Books.
______. 1976. *The Cultural Contradictions of Capitalism*. New York: Basic Books.
______. 1980. *The Winding Passage: Essays and Sociological Journeys, 1960–1980*. Cambridge, MA: Abt.
______. 1981. "First Love and Early Sorrows." *Partisan Review* 47(4):532–551.
Bellah, Robert. 1970. *Beyond Belief: Essays on Religion in a Post-Traditional World*, New York: Harper & Row.
______. 1996. Letter to President Clinton, reprinted in *New York Review of Books*, November 28, p. 65.

______. 2005. "McCarthyism at Harvard." *New York Review of Books,* February 10: 42–43.

Bellah, Robert, Richard Madsen, William M. Sullivan, Ann Swidler, and Steven M. Tipton. 1985. *Habits of the Heart: Individualism and Commitment in American Life.* Berkeley: University of California Press.

______. 1991. *The Good Society.* New York: Knopf.

______. 1996. "Individualism and the Crisis of Civic Membership." *Christian Century,* May 8, pp. 510–515.

Bender, Thomas. 1987. *New York Intellectuals.* New York: Knopf.

Bendix, Reinhard. 1960. *Max Weber: An Intellectual Portrait.* Garden City, NY: Doubleday.

Benhabib, Seyla. 1992. "Models of Public Space: Hannah Arendt, the Liberal Tradition, and Jürgen Habermas." Pp. 73–98 in *Habermas and the Public Sphere,* edited by C. Calhoun. Cambridge: MIT Press.

Berlin, Isaiah. 1963. *Karl Marx: His Life and Environment.* London: Oxford University Press.

Berman, Marshall. 1982. *All That Is Solid Melts Into Air: The Experience of Modernity.* New York: Random House.

Bernstein, Richard. 1972. *Praxis and Action.* London: Duckworth.

Besnard, Philippe. 1987. *L'Anomie, ses usages et fonction dans la discipline sociologique depuis Durkheim.* Paris: Presses Universitaires de France.

______. 1993. "Anomie and Fatalism in Durkheim's Theory of Regulation." Pp. 169–190 in *Émile Durkheim: Sociologist and Moralist,* edited by S. P. Turner. New York: Routledge.

Best, Steven and Douglas Kellner. 1991. *Postmodern Theory: Critical Interrogations.* New York: Guilford.

Bielharz, Peter. 2009. *Socialism and Modernity.* Minneapolis: University of Minnesota Press.

Birnbaum, Norman. 2009. "The Half-Forgotten Prophet." *The Nation,* March 30: 34–36.

Birnbaum, Pierre. 1970. *Sociologie de Tocqueville.* Paris: Presses Universitaires de France.

Blackburn, Robin. 2007. "Perishable Goods." *The Nation,* September 24:34–40.

Bluestone, Barry and Bennett Harrison. 1982. *The Deindustrialization of America: Plant Closings, Community Abandonment, and the Dismantling of Basic Industry.* New York: Basic Books.

Boltanski, Luc and Éve Chiapello. 2005. *The New Spirit of Capitalism.* London: Verso.

Bottomore, Tom. 1984. *The Frankfurt School.* London: Tavistock.

Bourdieu, Pierre. 1986. "The Forms of Capital." Pp. 241–258 in *Handbook of Theory and Research in the Sociology of Education,* edited by J. G. Richardson. Westport, CT: Greenwood.

______. 1993. *Sociology in Question.* Newbury Park, CA: Sage.

______. 2003. *Firing Back: Against the Tyranny of the Market 2.* New York: The New Press.

Bourdieu, Pierre and Loïc Wacquant. 1992. *An Invitation to Reflexive Sociology.* Chicago: University of Chicago Press.

Bourricauld, Francois. 1981. *The Sociology of Talcott Parsons.* Chicago: University of Chicago Press.

Brick, Howard. 1993. "The Reformist Dimension of Talcott Parsons's Early Social Theory." Pp. 357–396 in *The Culture of the Market: Historical Essays,* edited by T. L. Haskell and R. F. Teichgraeber III. Cambridge, UK: Cambridge University Press.

______. 2006. *Transcending Capitalism: Visions of a New Society in Modern American Thought.* Ithaca, NY: Cornell University Press.

Brint, Steven. 2001. "*Gemeinschaft* Revisited: A Critique and Reconstruction of the Community Concept." *Sociological Theory* 19(1):1–23.

Brogan, Hugh. 2008. *Alexis de Tocqueville: A Life.* New Haven, CT: Yale University Press.

Brown, Richard Harvey. 1989. *Social Science as Civic Discourse: Essays on the Invention, Legitimation, and Uses of Social Theory.* Chicago: University of Chicago Press.

Bryant, Christopher G. A. and David Jary, eds. 1991. *Giddens' Theory of Structuration: A Critical Appreciation.* London: Routledge.

Burnham, James. 1941. *The Managerial Revolution.* Bloomington: Indiana University Press.

Burns, Tom. 1992. *Erving Goffman.* London: Routledge.

Buxton, William. 1985. *Talcott Parsons and the Capitalist Nation-State.* Toronto: University of Toronto Press.

Cahnman, Werner J. 1995. *Weber and Toennies: Comparative Sociology in Historical Perspective,* edited by J. B. Maier, J. Marcus, and Z. Tarr. New Brunswick, NJ: Transaction.

Calhoun, Craig. 1993. "Civil Society and the Public Sphere." *Public Culture* 5:267–280.

______. 1994. *Neither Gods nor Emperors: Students and the Struggle for Democracy in China.* Berkeley: University of California Press.

Callinicos, Alex. 1989. *Against Postmodernism.* Cambridge, UK: Polity.

______. 2007. *Social Theory: A Historical Introduction,* 2nd edition. Cambridge, UK: Polity.

Camic, Charles. 1989. "Structure After 50 Years: The Anatomy of a Charter." *American Journal of Sociology* 95(1):38–107.

Cammett, John M. 1967. *Antonio Gramsci and the Origins of Italian Communism.* Stanford, CA: Stanford University Press.

Campbell, Colin. 1987. *The Romantic Ethic and the Spirit of Modern Consumerism.* Oxford, UK: Blackwell.

______. 2006. "Do Today's Sociologists Really Appreciate Weber's Essay *The Protestant Ethic and the Spirit of Capitalism*?" *The Sociological Review* 54(2):207–233.

Castells, Manuel. 1996–1998. *The Information Age: Economy, Society, and Culture.* Vols. 1–3. Malden, MA: Blackwell.

Chriss, James J. 1993. "Durkheim's Cult of the Individual as Civil Religion: Its Appropriation by Erving Goffman." *Sociological Spectrum* 13:251–275.

Cohen, Ira. 1989. *Structuration Theory: Anthony Giddens and the Constitution of Social Life*. New York: St. Martin's Press.

Cohen, Jere. 2002. *Protestantism and Capitalism: The Mechanisms of Influence*. New York: Aldine de Gruyter.

Collins, Randall. 1988. "The Theoretical Continuities in Goffman's Work." Pp. 41–63 in *Erving Goffman: Exploring the Interaction Order*, edited by P. Drew and A. Wootton. Boston: Northeastern University Press.

______. 2005. *Interaction Ritual Chains*. Princeton, NJ: Princeton University Press.

Connor, Steven. 2000. "Cultural Sociology and Cultural Sciences." Pp. 352–386 in *The Blackwell Companion to Social Theory*, 2d ed., edited by B. S. Turner. Malden, MA: Blackwell.

Cooley, Charles Horton. 1962. *Social Organization*. New York: Schocken.

Cormack, Patricia and Patrick Cormack. 2002. *Sociology and Mass Culture: Durkheim, Mills, and Baudrillard*. Toronto: University of Toronto Press.

Coser, Lewis A. 1971. *Masters of Sociological Thought*. New York: Harcourt Brace Jovanovich.

Coser, Rose Laub. 1975. "The Complexity of Roles as a Seedbox of Individual Autonomy." Pp. 237–263 in *The Idea of Social Structure: Papers in Honor of Robert K. Merton*, edited by L. A. Coser. New York: Harcourt Brace Jovanovich.

Craib, Ian. 1992. *Anthony Giddens*. London: Routledge.

Crothers, Charles. 1987. *Robert K. Merton*. New York: Tavistock.

Dahms, Harry F. 1995. "From Creative Action to the Social Rationalization of the Economy: Joseph A. Schumpeter's Social Theory." *Sociological Theory* 13(1):1–13.

Dandaneau, Steven P. 1998. "Critical Theory, Legitimation Crisis, and the Deindustrialization of Flint, Michigan." In *Illuminating Social Life*, edited by P. Kivisto. Thousand Oaks, CA: Pine Forge Press.

______. 2001. *Taking It Big: Defining Sociological Consciousness in Postmodern Times*. Thousand Oaks, CA: Pine Forge Press.

Debord, Guy. 1983. *Society of the Spectacle*. Detroit, MI: Black & Red.

Deegan, Mary Jo. 1988. *Jane Addams and the Men of the Chicago School*. New Brunswick, NJ: Transaction.

Delanty, Gerard. 2000. *Citizenship in a Global Age*. Buckingham, UK: Open University Press.

Denby, David. 2009. "Americans in Paris." *The New Yorker*, August 24:82–83.

Denzin, Norman. 1991. *Images of Postmodern Society: Social Theory and Contemporary Cinema*. Newbury Park, CA: Sage.

Derrida, Jacques. 1976. *Of Grammatology*. Baltimore: Johns Hopkins University Press.

______. 1978. *Writing and Difference*. Chicago: University of Chicago Press.

______. 1981. *Positions*. Chicago: University of Chicago Press.

______. 1994. *Specters of Marx: The State of the Debt, the Work of Mourning, and the New International*. New York: Routledge.

Diggins, John Patrick. 1988. *The Proud Decades: America in War and Peace: 1941–1960*. New York: Norton.

______. 1996. *Max Weber: Politics and the Spirit of Tragedy*. New York: Basic Books.

______. 1999. *Thorstein Veblen: Theorist of the Leisure Class*. Princeton, NJ: Princeton University Press.

Dorfman, Joseph. 1934. *Thorstein Veblen and His America*. New York: Viking.

Douglas, Jack D. 1967. *The Social Meanings of Suicide*. Princeton, NJ: Princeton University Press.

Dumont, Louis. 1977. *From Mandeville to Marx: The Genesis and Triumph of Economic Ideology*. Chicago: University of Chicago Press.

Dunbar, Paul Lawrence. 1974. "We Wear the Mask." P. 14 in *American Negro Poetry*, edited by Arna Bontemps. New York: Hall & Wang.

Durkheim, Émile. 1938. *The Rules of Sociological Method*. Chicago: University of Chicago Press.

______. [1897] 1951. *Suicide: A Study in Sociology*. Glencoe, IL: Free Press.

______. 1958a. *Professional Ethics and Civic Morals*. Translated by C. Brookfield. Glencoe, IL: Free Press.

______. 1958b. *Socialism and Saint-Simon*, edited by A. Gouldner. Yellow Springs, OH: Antioch.

______. 1961. *Moral Education*. Glencoe, IL: Free Press.

______. [1893] 1964. *The Division of Labor in Society*. Glencoe, IL: Free Press.

______. [1912] 1965. *The Elementary Forms of the Religious Life*. New York: Free Press.

______. [1898] 1969. "Individualism and the Intellectuals." *Political Studies* 17:14–30.

______. 1972. *Émile Durkheim: Selected Writings*, edited by A. Giddens. Cambridge, UK: Cambridge University Press.

______. [1924] 1974. *Sociology and Philosophy*. New York: Free Press.

______. [1899] 2008. "Anti-Semitism and Social Crisis." *Sociological Theory* 26(4):321–323.

Durkheim, Émile and Marcel Mauss. 1971. "Note on the Notion of Civilization." *Social Research* 38(4):808–813.

Eagleton, Terry. 2000. *The Idea of Culture*. Malden, MA: Blackwell.

Edemariam, Aida. 2007. "Professor with a Past." *The Guardian*, April 27:43.

Eden, Robert. 1984. *Political Leadership and Nihilism: A Study of Weber and Nietzsche*. Tampa: University Press of South Florida.

Edwards, Michael. 2004. *Civil Society*. Cambridge, UK: Polity.

Elias, Norbert. 1978. *What Is Sociology?* New York: Columbia University Press.

Elster, Jon. 1986. *An Introduction to Karl Marx*. Cambridge, UK: Cambridge University Press.

______. 2009. *Alexis de Tocqueville: The First Social Scientist*. New York: Cambridge University Press.

Emerson, Ralph Waldo. 1875. *The Prose Works of Ralph Waldo Emerson*. Vol. 1. New York: Osgood.

Engels, Friedrich. [1844] 1968. *The Condition of the Working Class in England*. Stanford, CA: Stanford University Press.

Etzioni, Amitai. 1993. *The Spirit of Community: Rights, Responsibilities, and the Communitarian Agenda*. New York: Crown.

Faist, Thomas. 1995. *Social Citizenship for Whom?* Brookfield, VT: Avebury.

Ferraro, Thomas J. 2001. *Social Action Systems: Foundation and Synthesis in Sociological Theory*. New York: Praeger.

Fine, Gary Alan and Philip Manning. 2000. "Erving Goffman." Pp. 457–485 in *The Blackwell Companion to Major Social Theorists*, edited by G. Ritzer. Malden, MA: Blackwell.

Foucault, Michel. 1988. *Politics, Philosophy, Culture: Interviews and Other Writings, 1977–1984*. New York: Routledge.

Fraser, Nancy. 1992. "Rethinking the Public Sphere: A Contribution to the Critique of Actually Existing Democracy." Pp. 109–142 in *Habermas and the Public Sphere*, edited by C. Calhoun. Cambridge: MIT Press.

Freund, Julien. 1968. *The Sociology of Max Weber*. New York: Pantheon.

_____. 1978. "German Sociology in the Time of Max Weber." Pp. 149–186 in *A History of Sociological Analysis*, edited by T. Bottomore and R. Nisbet. New York: Basic Books.

Frisby, David. 1981. *Sociological Impressionism: A Reassessment of Georg Simmel's Social Theory*. London: Heinemann.

_____. 1984. *Georg Simmel*. London: Tavistock.

_____. 1992. *Simmel and Since: Essays on Georg Simmel's Social Theory*. London: Routledge.

Fukuyama, Francis. 1992. *The End of History and the Last Man*. New York: Free Press.

Galbraith, John Kenneth. 1967. *The New Industrial State*. New York: New American Library.

Gane, Mike. 1991. *Baudrillard: Critical and Fatal Theory*. London: Routledge.

_____, ed. 1992. *The Radical Sociology of Durkheim and Mauss*. New York: Routledge.

Geary, Daniel. 2009. *Radical Ambition: C. Wright Mills, The Left, and American Social Thought*. Berkeley: University of California Press.

Giddens, Anthony. 1971. *Capitalism and Modern Social Theory: An Analysis of the Writings of Marx, Durkheim and Max Weber*. Cambridge, UK: Cambridge University Press.

_____. 1973. *The Class Structure of the Advanced Industrial Societies*. New York: Harper & Row.

_____. 1976. *The New Rules of Sociological Method: A Positive Critique of Interpretative Sociologies*. New York: Harper & Row.

_____. 1979. *Central Problems in Social Theory*. Berkeley: University of California Press.

_____. 1984. *The Constitution of Society: Outline of the Theory of Structuration*. Berkeley: University of California Press.

_____. 1987. *Social Theory and Modern Sociology*. Stanford, CA: Stanford University Press.

_____. 1990. *The Consequences of Modernity*. Stanford, CA: Stanford University Press.

_____. 1991a. *Introduction to Sociology*. New York: W.W. Norton.

_____. 1991b. *Modernity and Self-Identity*. Stanford, CA: Stanford University Press.

______. 1992. *The Transformation of Intimacy.* Stanford, CA: Stanford University Press.
______. 1994. *Beyond Left and Right: The Future of Radical Politics.* Stanford, CA: Stanford University Press.
______. 1995a. "In Defence of Sociology." *New Statesman and Society* 7:18–20.
______. 1995b. *Politics, Sociology and Social Theory.* Stanford, CA: Stanford University Press.
______. 1998. *The Third Way: The Renewal of Social Democracy.* Cambridge, UK: Polity.
______. 1999. *Runaway World: How Globalization Is Reshaping Our Lives.* London: Profile Books.
______. 2000. *The Third Way and Its Critics.* Cambridge, UK: Polity.
______. 2002. *Where Now for New Labour?* Cambridge, UK: Polity.
______. 2007. *Europe in the Global Age.* Cambridge, UK: Polity.
______. 2009. *The Politics of Climate Change.* Cambridge, UK: Polity.
Giddens, Anthony and Christopher Pierson. 1998. *Conversations With Anthony Giddens: Making Sense of Modernity.* Stanford, CA: Stanford University Press.
Gitlin, Todd. 1995. *The Twilight of Common Dreams: Why America Is Wracked by Culture Wars.* New York: Metropolitan.
Glassman, Ronald M., William H. Swatos, Jr., and Peter Kivisto. 1993. *For Democracy: The Noble Character and Tragic Flaws of the Middle Class.* Westport, CT: Greenwood.
Goffman, E. 1959. *The Presentation of Self in Everyday Life.* Garden City, NY: Doubleday.
______. 1961a. *Encounters: Two Studies in the Sociology of Interaction.* Indianapolis, IN: Bobbs-Merrill.
______. 1961b. *Asylums: Essays on the Social Situation of Mental Patients and Other Inmates.* Garden City, NY: Doubleday.
______. 1963. *Stigma: Notes on the Management of Spoiled Identity.* Englewood Cliffs, NJ: Prentice Hall.
______. 1967. *Interaction Ritual: Essays on Face-to-Face Behavior.* Garden City, NY: Doubleday.
______. 1971. *Relations in Public: Micro Studies of the Public Order.* New York: Harper & Row.
______. 1974. *Frame Analysis: An Essay on the Organization of Experience.* New York: Harper & Row.
Goldberg, Chad Alan. 2008. "Introduction to Emile Durkheim's 'Anti-Semitism and Social Crisis'." *Sociological Theory* 26(4):299–321.
Goodwyn, Lawrence. 1976. *Democratic Promise: The Populist Movement in America.* New York: Oxford University Press.
Gottdiener, Mark. 1993. "Ideology, Foundationalism, and Sociological Theory." *The Sociological Quarterly* 34(4):653–671.
Gouldner, Alvin. 1970. *The Coming Crisis of Western Sociology.* New York: Avon.
______. 1980. *The Two Marxisms: Contradictions and Anomalies in the Development of Theory.* New York: Seabury.

Graeff, Peter and Guido Mehlkop. 2007. "When Anomie Becomes a Reason for Suicide: A New Macro-sociological Approach in the Durkheimian Tradition." *European Sociological Review* 23(4):521–535.

Gramsci, Antonio. 1971. *Selections from the Prison Notebooks*. New York: International Publishers.

Guidry, John A., Michael D. Kennedy, and Mayer N. Zald. 2000. "Globalizations and Social Movements." Pp. 1–32 in *Globalizations and Social Movements*, edited by J. A. Guidry, M. D. Kennedy, and M. N. Zald. Ann Arbor: University of Michigan Press.

Gurnah, Ahmed and Alan Scott. 1992. *The Uncertain Science: Criticism of Sociological Formalism*. New York: Routledge.

Habermas, Jürgen. 1970. *Toward a Rational Society: Student Protest, Science, and Politics*. Boston: Beacon.

______. 1971. *Knowledge and Human Interests*. Boston: Beacon.

______. 1973. *Theory and Practice*. Boston: Beacon.

______. 1975. *Legitimation Crisis*. Boston: Beacon.

______. 1979. *Communication and the Evolution of Society*. Boston: Beacon.

______. 1984. *The Theory of Communicative Action*. Vol. 1. Boston: Beacon.

______. 1987. *The Theory of Communicative Action*. Vol. 2. Boston: Beacon.

______. 1989a. *The Structural Transformation of the Public Sphere*. Cambridge: MIT Press.

______. 1989b. *The New Conservatism*. Cambridge: MIT Press.

______. 1996. *Between Facts and Norms: Contributions to a Discourse Theory*. Cambridge: MIT Press.

______. 2002. *The Inclusion of the Other: Studies in Political Theory*. Cambridge, UK: Polity.

Halliday, Terence C. and Morris Janowitz, eds. 1992. *Sociology and Its Publics: Reforms and Fates of Disciplinary Organization*. Chicago: University of Chicago Press.

Halton, Eugene. 1995. *Bereft of Reason: On the Decline of Social Thought and Prospects for Its Renewal*. Chicago: University of Chicago Press.

Hamilton, Peter. 1983. *Talcott Parsons*. London: Tavistock.

Hannerz, Ulf. 1992. *Cultural Complexity: Studies in the Social Organization of Meaning*. New York: Columbia University Press.

Hardt, Michael and Antonio Negri. 2000. *Empire*. Cambridge, MA: Harvard University Press.

Harvey, David. 1989. *The Condition of Postmodernity: An Enquiry Into the Origins of Cultural Change*. Oxford, UK: Blackwell.

______. 1996. *Justice, Nature, and the Geography of Difference*. Malden, MA: Blackwell.

Haskell, Thomas. 1977. *The Emergence of Professional Social Science*. Bloomington: Indiana University Press.

Hawthorn, Geoffrey. 1976. *Enlightenment and Despair: A History of Sociology*. Cambridge, UK: Cambridge University Press.

Hayden, Tom. 2006. *Radical Nomad: C. Wright Mills and His Times*. Boulder, CO: Paradigm.

Heater, Derek. 2002. *World Citizenship: Cosmopolitan Thinking and Its Opponents.* New York: Continuum.

Heberle, Rudolf. 1968. "Ferdinand Toennies." Pp. 98–103 in *The International Encyclopedia of the Social Sciences,* vol. 16, edited by D. L. Sills. New York: Macmillan/Free Press.

Hillary, George. 1955. "Definitions of Community: Areas of Argument." *Rural Sociology* 20(1):111–123.

Hobsbawm, E. J. 1962. *The Age of Revolution, 1789–1848.* New York: New American Library.

_____. 1969. *Industry and Empire.* Middlesex, UK: Penguin.

_____. 1994. *Age of Extremes: The Short Twentieth Century, 1914–1991.* London: Abacus.

Hollinger, David A. 1996. *Science, Jews, and Secular Culture.* Princeton, NJ: Princeton University Press.

Holub, Robert C. 1991. *Jürgen Habermas: Critic in the Public Sphere.* London: Routledge.

Honigsheim, Paul. 1968. *On Max Weber.* New York: Free Press.

Horkheimer, Max and Theodor W. Adorno. [1948] 1971. *Dialectic of Enlightenment.* New York: Seabury.

Horowitz, Daniel. 1994. *Vance Packard and American Social Criticism.* Chapel Hill: University of North Carolina Press.

Horowitz, Irving Louis. 1983. *C. Wright Mills: An American Utopian.* New York: Free Press.

_____. 1993. *The Decomposition of Sociology.* New York: Oxford University Press.

Huff, Toby E. and Wolfgang Schluchter, eds. 1999. *Max Weber and Islam.* New Brunswick, NJ: Transaction.

Hughes, H. Stuart. 1961. *Consciousness and Society.* New York: Vintage.

_____. 1975. *The Sea Change: The Migration of Social Thought, 1930–1965.* New York: Harper & Row.

Huntington, Samuel P. 1976. "The Democratic Distemper." Pp. 9–38 in *The American Commonwealth,* edited by N. Glazer and I. Kristol. New York: Basic Books.

Illouz, Eva. 2007. *Cold Intimacies: The Making of Emotional Capitalism.* Cambridge, UK: Polity.

Ingram, David. 1987. *Habermas and the Dialectic of Reason.* New Haven, CT: Yale University Press.

Jacoby, Russell. 1987. *The Last Intellectuals: American Culture in the Age of Academe.* New York: Basic Books.

Jameson, Fredric. 1991. *Postmodernism, or, the Cultural Logic of Late Capitalism.* Durham, NC: Duke University Press.

Jamison, Andrew and Ron Eyerman. 1994. *Seeds of the Sixties.* Berkeley: University of California Press.

Jardin, André. 1989. *Tocqueville: A Biography.* Translated by L. Davis and R. Hemenway. New York: Farrar, Straus, & Giroux.

Jaspers, Karl. 1964. *Three Essays: Leonardo/Descartes/Max Weber.* New York: Harcourt, Brace, & World.

Jaworski, Gary D. 1997. *Georg Simmel and the American Prospect.* Albany: State University of New York Press.

Jay, Martin. 1973. *The Dialectical Imagination: A History of the Frankfort School and the Institute of Social Research, 1923–1950.* Boston: Little, Brown.

Jeffries, Stuart. 2005. "Modern Lover." *The Guardian,* November 12:31.

Johnson, Barclay. 1965. "Durkheim's One Cause of Suicide." *American Sociological Review* 30:875–886.

Jones, Robert Alun. 1986. *Émile Durkheim: An Introduction to Four Major Works.* Beverly Hills, CA: Sage.

______. 1999. *The Development of Durkheim's Social Realism.* Cambridge, UK: Cambridge University Press.

Joppke, Christian. 2009. *Veil: Mirror of Identity.* Cambridge, UK: Polity.

Judt, Tony. 2008. *Reappraisals: Reflections on the Forgotten Twentieth Century.* New York: Penguin.

Juergensmeyer, Mark. 2001. *Terror in the Mind of God: The Global Rise of Religious Violence.* Berkeley: University of California Press.

Kahan, Alan S. 2001. *Aristocratic Liberalism: The Social and Political Thought of Jacob Burckhardt, John Stuart Mill, and Alexis de Tocqueville.* New Brunswick, NJ: Transaction.

Kallen, Horace. 1924. *Culture and Democracy in the United States.* New York: Boni & Liveright.

Käsler, Dirk. 1988. *Max Weber: An Introduction to His Life and Work.* Chicago: University of Chicago Press.

Kateb, George. 1989. "Individualism, Communitarianism, and Docility." *Social Research* 56(Winter):921–942.

Keen, Mike F. 1993. "No One Above Suspicion: Talcott Parsons Under Surveillance." *The American Sociologist* Fall/Winter:37–54.

Keene, John. 2003. *Global Civil Society?* Cambridge, UK: Cambridge University Press.

Kellner, Douglas. 2000. "Jean Baudrillard." Pp. 731–753 in *The Blackwell Companion to Major Social Theorists*, edited by G. Ritzer. Malden, MA: Blackwell.

Kivisto, Peter. 1980/1981. "Touraine's Post-Industrial Society." *Humboldt Journal of Social Relations* 8(1):25–43.

______. 1981. "The Theorist as Seer: The Case of Bell's Post-Industrial Society." *Quarterly Journal of Ideology* 5(2):39–43.

______. 1984. "Contemporary Social Movements in Advanced Industrial Societies and Sociological Intervention." *Acta Sociologica* 27:355–366.

______. 1989. "The Critic's Weapons: Comment on Sica." *The American Sociologist* Fall:246–248.

______. 1990. "The Transplanted Then and Now: The Reorientation of Immigration Studies From the Chicago School to the New Social History." *Ethnic and Racial Studies* 13(4):455–481.

______. 1993. "A Dialectic of Racial Enlightenment." *International Journal of Politics, Culture, and Society* 7(1):121–131.

______. 1994. "Toward an Antifoundational yet Relevant Sociology: Can Gottdiener Have It Both Ways?" *The Sociological Quarterly* 35(4):723–728.

______. 2001. "Theorizing Transnational Immigration: A Critical Review of Current Efforts." *Ethnic and Racial Studies* 24(4):549–577.

______. 2002. *Multiculturalism in a Global Society.* Malden, MA: Blackwell.

______. 2003a. "Social Spaces, Transnational Immigrant Communities, and the Politics of Incorporation." *Ethnicities* 3(1):35–58.

______. 2003b. "The View From America: Comments on Banton." *Ethnic and Racial Studies* 26(3):526–534.

______. 2005. "The Revival of Assimilation in Historical Perspective." Pp. 3–29 in *Incorporating Diversity: Rethinking Assimilation in a Multicultural Age,* edited by P. Kivisto. Boulder, CO: Paradigm.

______. 2007. "In Search of the Social Space for Solidarity and Justice." *Thesis Eleven* No. 91:110–127.

Kivisto, Peter and Thomas Faist. 2007. *Citizenship: Discourse, Theory, and Transnational Prospects.* Malden, MA: Blackwell.

______. 2010. *Beyond a Border: The Causes and Consequences of Contemporary Immigration.* Thousand Oaks, CA: Pine Forge.

Kolakowski, Leszek. 2008. *Main Currents of Marxism: The Founders—The Golden Age—The Breakdown.* New York: W. W. Norton.

Kolbert, Elizabeth. 2004. "Why Work? A Hundred Years of 'The Protestant Ethic'." *The New Yorker,* November 29:154–160.

Korpi, Walter. 1982. *The Democratic Class Struggle.* London: Routledge.

Kracauer, Siegfried. 1995. *The Mass Ornament: Weimar Essays.* Cambridge, MA: Harvard University Press.

Kumar, Krishan. 1988. *The Rise of Modern Society: Aspects of the Social and Political Development of the West.* Cambridge, MA: Blackwell.

______. 1993. "Civil Society: An Inquiry Into the Usefulness of an Historical Term." *British Journal of Sociology* 44(3):375–395.

Lal, Barbara Ballis. 1990. *The Romance of Culture in an Urban Civilization: Robert E. Park on Race and Ethnic Relations in Cities.* London: Routledge.

Lash, Scott. 1990. *Sociology of Postmodernism.* London: Routledge.

Lash, Scott and John Urry. 1987. *The End of Organized Capitalism.* Cambridge, UK: Polity.

Lassman, Peter and Irving Velody. 1998. *Max Weber and the Fate of Politics.* New York: Routledge.

Latour, Bruno. 1993. *We Have Never Been Modern.* Cambridge, MA: Harvard University Press.

Lechner, Frank. 2005. "Globalization." Pp. 330–333 in *The Encyclopedia of Social Theory,* vol. 1, edited by G. Ritzer. Thousand Oaks, CA: Sage.

Leck, Ralph M. 2000. *Georg Simmel and Avant-Garde Sociology.* New York: Humanities Press.

LeFeber, Walter. 2002. *Michael Jordan and the New Global Capitalism.* New York: Norton.

Lehmann, Jennifer M. 1993. *Deconstructing Durkheim: A Post-Post-Structuralist Critique*. New York: Routledge.

______. 1995. "Durkheim's Theories of Deviance and Suicide: A Feminist Reconsideration." *American Journal of Sociology* 100(4):904–930.

Lemert, Charles. 1995. *Sociology After the Crisis*. Boulder, CO: Westview.

______. 2005. *Postmodernism Is Not What You Think*. Boulder, CO: Paradigm.

______. 2006. *Durkheim's Ghosts: Cultural Logics and Social Things*. New York: Cambridge University Press.

Lenin, Vladimir Ilyich. 1969. *The Lenin Reader*. Chicago: Henry Regnery.

Lepenies, Wolf. 1988. *Between Literature and Science: The Rise of Sociology*. Cambridge, UK: Cambridge University Press.

Lerner, Max. 1994. *Tocqueville and American Civilization*. New Brunswick, NJ: Transaction.

Levine, Donald. 1985. *The Flight From Ambiguity: Essays in Social and Cultural Theory*. Chicago: University of Chicago Press.

______. 1995. *Visions of the Sociological Tradition*. Chicago: University of Chicago Press.

______. 2000. "On the Critique of 'Utilitarian' Theories of Action: Newly Identified Convergences Among Simmel, Weber, and Parsons." *Theory, Culture, and Society* 17(1):63–78.

Liebersohn, Harry. 1988. *Fate and Utopia in German Sociology, 1870–1923*. Cambridge: MIT Press.

Linder, Rolf. 2006. *Reportage of Urban Culture: Robert Park and the Chicago School*, translated by A. Morris. Cambridge, UK: Cambridge University Press.

Lipovetsky, Gilles. 1994. *The Empire of Fashion: Dressing Modern Democracy*. Princeton, NJ: Princeton University Press.

Lipset, Seymour Martin. 1950. *Agrarian Socialism: The Cooperative Commonwealth Federation in Saskatchewan*. Berkeley: University of California Press.

______. 1963a. *Political Man: The Social Bases of Politics*. Garden City, NY: Anchor.

______. 1963b. *First New Nation*. New York: Basic Books.

______. 1964. "The Biography of a Research Project: Union Democracy." Pp. 96–120 in *Sociologists at Work*, edited by P. E. Hammond. New York: Basic Books.

______. 1970. *The Politics of Unreason*. New York: Harper & Row.

______. 1994. "The Social Requisites of Democracy Revisited." *American Sociological Review* 59(1):1–22.

Lipset, Seymour Martin and Gary Marks. 2000. *It Didn't Happen Here: Why Socialism Failed in the United States*. New York: Norton.

Lipset, Seymour Martin and Gerald M. Schaflander. 1971. *Passion and Politics: Student Activism in America*. Boston: Little, Brown.

Lipset, Seymour Martin, Martin Trow, and James Coleman. 1956. *Union Democracy: The Internal Politics of the International Typographical Union*. Garden City, NY: Anchor.

Loewenstein, Karl. 1966. *Max Weber's Political Ideas in the Perspective of Our Time*. Amherst: University of Massachusetts Press.

Lofland, John. 1980. "Early Goffman: Style, Structure, Substance, Soul." Pp. 24–51 in *The View From Goffman*, edited by J. Ditton. New York: St. Martin's Press.

Lowenthal, Richard. 1976. "Social Transformation and Democratic Legitimacy." *Social Research* 43(2):423–434.

Lukács, Georg. [1923] 1971. *History and Class Consciousness: Studies in Marxist Dialectics*. Cambridge: MIT Press.

Lukes, Steven. 1972. *Emile Durkheim: His Life and Work*. New York: Harper & Row.

Lybrand, G. Steven. 1996. "Confusion at the Hermeneutic Cafe: How Sociologists (Mis)Read the Texts of Their Ancestors." Presented at the annual meeting of the Midwest Sociological Society, April, Chicago.

Lyman, Stanford M. 1968. "The Race Relations Cycle of Robert E. Park." *Pacific Sociological Review* 11(2):16–22.

______. 1973. "Civilization: Contents, Discontents, Malcontents." *Contemporary Sociology* 2:360–366.

______. 1992. *Militarism, Imperialism, and Racial Accommodation: An Analysis and Interpretation of the Early Writings of Robert E. Park*. Fayetteville: University of Arkansas Press.

Lyman, Stanford M. and Marvin B. Scott. 1975. *The Drama of Social Reality*. New York: Oxford University Press.

Lynd, Robert and Helen Lynd. 1929. *Middletown*. New York: Harcourt, Brace, & World.

______. 1937. *Middletown in Transition: A Study in Cultural Conflicts*. New York: Harcourt, Brace, & World.

Lyon, David. 1994. *Postmodernity*. Minneapolis: University of Minnesota Press.

Lyotard, Jean-Francois. 1979. *The Postmodern Condition: A Report on Knowledge*. Minneapolis: University of Minnesota Press.

Macdonald, Dwight. 1974. *Discriminations: Essays and Afterthoughts, 1938–1974*. New York: Viking.

Manning, Philip. 1992. *Erving Goffman and Modern Sociology*. Stanford, CA: Stanford University Press.

______. 2005. *Freud and American Sociology*. Cambridge, UK: Polity.

Manuel, Frank. 1995. *A Requiem for Karl Marx*. Cambridge, MA: Harvard University Press.

Marcuse, Herbert. 1964. *One-Dimensional Man*. Boston: Beacon.

Markoff, John. 1996. *Waves of Democracy*. Thousand Oaks, CA: Pine Forge Press.

Marshall, Gordon. 1982. *In Search of the Spirit of Capitalism: An Essay on Max Weber's Protestant Ethic Thesis*. New York: Columbia University Press.

Marshall, T. H. 1964. *Class, Citizenship, and Social Development*. Garden City, NY: Doubleday.

Martinelli, Alberto. 2002. "Markets, Governments, Communities, and Global Governance." Presidential address at the International Sociological Association XV Congress, July 8, Brisbane, Australia.

Marx, Karl. [1847] 1963. *The Poverty of Philosophy*. New York: International Publishers.

______. [1862/1863] 1963. *Theories of Surplus Value.* New York: International Publishers.

______. 1964. *Early Writings*, edited by T. B. Bottomore. New York: McGraw-Hill.

______. [1857/1858] 1965. *Pre-Capitalist Economic Formations*, edited by E. J. Hobsbawm. New York: International Publishers.

______. [1867] 1967. *Capital.* 3 vols. New York: International Publishers.

______. [1862/1863] 1968. *Theories of Surplus Value.* New York: International Publishers.

______. [1895] 1970. *The Class Struggles in France.* New York: International Publishers.

______. 1971. *Economic and Philosophical Manuscripts of 1844*, edited by D. J. Struick. New York: International Publishers.

______. [1857/1858] 1974. *The Grundrisse: Foundations of a Critique of Political Economy.* New York: Random House.

______. [1852] 1996. *Later Political Writings.* Cambridge, UK: Cambridge University Press.

Marx, Karl and Friedrich Engels. [1848] 1967. *The Communist Manifesto.* New York: Penguin.

Matthews, Fred. 1977. *Quest for an American Sociology: Robert E. Park and the Chicago School.* Montreal: McGill-Queen's University Press.

Mazlish, Bruce. 1989. *A New Science: The Breakdown of Connections and the Birth of Sociology.* New York: Oxford University Press.

McClay, Wilfred M. 1993. "The Strange Career of *The Lonely Crowd*: Or, the Antinomies of Autonomy." Pp. 397–440 in *The Culture of the Market: Historical Essays*, edited by T. L. Haskell and R. F. Teichbraeher III. Cambridge, UK: Cambridge University Press.

______. 1994. *The Masterless: Self and Society in Modern America.* Chapel Hill: University of North Carolina Press.

McCloskey, Donald. 1994. *Knowledge and Persuasion in Economics.* Cambridge, UK: Cambridge University Press.

McCraw, Thomas K. 2007. *Prophet of Innovation: Joseph Schumpeter and Creative Destruction.* Cambridge, MA: The Belknap Press of Harvard University Press.

McLellan, David. 1975. *Karl Marx.* New York: Viking.

McLuhan, Marshall. 1964. *Understanding Media.* London: Routledge.

Merton, Robert K. 1938. "Social Structure and Anomie." *American Sociological Review* 3(3):672–682.

______. 1968. *Social Theory and Social Structure.* New York: Free Press.

______. 1976. *Sociological Ambivalence and Other Essays.* New York: Free Press.

______. 1994. "A Life of Learning." Occasional Paper No. 25, American Council of Learned Societies, New York.

Mestrovíc, Stjepan G. 1988. *Émile Durkheim and the Reformation of Sociology.* Totowa, NJ: Rowman & Littlefield.

Mestrovíc, Stjepan G. and Helene M. Brown. 1985. "Durkheim's Concept of Anomie as *Dérèglement.*" *Social Problems* 33(2):81–99.

Mészáros, István. 1970. *Marx's Theory of Alienation.* London: Merlin.

Meyer, John, John Boli, George M. Thomas, and Francisco O. Ramirez. 1997. "World Society and the Nation-State." *American Journal of Sociology* 103(1):144–181.

Michels, Robert. 1958. *Political Parties*. New York: Free Press.

Mills, C. Wright. 1948. *The New Men of Power.* New York: Harcourt, Brace & World.

______. 1951. *White Collar: The American Middle Class*. New York: Oxford University Press.

______. 1956. *The Power Elite*. New York: Oxford University Press.

______. 1959. *The Sociological Imagination*. New York: Grove.

______. 1963. *Power, Politics, and People*, edited by I. L. Horowitz. New York: Oxford University Press.

______. 2000. *C. Wright Mills: Letters and Autobiographical Writings*, edited by Kathryn Mills with Pamela Mills. Berkeley: University of California Press.

Mitchell, Harvey. 2002. *American After Tocqueville: Democracy Against Difference*. Cambridge, UK: Cambridge University Press.

Mitzman, Arthur. 1970. *The Iron Cage: An Historical Interpretation of Max Weber.* New York: Knopf.

______. 1973. *Sociology and Estrangement: Three Sociologists of Imperial Germany.* New York: Knopf.

Mommsen, Wolfgang. 1974. *The Age of Bureaucracy: Perspectives on the Political Sociology of Max Weber.* New York: Harper & Row.

______. 1984. *Max Weber and German Politics, 1890–1920*. Chicago: University of Chicago Press.

______. 1987. "Max Weber and the Crisis of Liberal Democracy." Pp. 39–45 in *Bureaucracy Against Democracy and Socialism*, edited by R. M. Glassman, W. H. Swatos, Jr., and P. L. Rosen. New York: Greenwood.

______. 1989. *The Political and Social Theory of Max Weber.* Chicago: University of Chicago Press.

Morris-Reich, Amos. 2008. *The Quest for Jewish Assimilation in Modern Social Science*. New York: Routledge.

Nealon, Jeffrey T., ed. 2002. *Rethinking the Frankfurt School: Alternative Legacies of Cultural Critique*. Albany: State University of New York Press.

Nedelmann, Birgitta. 1990. "Georg Simmel as an Analyst of Autonomous Dynamics: The Merry-Go-Round of Fashion." Pp. 243–257 in *Georg Simmel and Contemporary Sociology*, edited by M. Kaern, B. S. Phillips, and R. S. Cohen. Dordrecht, The Netherlands: Kluwer.

______. 1991. "Individualization, Exaggeration, and Paralysation: Simmel's Three Problems of Culture." *Theory, Culture, and Society* 8:169–194.

Nelson, Benjamin. 1973. "Civilizational Complexes and Inter-Civilizational Encounters." *Sociological Analysis* 34(2):79–105.

Nielsen, Donald A. 1999. *Three Faces of God: Society, Religion, and Categories of Totality in the Philosophy of Émile Durkheim*. Albany: State University of New York Press.

Nielsen, Jens Kaalhauge. 1991. "The Political Orientation of Talcott Parsons: The Second World War and Its Aftermath." Pp. 217–233 in *Talcott Parsons: Theorist of Modernity*, edited by R. Robertson and B. S. Turner. Newbury Park, CA: Sage.

Nisbet, Robert. 1974. *The Sociology of Émile Durkheim*. New York: Oxford University Press.

______. 1976. *Sociology as an Art Form*. New York: Oxford University Press.

Nove, Alec. 1972. *An Economic History of the U.S.S.R.* Harmondsworth, UK: Penguin.

Oakes, Guy and Arthur J. Vidich. 1999. *Collaboration, Reputation, and Ethics in American Academic Life: Hans H. Gerth and C. Wright Mills*. Urbana: University of Illinois Press.

Oberschall, Anthony. 1965. *Empirical Social Research in Germany, 1848–1914*. New York: Humanities Press.

O'Neill, John. 1995. *The Poverty of Postmodernism*. London: Routledge.

Ong, Aihwa. 1999. *Flexible Citizenship: The Cultural Logic of Transnationality*. Durham, NC: Duke University Press.

Pachter, Henry. 1984. *Socialism and History*. New York: Columbia University Press.

Padover, Saul K. 1978. *Karl Marx: An Intimate Biography*. New York: McGraw-Hill.

Page, Charles H. 1982. *Fifty Years in the Sociological Enterprise: A Lucky Journey*. Amherst: University of Massachusetts Press.

Park, Robert E. 1914. "Racial Assimilation in Secondary Groups, With Particular Reference to the Negro." *American Journal of Sociology* 19(5):606–623.

______. 1922. *The Immigrant Press and Its Control*. New York: Harper & Brothers.

______. 1950. *Race and Culture*. Glencoe, IL: Free Press.

______. 1952. *Human Communities*. Glencoe, IL: Free Press.

______. 1972. *The Crowd and the Public, and Other Essays*. Chicago: University of Chicago Press.

Park, Robert E., Ernest W. Burgess, and Roderick D. McKenzie. 1925. *The City*. Chicago: University of Chicago Press.

Park, Robert E. and Herbert A. Miller. 1921. *Old World Traits Transplanted*. New York: Harper & Brothers.

Parkin, Frank. 1979. *Marxism and Class Theory: A Bourgeois Critique*. New York: Columbia University Press.

Parsons, Talcott. 1937. *The Structure of Social Action*. Vol. 1. New York: McGraw-Hill.

______. 1954. *Essays in Sociological Theory*. New York: Free Press.

______. 1959. "A Short Account of My Intellectual Development." *Alpha Kappa Deltan* 29(1):3–12.

______. 1967. *Sociological Theory and Modern Society*. New York: Free Press.

______. 1971. *The System of Modern Societies*. Englewood Cliffs, NJ: Prentice Hall.

______. 1990. "Beyond Coercion and Crisis: The Coming of an Era of Voluntary Community." Pp. 298–305 in *Culture and Society*, edited by J. C. Alexander and S. Seidman. Cambridge, UK: Cambridge University Press.

______. 1991. *The Early Essays*, edited by C. Camic. Chicago: University of Chicago Press.

______. 1993. *Talcott Parsons on National Socialism*, edited by U. Gerhardt. New York: Aldine.

______. 2007. *American Society: A Theory of the Societal Community*, edited by Giuseppe Sciortino. Boulder, CO: Paradigm.

Patterson, Orlando. 2000. "Ecumenical America: Global Culture and the American Cosmos." Pp. 465–480 in *Multiculturalism in the United States*, edited by P. Kivisto and G. Rundblad. Thousand Oaks, CA: Pine Forge Press.

Pearce, Frank. 1989. *The Radical Durkheim.* Winchester, MA: Unwin Hyman.

Pescosolido, Bernice A. and Beth A. Rubin. 2000. "The Web of Group Affiliations Revisited: Social Life, Postmodernism, and Sociology." *American Sociological Review* 65(1):52–76.

Piore, Michael and Charles Sabel. 1984. *The Second Industrial Divide: Possibilities for Prosperity*. New York: Basic Books.

Poggi, Gianfranco. 1983. *Calvinism and the Capitalist Spirit: Max Weber's Protestant Ethic.* Amherst: University of Massachusetts Press.

______. 1993. *Georg Simmel's Philosophy of Money.* Berkeley: University of California Press.

______. 2000. *Durkheim.* New York: Oxford University Press.

Pope, Whitney. 1976. *Durkheim's* Suicide: *A Classic Analyzed.* Chicago: University of Chicago Press.

Portes, Edward Bryan. 1986. *Max Weber and Political Commitment.* Philadelphia: Temple University Press.

Proudhon, Pierre-Joseph. 1969. *Selected Writings.* Garden City, NY: Anchor.

Putnam, Robert D. 1995. "Bowling Alone: America's Declining Social Capital." *Journal of Democracy* 6(1):65–78.

______. 2000. *Bowling Alone: The Collapse and Revival of American Community.* New York: Simon & Schuster.

______, ed. 2002. *Democracies in Flux: The Evolution of Social Capital in Contemporary Society*. New York: Oxford University Press.

Radkau, Joachim, 2009. *Max Weber: A Biography.* Cambridge, UK: Polity.

Raushenbush, Winifred. 1979. *Robert E. Park: Biography of a Sociologist.* Durham, NC: Duke University Press.

Richman, Michele H. 2002. *Sacred Revolutions: Durkheim and the College de Sociologie*. Minneapolis: University of Minnesota Press.

Rieff, Philip. 1966. *The Triumph of the Therapeutic: Uses of Faith After Freud.* New York: Harper & Row.

Riesman, David. 1953. *Thorstein Veblen: A Critical Interpretation.* New York: Scribner.

______. 1954. *Individualism Reconsidered.* Garden City, NY: Doubleday.

______. 1990. "Becoming an Academic Man." Pp. 22–74 in *Authors of Their Own Lives: Intellectual Autobiographies by Twenty American Sociologists*, edited by B. M. Berger. Berkeley: University of California Press.

Riesman, David, with Nathan Glazer and Reuel Denney. [1950] 1989. *The Lonely Crowd.* New Haven, CT: Yale University Press.

Rittersporn, Gábor Tómas. 1991. *Stalinist Simplifications and Soviet Complications.* Chur, Switzerland: Harwood.

Ritzer, George. 1996. *The McDonaldization of Society.* Thousand Oaks, CA: Pine Forge Press.

______. 1999. *Enchanting a Disenchanted World: Revolutionizing the Means of Consumption.* Thousand Oaks, CA: Pine Forge Press.

_____, ed. 2007. *The Blackwell Companion to Globalization.* Malden, MA: Blackwell.

Robertson, Roland. 1992. *Globalization.* Newbury Park, CA: Sage.

Rojek, Chris and Bryan S. Turner. 1993. *Forget Baudrillard?* London: Routledge.

Rosenau, Pauline Marie. 1992. *Post-Modernism and the Social Sciences: Insights, Inroads and Intrusions.* Princeton, NJ: Princeton University Press.

Rosenberg, Nathan. 2000. *Schumpeter and the Endogeneity of Technology: Some American Perspectives.* London: Routledge.

Ross, Dorothy. 1991. *The Origins of American Social Science.* Cambridge, UK: Cambridge University Press.

Roth, Guenther. 1963. *The Social Democrats in Imperial Germany: A Study in Working-Class Isolation and National Integration.* New York: Bedminster.

Rowe, Dorothy. 2005. "Money, Modernity, and Melancholy: The Writings of Georg Simmel." *Critical Studies* 25:27–38.

Rueschemeyer, Dietrich, Evelyne Huber Stephens, and John D. Stephens. 1992. *Capitalist Development and Democracy.* Chicago: University of Chicago Press.

Rushdie, Salman. 1989. *The Satanic Verses.* New York: Viking.

Ryan, Alan. 2003. "The Power of Positive Thinking." *New York Review of Books* L(1):43–46.

_____. 2007. "Tocqueville: The Flaws of Genius." *New York Review of Books,* November 22:53–56.

Sartre, Jean-Paul. 1976. *Critique of Dialectical Reason.* London: New Left Books.

Sassen, Saskia. 1994. *Cities in a World Economy.* Thousand Oaks, CA: Pine Forge Press.

_____. 1996. *Losing Control? Sovereignty in an Age of Globalization.* New York: Columbia University Press.

Savage, Stephen P. 1981. *The Theories of Talcott Parsons: The Social Relations of Action.* New York: St. Martin's Press.

Scaff, Lawrence A. 1989. *Fleeing the Iron Cage: Culture, Politics, and Modernity in the Thought of Max Weber.* Berkeley: University of California Press.

_____. 2000. "Georg Simmel." Pp. 215–278 in *The Blackwell Companion to Major Social Theorists,* edited by George Ritzer. Malden, MA: Blackwell.

Scheff, Thomas J. 2006. *Goffman Unbound: A New Paradigm for Social Science.* Boulder, CO: Paradigm.

Schluchter, Wolfgang. 1989. *Rationalism, Religion, and Domination: A Weberian Perspective.* Berkeley: University of California Press.

Schumpeter, Joseph A. 1928. "The Instability of Capitalism." *Economic Journal* 38:361–386.

_____. 1942. *Capitalism, Socialism, and Democracy.* New York: Harper & Brothers.

Scimecca, Joseph A. 1977. *The Sociological Theory of C. Wright Mills.* Port Washington, NY: Kennikat.

Sciortino, Giuseppe. 2005. "How Different Can We Be? Parsons's Societal Community, Pluralism, and the Multicultural Debate." Pp. 111–136 in *After Parsons: A Theory of Social Action for the Twenty-First Century,* edited by Renée C. Fox, Victor Lidz, and Harold J. Bershady. New York: Russell Sage Foundation.

Sciulli, David and Dean Gernstein. 1985. "Social Theory and Talcott Parsons in the 1980s." *Annual Review of Sociology* 11:369–387.

Seeley, John R., R. Alexander Sim, and Elizabeth W. Loosley. 1956. *Crestwood Heights.* New York: Basic Books.

Seidman, Steven. 1983. *Liberalism and the Origins of European Social Theory.* Berkeley: University of California Press.

______. 1994. *Contested Knowledge: Social Theory in the Postmodern Era.* Cambridge, MA: Blackwell.

Seigel, Jerrold. 1978. *Marx's Fate: The Shape of a Life.* Princeton, NJ: Princeton University Press.

Sellerberg, Ann-Marie. 1994. *A Blend of Contradictions: Georg Simmel in Theory and Practice.* New Brunswick, NJ: Transaction.

Sennett, Richard. 1998. *The Corrosion of Character: The Personal Consequences of Work in the New Capitalism.* New York: Norton.

______. 2003. *Respect in a World of Inequality.* New York: Norton.

______. 2006. *The New Culture of Capitalism.* New Haven, CT: Yale University Press.

Shapin, Steven. 2007. "Man with a Plan: Herbert Spencer's Theory of Everything." *The New Yorker,* August 13, 75–79.

Shils, Edward. 1981. *The Calling of Sociology and Other Essays on the Pursuit of Learning.* Chicago: University of Chicago Press.

Sica, Alan. 1989. "Social Theory's Constituency." *The American Sociologist* Fall:227–241.

______. 2003. *Max Weber and the New Century.* New Brunswick, NJ: Transaction.

Simmel, Georg. 1950. *The Sociology of Georg Simmel*, edited by K. H. Wolff. New York: Free Press.

______. [1908] 1955. *Conflict and the Web of Group Affiliations.* New York: Free Press.

______. 1959. *Georg Simmel, 1858–1918*, edited by K. Wolff. Columbus: Ohio State University Press.

______. 1971. *On Individuality and Social Forms*, edited by D. N. Levine. Chicago: University of Chicago Press.

______. [1892] 1977. *The Problems of the Philosophy of History: An Epistemological Essay*, edited by G. Oakes. New York: Free Press.

______. 1984. *Georg Simmel: On Women, Sexuality, and Love.* Translated and introduced by G. Oakes. New Haven, CT: Yale University Press.

______. [1907] 1991. *The Philosophy of Money.* London: Routledge.

Sklair, Leslie. 1995. *Sociology of the Global System.* Baltimore: Johns Hopkins University Press.

______. 2001. *The Transnational Capitalist Class.* Malden, MA: Blackwell.

Slater, Philip. 1970. *The Pursuit of Loneliness: American Culture at the Breaking Point.* Boston: Beacon.

Smart, Barry. 1992. *Modern Conditions, Postmodern Controversies.* London: Routledge.

Smelser, Neil J. and R. Stephen Warner. 1976. *Sociological Theory: Historical and Formal.* Morristown, NJ: General Learning Press.

Smith, Dennis. 1988. *The Chicago School: A Liberal Critique of Capitalism.* New York: St. Martin's Press.
Soysal, Yasemin. 1994. *Limits of Citizenship: Migrants and Postnational Membership in Europe.* Chicago: University of Chicago Press.
Spinner, Jeff. 1994. *The Boundaries of Citizenship: Race, Ethnicity, and Nationality in the Liberal State.* Baltimore: Johns Hopkins University Press.
Spinner-Halev, Jeff. 1999. "Cultural Pluralism and Partial Citizenship." Pp. 65–86 in *Multicultural Questions*, edited by C. Joppke and S. Lukes. Oxford, UK: Oxford University Press.
Spivak, Gayatri. 1988. "Can the Subaltern Speak." Pp. 271–313 in *Marxism and the Interpretation of Culture*, edited by C. Nelson and L. Grossberg. Urbana: University of Illinois Press.
Stedman Jones, Susan. 2001. *Durkheim Reconsidered.* Cambridge, UK: Polity.
Stein, Maurice. 1960. *The Eclipse of Community: An Interpretation of American Studies.* Princeton, NJ: Princeton University Press.
Steinmeier, Frank-Walter. 2009. Habermas, Germany's greatest living philosopher, turns 80. *Newsletter.* German Embassy London. Retrieved December 7, 2009 (www.london.diplo.de/Vertretung/london/en/05/_Cultural_20News/2009/Habermas).
Stolper, Wolfgang. 1968. "Joseph A. Schumpeter." Pp. 67–72 in *The International Encyclopedia of the Social Sciences*, edited by D. L. Sills. New York: Macmillan/Free Press.
Strenski, Ivan. 1997. *Durkheim and the Jews of France.* Chicago: University of Chicago Press.
Sumner, Colin. 1994. *The Sociology of Deviance: An Obituary.* New York: Continuum.
Swatos, William H., Jr. and Peter Kivisto. 1991a. "Max Weber as Christian Sociologist." *Journal for the Scientific Study of Religion* 30(4):347–362.
_____. 1991b. "Beyond *Wertfreiheit:* Max Weber and Moral Order." *Sociological Focus* 24(2):117–128.
Szakolczai, Arpad. 1998. *Max Weber and Michel Foucault: Parallel Life-Works.* London: Routledge.
Sztompka, Piotr. 1986. *Robert K. Merton: An Intellectual Profile.* New York: St. Martin's Press.
_____. 1993. *The Sociology of Social Change.* Cambridge, MA: Blackwell.
Tar, Zolton. 1977. *The Frankfurt School: The Critical Theories of Max Horkheimer and Theodore W. Adorno.* New York: John Wiley.
Tawney, R.H. [1926] 1958. *Religion and the Rise of Capitalism: A Historical Study.* New York: New American Library.
Therborn, Göran. 1976. *Science, Class, and Society.* London: New Left Books.
_____. 1995. *European Modernity and Beyond.* Thousand Oaks, CA: Sage.
Thompson, Kenneth. 1982. *Emile Durkheim.* New York: Tavistock.
Tilman, Rick. 1984. *C. Wright Mills: A Native Radical and His American Intellectual Roots.* University Park: Pennsylvania State University Press.
_____. 1992. *Thorstein Veblen and His Critics, 1891–1963.* Princeton, NJ: Princeton University Press.

Tiryakian, Edward. 1978. "Emile Durkheim." Pp. 187–236 in *A History of Sociological Analysis*, edited by T. Bottomore and R. Nisbet. New York: Basic Books.

Tocqueville, Alexis de. [1856] 1955. *The Old Regime and the French Revolution.* Translated by S. Gilbert. Garden City, NY: Doubleday.

______. [1853] 1969. *Democracy in America*, edited by J. P. Mayer. Garden City, NY: Doubleday.

Toennies, Ferdinand. [1887] 1957. *Community and Society*, edited and translated by C. P. Loomis. New York: Harper & Row.

Tole, Lise Ann. 1993. "Durkheim on Religion and Moral Community in Modernity." *Sociological Inquiry* 63(1):1–29.

Touraine, Alain. 1971. *Post-Industrial Society.* New York: Random House.

______. 1977. "What Is Daniel Bell Afraid Of?" *American Journal of Sociology* 83(2):469–473.

______. 1995. *Critique of Modernity.* Cambridge, MA: Blackwell.

______. 2000. *Can We Live Together?* Stanford, CA: Stanford University Press.

______. 2001. *Beyond Neoliberalism.* Cambridge, UK: Polity.

Trevino, A. Javier, ed. 2001. *Talcott Parsons Today: His Theory and Legacy in Contemporary Sociology*. Lanham, MD: Rowman & Littlefield.

Turner, Stephen, ed. 1993. *Émile Durkheim: Sociologist and Moralist.* New York: Routledge.

Turner, Steven Park and Jonathan H. Turner. 1990. *The Impossible Science: An Institutional Analysis of American Sociology.* Newbury Park, CA: Sage.

Urry, John. 2000. *Sociology Beyond Societies: Mobilities for the Twenty-First Century*. London: Routledge.

Veblen, Thorstein. 1904. *The Theory of Business Enterprise.* New York: Scribner.

______. 1921. *The Engineers and the Price System.* New York: Viking.

______. [1899] 1924. *The Theory of the Leisure Class: An Economic Study of Institutions.* New York: Huebsch.

______. [1924] 1993. *The Higher Learning in America.* New Brunswick, NJ: Transaction.

Vidich, Arthur J. and Joseph Bensman. 1958. *Small Town in Mass Society: Class, Power, and Religion in a Rural Community.* Princeton NJ: Princeton University Press.

Vidich, Arthur J. and Stanford M. Lyman. 1985. *American Sociology: Worldly Rejections of Religion and Their Directions.* New Haven, CT: Yale University Press.

Vromen, Suzanne. 1990. "Georg Simmel and the Cultural Dilemmas of Women." Pp. 319–339 in *Georg Simmel and Contemporary Sociology,* edited by Michael Kaern, Bernard Phillips, and Robert Cohen. Dordrecht, The Netherlands: Kluwer.

Wagner, Peter. 2008. *Modernity as Experience and Interpretation: A New Sociology of Modernity.* Cambridge, UK: Polity.

Wallerstein, Immanuel. 1974. *The Modern World-System: Capitalist Agriculture and the Origins of the European World-Economy in the 16th Century*. New York: Academic Press.

______. 1980. *The Modern World-System II: Mercantilism and the Consolidation of the European World-Economy, 1600–1750.* New York: Academic Press.

______. 1989. *The Modern World-System III: The Second Era of Great Expansion of the Capitalist World-Economy, 1730–1840*. New York: Academic Press.

______. 1991. *Unthinking Social Science: The Limits of Nineteenth Century Paradigms*. Cambridge, MA: Polity.

______. 1998. *Utopistics: Or, Historical Choices for the Twenty-First Century*. New York: New Press.

Warner, W. Lloyd and Paul S. Lunt. 1941. *The Social Life of a Modern Community*. New Haven, CT: Yale University Press.

Waters, Malcolm. 1996. *Daniel Bell*. London: Routledge.

______. 2001. *Globalization*. 2d ed. London: Routledge.

Wearne, Bruce C. 1989. *The Theory and Scholarship of Talcott Parsons to 1951*. Cambridge, UK: Cambridge University Press.

Weber, Marianne. 1988. *Max Weber: A Biography*, edited and translated by H. Zohn. New Brunswick, NJ: Transaction.

Weber, Max. [1916] 1951. *The Religion of China: Confucianism and Taoism*. Glencoe, IL: Free Press.

______. [1904/1905] 1958. *The Protestant Ethic and the Spirit of Capitalism*. New York: Scribner.

______. [1921] 1968. *Economy and Society*. Vols. 1–3. Berkeley: University of California Press.

______. 1978. *Weber: Selections in Translation*, edited by W. G. Runciman. Cambridge, UK: Cambridge University Press.

______. 1994. *Political Writings*, edited by P. Lassman and R. Speirs. Cambridge, UK: Cambridge University Press.

______. 2002. *The Protestant Ethic and the Spirit of Capitalism*. Translated by Stephen Kalberg. Los Angeles: Roxbury.

Webster, Frank. 1995. *Theories of the Information Society*. London: Routledge.

Weingartner, Rudolph H. 1960. *Experience and Culture: The Philosophy of Georg Simmel*. Middletown, CT: Wesleyan University Press.

Weinstein, Deena and Michael A. Weinstein. 1993. *Post-Modern(ized) Simmel*. London: Routledge.

Welch, Cheryl B. 2001. *De Tocqueville*. Oxford, UK: Oxford University Press.

Wheatland, Thomas. 2009. *The Frankfurt School in Exile*. Minneapolis: University of Minnesota Press.

Wheen, Francis. 1999. *Karl Marx*. London: Fourth Estate.

______. 2008. *Marx's* Das Kapital: *A Biography*. New York: Grove Press.

Whyte, William H., Jr. 1956. *The Organization Man*. Garden City, NY: Doubleday.

Wiggershaus, Rolf. 1994. *The Frankfurt School: Its History, Theories, and Political Significance*. Cambridge: MIT Press.

Wiley, Norbert. 1994. *The Semiotic Self*. Chicago: University of Chicago Press.

Williams, Raymond. 1976. *Keywords: A Vocabulary of Culture and Society*. New York: Oxford University Press.

Wills, Garry. 2004. "Did Tocqueville 'Get' America?" *New York Review of Books*, April 29:52–56.

Winant, Howard. 2000. "Race and Race Theory." *Annual Review of Sociology* 26:169–185.

Wolfe, Alan. 1993. *The Human Difference: Animals, Computers, and the Necessity of Social Science.* Berkeley: University of California Press.

______. 1995. "Realism and Romanticism in Sociology." *Society* January/February: 56–63.

______. 1996. *Marginalized in the Middle.* Chicago: University of Chicago Press.

Wolff, Jonathan. 2002. *Why Read Marx Today?* Oxford, UK: Oxford University Press.

Wolin, Sheldon S. 2001. *Between Two Worlds: The Making of a Political and Theoretical Life.* Princeton, NJ: Princeton University Press.

______. 2008. *Democracy Inc.: Managed Democracy and the Specter of Inverted Totalitarianism.* Princeton, NJ: Princeton University Press.

Wright, Erik Olin. 2000. *Class Matters: Student Edition.* Cambridge, UK: Cambridge University Press.

Wuthnow, Robert. 1994. *Sharing the Journey: Support Groups and America's New Quest for Community.* New York: Free Press.

Young, Iris Marion. 1997. *Intersecting Voices: Dilemmas of Gender, Political Philosophy, and Policy.* Princeton, NJ: Princeton University Press.

Žižek, Slavoj. 2002. *Welcome to the Desert of the Real.* London: Verso.

______. 2008. *In Defense of Lost Causes.* London: Verso.

Index

About the Author

Peter Kivisto is the Richard Swanson Professor of Social Thought and chair of Sociology at Augustana College and Finland Distinguished Professor at the University of Turku. Among his recent books are *Beyond a Border* (2010, with Thomas Faist), *Social Theory: Roots and Branches* (4th ed.; 2010), *Citizenship: Discourse, Theory, and Transnational Prospects* (2007, with Thomas Faist), *Dual Citizenship in Global Perspective* (2007, with Thomas Faist), and *Multiculturalism in a Global Society* (2002). His primary scholarly and teaching interests concern social theory and ethnic studies. He has served as secretary-treasurer of the American Sociological Association's Theory and International Migration Sections and is the immediate past editor of *The Sociological Quarterly.* He is currently president of the Midwest Sociological Society.